ב"ה

Decoding the Talmud

Cover Art: *Preparing the Shiur* (detail)
Chava Roth, oil on canvas, New York, 1999

Printed in the United States of America

832 Eastern Parkway, Brooklyn, NY 11213

718-221-6900
WWW.MYJLI.COM

Decoding the Talmud

Inside the Story, Substance, and Significance of the Book That Defines Judaism

COURSE TEXTBOOK

ADVISORY BOARD *of* GOVERNORS

Yaakov and Karen Cohen
Potomac, MD

Yitzchok and Julie Gniwisch
Montreal, QC

Barbara Hines
Aspen, CO

Ellen Marks
S. Diego, CA

David Mintz, OBM
Tenafly, NJ

George Rohr
New York, NY

Dr. Stephen F. Serbin
Columbia, SC

Leonard A. Wien, Jr.
Miami Beach, FL

PARTNERING FOUNDATIONS

Beinoni Foundation

David Samuel Rock Foundation

Diamond Foundation

Estate of Elliot James Belkin

Francine Gani Charitable Fund

Goldstein Family Foundation

The Harvey L. Miller Family Foundation

Kohelet Foundation

Kosins Family Foundation

Leticia and Eduardo Azar Foundation

Lion Heritage Fund at Rose Foundation

Meromim Foundation

Myra Reinhard Family Foundation

Robbins Family Foundation

Ruderman Family Foundation

Schulich Foundation

William Davidson Foundation

World Zionist Organization

Yehuda and Anne Neuberger Philanthropic Fund

Zalik Foundation

PRINCIPAL BENEFACTOR

George Rohr
New York, NY

PILLARS *of* JEWISH LITERACY

Shaya and Sarah Boymelgreen
Miami Beach, FL

Pablo and Sara Briman
Mexico City, Mexico

Zalman and Mimi Fellig
Miami Beach, FL

Edwin and Arlene Goldstein
Cincinnati, OH

Yosef and Chana Malka Gorowitz
Redondo Beach, CA

Shloimy and Mirele Greenwald
Brooklyn, NY

Dr. Vera Koch Groszmann
S. Paulo, Brazil

Carolyn Starman Hessel
Great Neck, NY

Edward and Inna Kholodenko
Toronto, ON

David and Debra Magerman
Gladwyne, PA

Yitzchak Mirilashvili
Herzliya, Israel

David and Harriet Moldau
Longwood, FL

Ben Nash
Sunny Isles Beach, FL

Eyal and Aviva Postelnik
Marietta, GA

Clive and Zoe Rock
Irvine, CA

Michael and Fiona Scharf
Palm Beach, FL

Lee and Patti Schear
Dayton, OH

Isadore and Roberta Schoen
Fairfax, VA

Rabbi Roberto and Margie Szerer
Aventura, FL

SPONSORS

Moshe and Rebecca Bolinsky
Long Beach, NY

Dr. Stephen and Bella Brenner
New York, NY

Rabbi Meyer and Leah Eichler
Brooklyn, NY

Yechiel and Nechy Eisenstadt
Brooklyn, NY

Steve and Esther Feder
Los Angeles, CA

Yoel Gabay
Brooklyn, NY

Dr. Gerald Gilbert Glass
Sunrise, FL

Shmuel and Sharone Goodman
Chicago, IL

Marc Kulick
New York, NY

Michael and Andrea Leven
Atlanta, GA

Joe and Shira Lipsey
Aspen, CO

Josef and Yael Michelashvili
Brooklyn, NY

Jack and Judy Miller
Boca Raton, FL

Rachelle Nedow
El Paso, TX

Peter and Hazel Pflaum
Newport Beach, CA

Abraham Podolak
Princeton Junction, NJ

Dr. Ze'ev and Varda Rav-Noy
Los Angeles, CA

Arthur Isaac Resetschnig
Vienna, Austria

Zvi Ryzman
Los Angeles, CA

Larry Sifen
Virginia Beach, VA

Myrna Zisman
Cedarhurst, NY

Janice and Ivan Zuckerman
Coral Gables, FL

The Rohr Jewish Learning Institute
gratefully acknowledges the pioneering
and ongoing support of

George and Pamela Rohr

Since its inception, the Rohr JLI has been
a beneficiary of the vision, generosity, care,
and concern of the Rohr family.

In the merit of the tens of thousands of hours
of Torah study by JLI students worldwide,
may they be blessed with health, *Yiddishe
nachas* from all their loved ones, and
extraordinary success in all their endeavors.

IN TRIBUTE TO

Rabbi Moshe Kotlarsky

of blessed memory

הרב החסיד ר' משה יהודא ב"ר צבי יוסף ע"ה

Our longstanding visionary chairman, entrusted and empowered by the Rebbe to facilitate the growth and expansion of the network of Chabad *shluchim* and its institutions worldwide.

יהא זכרו ברוך

THIS COURSE IS DEDICATED TO OUR
DEAR FRIENDS AND PARTNERS

Reb Meyer and Leah Eichler

who embody the values of Jewish education, community, family, and heartfelt generosity.

Their partnership with JLI has brought Torah study to all corners of the world.

May they go from strength to strength and enjoy good health, happiness, *nachas* from their loved ones, and success in all their endeavors לאורך ימים ושנים טובות.

AND IN LOVING MEMORY OF

הרב צבי אריה ב"ר אהרן אליהו
מרת עלקא בת ר' שלמה שמואל

May the Torah studied and exchanged in this JLI series across the globe merit that their souls ascend ever higher and yield blessing for their entire family.

Citation Types

SCRIPTURE

The icon for Scripture is based on the images of a scroll and a spiral. The scroll is a literal reference; the spiral symbolizes Scripture's role as the singular source from which all subsequent Torah knowledge emanates.

SCRIPTURAL COMMENTARY

Throughout the ages, Jews have scrutinized the Torah's text, generating many commentaries.

TALMUD AND MIDRASH

The Talmud and Midrash record the teachings of the sages—fundamental links in the unbroken chain of the Torah's transmission going back to Mount Sinai.

TALMUDIC COMMENTARY

The layers of Talmudic teaching have been rigorously excavated in each era, resulting in a library of insightful commentaries.

JEWISH MYSTICISM

The mystics explore the inner, esoteric depths. The icon for mystical texts reflects the "*sefirot* tree" commonly present in kabbalistic charts.

CHARACTER AND VIRTUE

Often called *musar*, this literature provides character refinement and personal development strategies.

JEWISH PHILOSOPHY

Jewish philosophic texts shed light on life's big questions and demonstrate the relevance of Jewish teachings even as the sands of societal values continuously shift.

JEWISH LAW AND CUSTOM

The guidance that emerges from Scripture and the Talmud finds practical expression in Jewish law, known as *Halachah* ("the way"), alongside customs adopted by Jewish communities through the generations.

CHASIDUT

Chasidism's advent in the eighteenth century brought major, encouraging changes to Jewish life and outlook. Its teachings are akin to refreshing, life-sustaining waters from a continuously flowing well of the profoundest insights.

LITURGY

The texts of the Jewish prayer book burst with the full spectrum of human emotion, from joy to longing to contrition and to hope. They all share the authentic search for a meaningful encounter with G-d.

PERSPECTIVES

Personal, professional, and academic perspectives, expressed in essays, research papers, diaries, and other works, can often enhance appreciation for Torah ideas and the totality of the Jewish experience.

Contents

Foreword

BEN BAG BAG SAID: TURN IT OVER, AND TURN IT OVER AGAIN, FOR IT CONTAINS EVERYTHING. LOOK INTO IT; GROW GRAY AND OLD OVER IT, AND DO NOT BUDGE FROM IT, FOR YOU HAVE NO BETTER PORTION THAN IT.

—MISHNAH, AVOT 5:22

"The Sages of the Talmud"..."Talmudic Wisdom"... "Talmudic Reasoning"...

Almost every Jew has heard of the Talmud. While many might recognize it as an important text in Jewish tradition, few have a clear understanding of what the Talmud truly is. Some may picture it as a collection of philosophical insights about G-d or as a compilation of religious, ethical, and moral teachings. Others may know that it contains rabbinic debates. However, without the experience of studying the Talmud firsthand, it's challenging to grasp what the Talmud is and why it holds such a central place in Judaism.

The course you are beginning today, *Decoding the Talmud*, offers a direct introduction to the Talmud. Together we will explore its primary themes, trace its development over centuries, and learn about the scholars whose intellect and creativity it preserves. We will delve into the distinctive thinking that has embedded itself into Jewish culture and discover that, in many ways, the Talmud *is* Judaism.

The metaphor of the "Sea of the Talmud" has often been used to describe this vast and profound work. Borrowing from this imagery, our course will not just talk about journeys on this sea—it will actually give you a chance to get out on the water yourself. By engaging with a selection of Talmudic discussions, we will make the theory real, immersing you directly in the experience.

Whether you have some prior experience with Talmud study, are simply curious about one of Judaism's greatest cultural and spiritual treasures, or are beginning a lifelong journey into the Talmud's depths, this course is designed with you in mind. For those with background knowledge, we will offer new insights and historical context that may be unfamiliar. For the curious, these six lessons will provide a captivating overview of the Talmud's story. And for those starting out, we hope today is just the beginning of a meaningful and lasting journey through the Sea of the Talmud!

LESSON

1

THE JEWISH PEOPLE AND THE TALMUD

Why Jewish life orbits a book of law

Jewish law's ultimate record is the Talmud, but what is Jewish law? Explore its nature, scope, and roots in the written Torah and Oral Law—and see learning's central role in Jewish practice and culture.

SABBATH AFTERNOON
Moritz Daniel Oppenheim, oil on canvas, Frankfurt, Germany, 1866

I. THE TREASURE OF THE JEWISH NATION

The Talmud is an enormous compendium of ancient Jewish teaching, dozens of volumes in size. However, it is much more than mere inked words. Rather, it is the very basis of the Jewish religion, it has been the source of unique Jewish delight for millennia, and it has preserved our people—against all odds—through thousands of years of tumultuous exile. Today's study explores the nature and role of the Talmud, with a focus on the outsized role this compendium has played in Jewish practice, thought, and survival.

REGENERATION
Yossi Rosenstein, oil on canvas, Israel, 1999

TEXT 1

Burned Treasure

Rabbi Meir of Rothenburg, *Shaali Serufah Ba'esh*, *Kinot* of Tishah Be'Av

אוֹרִיד דְּמָעוֹת
עֲדֵי יִהְיוּ כְּנַחַל
וְיַגִּיעוּ לְקִבְרוֹת
שְׁנֵי שָׂרֵי אֲצִילָיִךְ
מֹשֶׁה וְאַהֲרֹן בְּהֹר הָהָר
וְאֶשְׁאַל
הֲיֵשׁ תּוֹרָה חֲדָשָׁה
בְּכֵן נִשְׂרְפוּ גְּלִילָיִךְ . . .
אֶתְמַהּ לְנַפְשִׁי
וְאֵיךְ יֶעֱרַב לְחִכִּי אֲכוֹל,
אַחֲרֵי רְאוֹתִי
אֲשֶׁר אָסְפוּ שְׁלָלָיִךְ
אֶל־תּוֹךְ רְחוֹבָהּ כְּנִדַּחַת,
וְשָׂרְפוּ שְׁלַל עֶלְיוֹן.

I will shed tears

Until they surge like a stream

RABBI MEIR OF ROTHENBURG
C. 1220-1293

Halachic authority. Born in Worms, Germany, Rabbi Meir studied under the famous Tosafist scholars in Germany and France. Settling in Rothenburg, Germany, Rabbi Meir became the leading Halachic authority for Ashkenazi Jewry. After attempting to flee increasing persecution of the Jews in Germany, Rabbi Meir was imprisoned, heroically refusing to be ransomed for an exorbitant price and dying in captivity. Hundreds of his Halachic responsa are collected in *Shu"t Maharm Mirothenburg*, and his rulings helped shape Halachah and define Ashkenazi custom.

That will reach the graves

Of Your two noble princes

Moses and Aaron

On the mountain of Hor

And I will inquire [of them]:

Will a new [version of the] Torah [be given]?

Is that why your columns were
[permitted to be] burned?...

My soul is astonished!

Can edibles ever taste sweet to my palate

Now that I have watched

How they gathered Your treasure

Into the city square—

Like [the penalty of] a [Jewish] city
that strayed [to idolatry]—

And burned the supernal treasure!

TEXT 2

The Delight of Torah

Psalms 119:92–93

לוּלֵי תוֹרָתְךָ שַׁעֲשֻׁעָי, אָז אָבַדְתִּי בְעָנְיִי.

לְעוֹלָם לֹא אֶשְׁכַּח פִּקּוּדֶיךָ, כִּי בָם חִיִּיתָנִי.

Had Your Torah not been my delight, I would have perished in my suffering.

I will never forget Your precepts, for through them You preserved my life.

PSALMS

Biblical book. The book of Psalms contains 150 psalms expressing praise for G-d, faith in G-d, and laments over tragedies. The primary author of the psalms was King David, who lived in the 9th century BCE. Psalms also contains material from earlier figures. The feelings and circumstances expressed in the psalms resonate throughout the generations, and they have become an important part of communal and personal prayer.

BUBBY RECITING *TEHILLIM* (PSALMS)
Elie Benzaquen, oil on canvas, Ottawa, Canada, 1999

TEXT 3

Home in a Book

Cecil Roth, *A Short History of the Jewish People* (London: East and West Library, 1948), p. 132

The importance in Jewish life of the Talmud is not by any means purely academic. It comprises the accumulated wisdom of the Jewish people over many generations. . . .

The period of its redaction coincided with the growth of independent centers of life in far-distant regions, cut off politically and linguistically from the former nuclei. The Jewish people was about to enter on an entirely different phase of its being, in countries of which their fathers had never heard . . . in the face of difficulties hitherto unimaginable. But they possessed, to bring with them into their new existence, a code, not merely of religion or of law, but of civilisation. . . .

[The Talmud] gave [the Jew] a fatherland which he could carry about with him when his own land was lost. And, if he was able to maintain his identity in the course of the long centuries to come, under conditions such as no other people has ever been able to surmount, it is with the Talmud, above all, that the credit lies.

CECIL ROTH
1899–1970

British Jewish historian. Dr. Roth was a professor of Jewish studies at Oxford University and later served as visiting professor at Bar-Ilan University in Israel and at the City University of New York. A prolific author, he wrote more than 600 historical works on Jewish topics, such as the Dead Sea Scrolls and Jewish art. Roth served as editor of the *Encyclopedia Judaica* from 1965 until his passing.

II. WHAT IS THE TALMUD?

The Talmud is a vast treasury of information and covers an astonishing variety of topics. The immediate concern of the bulk of its material is on preserving a record of Halachah, Jewish law, through reporting the deliberations over its many particulars. These laws cover literally every facet of Jewish life.

THE TRANSMISSION OF MEMORIES
Walter Spitzer (1927 [Cieszyn, Poland]–2021 [Paris, France]), oil on canvas

FIGURE 1.1

Ten Useful Facts about the Talmud

1.	The Talmud is a combination of two books, the Mishnah and the Gemara, with the latter styled as a commentary, elaboration, and analysis of the former.
2.	The Mishnah was composed around 200 CE, in northern Israel.
3.	There are two versions of the Gemara. The first is the Jerusalem Talmud (*Talmud Yerushalmi*) and the second is the Babylonian Talmud (*Talmud Bavli*).
4.	The Jerusalem Talmud was completed in the mid-4th century, in northern Israel. The Babylonian Talmud was completed in the 5th century, in Babylonia (*Bavel*, located in the region of modern-day Iraq).
5.	The Mishnah compiles the teachings of approximately 120 sages, referred to as the *tana'im*.
6.	The Gemara compiles the teachings of approximately 800 sages, referred to as the *amora'im*.
7.	The Talmud is divided into 63 sections or books, referred to as *masechtot*, "tractates."
8.	Every tractate contains teachings of the Mishnah, but not every tractate features the teachings of the Gemara. Some tractates are treated in the Babylonian Talmud, some in the Jerusalem Talmud, some in both, and some in neither.
9.	The universal standard print of the Babylonian Talmud is the 19th-century "Vilna *Shas*," which includes several primary commentaries and fills 2,711 double-sided pages (folios).
10.	Talmudic citations in English writings typically include 1) a tractate name; 2) a folio number; and 3) a letter indicating the folio side ("a" or "b"). For example, the citation "Pesachim 99b" indicates that the passage cited is sourced in the tractate entitled Pesachim, on the reverse side of its 99th folio. Unless otherwise specified, all such references refer to the heavily studied Babylonian Talmud, and not the Jerusalem Talmud, the study of which is more limited.

KEY TERM 1.1

HEBREW TERM	הֲלָכָה
TRANSLITERATION	*Halachah*
PRONUNCIATION	Ha-LA-khah
LITERAL MEANING	***way* or *path***
MEANING	Jewish law

TEXT 4A

Time for Matzah

Talmud, Pesachim 99b

עַרְבֵי פְסָחִים סָמוּךְ לַמִּנְחָה, לֹא יֹאכַל אָדָם עַד שֶׁתֶּחְשַׁךְ.

On the eve of Passover, we may not eat from close to the time of Minchah until it is dark [to ensure a hearty appetite for eating matzah at the Passover *seder* later that night].

BABYLONIAN TALMUD

A literary work of monumental proportions that draws upon the legal, spiritual, intellectual, ethical, and historical traditions of Judaism. The 37 tractates of the Babylonian Talmud contain the teachings of the Jewish sages from the period after the destruction of the 2nd Temple through the 5th century CE. It has served as the primary vehicle for the transmission of the Oral Law and the education of Jews over the centuries; it is the entry point for all subsequent legal, ethical, and theological Jewish scholarship.

TEXT 4B

Right to Gripe

Talmud, Bava Metzi'a 75b

הַשּׂוֹכֵר אֶת הָאֻמָּנִין וְהִטְעוּ זֶה אֶת זֶה,
אֵין לָהֶם זֶה עַל זֶה אֶלָּא תַּרְעֹמֶת.

If one hires skilled workers, and they deceived each other, they have only a right to complain [but not to pursue a financial claim].

TEXT 4C

Immersion Times

Talmud, Yoma 6a

כָּל חַיָּיבֵי טְבִילוֹת טְבִילָתָן בַּיּוֹם, נִדָּה וְיוֹלֶדֶת טְבִילָתָן בַּלַּיְלָה.

All who are obligated to ritually immerse must do so during the day, with the exception of [a woman who is] a *nidah* or a *yoledet* (post-menstruation or post-birth), who must ritually immerse at night.

TEXT 4D

A Place for Everyone

Talmud, Sanhedrin 90a

כָּל יִשְׂרָאֵל יֵשׁ לָהֶם חֵלֶק לָעוֹלָם הַבָּא, שֶׁנֶּאֱמַר: וְעַמֵּךְ כּוּלָּם
צַדִּיקִים לְעוֹלָם יִירְשׁוּ אָרֶץ, נֵצֶר מַטָּעַי מַעֲשֵׂה יָדַי לְהִתְפָּאֵר.

Every Jewish individual has a share in the World to Come, as it is stated, "Your people are all righteous—they will inherit the land forever; [they are] the branch of My planting, the work of My hands, in which I take pride" (ISAIAH 60:21).

KEY TERM 1.2

HEBREW TERM	אַגָדָה
ARAMAIC	אַגָדְתָא
TRANSLITERATION	*agadah or agadeta*
PRONUNCIATION	ah-GAH-dah / ah-gah-deh-TAH
LITERAL MEANING	***retelling* or *relating***
MEANING	Nonlegal sections of the Talmud. Topics covered include records of historical and contemporary events; homiletic interpretations of biblical texts; and ethical, spiritual, medicinal, and practical teachings and advice.

SEFER
Mark Podwal, aquatint color print on paper, New York, 1980

III. THE ORAL LAW

The extensive presentations and clarification of Jewish law that the Talmud records is referred to collectively as "the Oral Law." As its name suggests, this information was not explicitly recorded in the Five Books of Moses (referred to by contrast as "the Written Law"). A large portion of this material was legislated by sages who lived several or many generations after Moses. Judaism views the entire body of the Oral Law as binding upon us as an integral part of our biblical covenant with G-d.*

THE ORAL TORAH
Loren Hodes, charcoal on paper, Johannesburg, 2004

*Throughout this book, "G-d" and "L-rd" are written with a hyphen instead of an "o" (both in our own translations and when quoting others). This is one way we accord reverence to the sacred Divine name. This also reminds us that, even as we seek G-d, He transcends any human effort to describe His reality.

TEXT 5

Written and Oral

Maimonides, *Mishneh Torah*, introduction

כָּל הַמִצְווֹת שֶׁנִתְּנוּ לוֹ לְמֹשֶׁה בְּסִינַי - בְּפֵרוּשָׁן נִתְּנוּ.

שֶׁנֶאֱמַר: "וְאֶתְּנָה לְךָ אֶת לֻחֹת הָאֶבֶן, וְהַתּוֹרָה וְהַמִצְוָה" (שְׁמוֹת כד, יב): "תּוֹרָה", זוֹ תּוֹרָה שֶׁבִּכְתָב; וְ"מִצְוָה", זֶה פֵּרוּשָׁהּ.

וְצִוָנוּ לַעֲשׂוֹת הַתּוֹרָה עַל פִּי הַמִצְוָה. וּמִצְוָה זוֹ, הִיא הַנִקְרֵאת תּוֹרָה שֶׁבְּעַל פֶּה.

All of the commandments that were given by G-d to Moses at Mount Sinai [and recorded in the Five Books of Moses] were presented to Moses along with their [detailed] explanations [that were not recorded in those books].

The Torah itself refers to this in its statement, "I will give you the tablets of stone, and the Torah, and the *mitzvah*" (EXODUS 24:12). In this context, the phrase "the Torah" refers to the Written Law. The phrase "the *mitzvah*" refers to the explanation [of the Written Law].

G-d commanded us to fulfill "the Torah" in accordance with "the *mitzvah*." It is the latter instructions that we refer to as the Oral Law.

RABBI MOSHE BEN MAIMON (MAIMONIDES, RAMBAM) 1135–1204

Halachist, philosopher, author, and physician. Maimonides was born in Córdoba, Spain. After the conquest of Córdoba by the Almohads, he fled Spain and eventually settled in Cairo, Egypt. There, he became the leader of the Jewish community and served as court physician to the vizier of Egypt. He is most noted for authoring the *Mishneh Torah*, an encyclopedic arrangement of Jewish law; and for his philosophical work, *Guide for the Perplexed*. His rulings on Jewish law are integral to the formation of Halachic consensus.

TEXT 6

Legal Authority

Deuteronomy 17:8–11

כִּי יִפָּלֵא מִמְּךָ דָבָר לַמִּשְׁפָּט, בֵּין דָּם לְדָם בֵּין דִּין
לְדִין וּבֵין נֶגַע לָנֶגַע דִּבְרֵי רִיבֹת בִּשְׁעָרֶיךָ, וְקַמְתָּ
וְעָלִיתָ . . . אֶל הַשֹּׁפֵט אֲשֶׁר יִהְיֶה בַּיָּמִים הָהֵם,
וְדָרַשְׁתָּ וְהִגִּידוּ לְךָ אֵת דְּבַר הַמִּשְׁפָּט.

וְעָשִׂיתָ עַל פִּי הַדָּבָר אֲשֶׁר יַגִּידוּ לְךָ . . .
וְשָׁמַרְתָּ לַעֲשׂוֹת כְּכֹל אֲשֶׁר יוֹרוּךָ.

עַל פִּי הַתּוֹרָה אֲשֶׁר יוֹרוּךָ וְעַל הַמִּשְׁפָּט אֲשֶׁר יֹאמְרוּ לְךָ
תַּעֲשֶׂה, לֹא תָסוּר מִן הַדָּבָר אֲשֶׁר יַגִּידוּ לְךָ יָמִין וּשְׂמֹאל.

If, regarding matters of dispute within your [local] courts, a case is too baffling for you to decide, be it a controversy over blood, civil law, or lesions, you must rise up and ascend . . . to the supreme judge in that era. You should inquire, and they must inform you of the [correct] verdict in the case.

You must carry out the verdict that is announced to you . . . observing scrupulously all their instructions to you.

You must act in accordance with the instructions they give you and the ruling handed down to you. You must not deviate to the right or to the left from the rulings that they announce to you.

TEXT 7

Matzah Date

Exodus 12:18

בָּרִאשֹׁן בְּאַרְבָּעָה עָשָׂר יוֹם לַחֹדֶשׁ בָּעֶרֶב תֹּאכְלוּ מַצֹּת.

In the first [month], on the fourteenth day of that month, in the evening, you shall eat *matzot*.

FIGURE 1.2

The Parts of Jewish Law

	WRITTEN	RECEIVED	DERIVED	LEGISLATED
DEFINITIONS	Laws recorded in the Torah's text—the "lecture notes."	Laws *received* by Moses together with the Torah's text—the "full lecture."	Laws *derived* by the sages subsequent to Moses, directly from the Torah's text using the received hermeneutical methods.	Laws *legislated* by the sages throughout Jewish history, relying on their own initiative.
EXAMPLES	Eat matzah on the night of Passover.	A minimum of an olive-sized quantity of matzah must be eaten.	Passover matzah can only be baked from types of flour that can possibly turn into leavened bread.	On the night of Passover, the matzah must be eaten while reclining.

TEXT 8

Observing the Covenant

Exodus 19:5, 8

וְעַתָּה אִם שָׁמוֹעַ תִּשְׁמְעוּ בְּקֹלִי וּשְׁמַרְתֶּם אֶת בְּרִיתִי, וִהְיִיתֶם לִי סְגֻלָּה מִכָּל הָעַמִּים . . . וַיַּעֲנוּ כָל הָעָם יַחְדָּו וַיֹּאמְרוּ, כֹּל אֲשֶׁר דִּבֶּר ה' נַעֲשֶׂה.

If you listen to My voice and carefully observe My covenant, you will be a treasure to Me from among all the nations. . . . All the people responded in unison, and they proclaimed, "All that G-d has spoken, we will do!"

MATAN TORAH
Art by Abish, digital painting, 2023

IV. WHY DO JEWS STUDY SO MUCH LAW?

The study of the Torah has always been a central feature of Jewish life. For the past two millennia, the lion's share of that study has traditionally been dedicated to the study of Jewish law as presented in the Talmud. In part, this is because Judaism places primary focus on action; consequently, the parts of the Torah devoted to clarifying that action are heavily prioritized.

PLEADING BEFORE THE RABBINIC COURT
Artist unknown, oil on canvas, c. 1900, Vienna, Austria (Photo Credit: Menachem Adelman)

TEXT 9

Tripart Foundation

Mishnah, Avot 1:2

שִׁמְעוֹן הַצַּדִּיק הָיָה מִשְּׁיָרֵי כְנֶסֶת הַגְּדוֹלָה. הוּא הָיָה אוֹמֵר: עַל שְׁלֹשָׁה דְבָרִים הָעוֹלָם עוֹמֵד, עַל הַתּוֹרָה וְעַל הָעֲבוֹדָה וְעַל גְּמִילוּת חֲסָדִים.

Shimon the Righteous was one of the last surviving figures of the Men of the Great Assembly. He used to say, "The world stands upon three things: the Torah, the [Temple] service, and acts of lovingkindness."

THREE PILLARS
Yoram Raanan (b. 1953), acrylic on canvas, Israel

EXERCISE 1.1

Identify the last three efforts you made to study material that was not from the Torah or other Jewish learning: perhaps an educational book, video, or course. In the following chart, briefly summarize (a) the nature of the material, and (b) your purpose in pursuing that information.

TOPIC	PURPOSE

TEXT 10

Study Plan

Maimonides, *Mishneh Torah*, Laws of Torah Study 1:11

וְחַיָּב לְשַׁלֵּשׁ אֶת זְמַן לְמִידָתוֹ.

שְׁלִישׁ בַּתּוֹרָה שֶׁבִּכְתָב, וּשְׁלִישׁ בַּתּוֹרָה שֶׁבְּעַל פֶּה, וּשְׁלִישׁ יָבִין וְיַשְׂכִּיל אַחֲרִית דָּבָר מֵרֵאשִׁיתוֹ, וְיוֹצִיא דָּבָר מִדָּבָר, וִידַמֶּה דָּבָר לְדָבָר וְיָבִין בַּמִּדּוֹת שֶׁהַתּוֹרָה נִדְרֶשֶׁת בָּהֶן, עַד שֶׁיֵּדַע הֵיאַךְ הוּא עִקַּר הַמִּדּוֹת וְהֵיאַךְ יוֹצִיא הָאָסוּר וְהַמֻּתָּר וְכַיּוֹצֵא בָּהֶן מִדְּבָרִים שֶׁלָּמַד מִפִּי הַשְּׁמוּעָה.

וְעִנְיָן זֶה הוּא הַנִּקְרָא גְּמָרָא.

The time allotted to study should be divided into three parts:

A third should be devoted to the Written Law; a third to the Oral Law; and the last third should be spent in reflection, deducing conclusions from premises, developing implications of statements, comparing statements, and studying the hermeneutical principles by which the Torah is interpreted, until one knows the essence of these principles and how to deduce what is permitted and what is forbidden from what one has learned by tradition.

The latter topic is called *Gemara*.

TEXT 11

Primacy of Action

Mishnah, Avot 1:17

וְלֹא הַמִּדְרָשׁ עִקָּר, אֶלָּא הַמַּעֲשֶׂה.

The study is not the principal goal, but rather, the action.

WALKING TO THE SYNAGOGUE
Zvi Malnovitzer, oil on canvas, Benei Berak, Israel, 2005

V. THE SPIRITUAL BENEFITS OF TALMUD STUDY

Judaism views the Torah's laws as beyond merely informing our activity and choices. Rather, they are cherished as direct manifestations of G-d's will and wisdom. We therefore value the study of the Talmud for facilitating a profound connection with G-d and delivering G-d's holiness into the elements of our lives that are governed by the specific laws we study.

TORAH STUDY
Lesya Bershov (b. 1975, Ukrainian, Israeli), oil on canvas, Israel

TEXT 12

Double Service

Rabbi Shneur Zalman of Liadi, *Igrot Kodesh*, p. 210

מָה שֶׁנִקְרָא בִּלְשׁוֹן רוּסְיָה דִמְדִינָתֵינוּ "בָּאהַא מַאלִיצַא", עִנְיָן זֶה נֶחֱלָק אֶצְלֵנוּ כְּלַל הַיְהוּדִים לִשְׁנֵי עִנְיָינִים

עִנְיָן א' לִימוּד וּקְרִיאָה בְּתָנָ"ךְ וְתַלְמוּד וּמִדְרָשִׁים וּמְפָרְשֵׁיהֶם, וּבַפּוֹסְקִים הַמְקַצְּרִים דִינֵי הַתַּלְמוּד . . .

עִנְיָן ב' הִיא הַתְּפִלָּה.

That which we refer to in our Russian language as *Boga malizia* (Divine service) is divided by all of us Jews into two parts:

The first is the reading and studying of the Scriptures, Talmud, Midrashim, and their commentaries—as well as the study of the legal codes that summarize the laws of the Talmud. . . .

The second aspect is the concept of prayer.

RABBI SHNEUR ZALMAN OF LIADI (ALTER REBBE) 1745–1812

Chasidic rebbe, Halachic authority, and founder of the Chabad movement. The Alter Rebbe was born in Liozna, Belarus, and was among the principal students of the Magid of Mezeritch. His numerous works include the *Tanya*, an early classic containing the fundamentals of Chabad Chasidism; and *Shulchan Aruch HaRav*, an expanded and reworked code of Jewish law.

TEXT 13

Knowing the Unknowable

Rabbi Shneur Zalman of Liadi, *Tanya*, *Likutei Amarim*, ch. 5

הֲלָכָה זוֹ, הִיא חָכְמָתוֹ וּרְצוֹנוֹ שֶׁל הַקָּדוֹשׁ בָּרוּךְ הוּא, שֶׁעָלָה בִּרְצוֹנוֹ, שֶׁכְּשֶׁיִּטְעוֹן רְאוּבֵן כָּךְ וְכָךְ דֶּרֶךְ מָשָׁל וְשִׁמְעוֹן כָּךְ וְכָךְ - יִהְיֶה הַפְּסַק בֵּינֵיהֶם כָּךְ וְכָךְ.

וְאַף אִם לֹא הָיָה וְלֹא יִהְיֶה הַדָּבָר הַזֶּה לְעוֹלָם, לָבֹא לְמִשְׁפָּט עַל טְעָנוֹת וּתְבִיעוֹת אֵלוּ, מִכָּל מָקוֹם, מֵאַחַר שֶׁכָּךְ עָלָה בִּרְצוֹנוֹ וְחָכְמָתוֹ שֶׁל הַקָּדוֹשׁ בָּרוּךְ הוּא, שֶׁאִם יִטְעוֹן זֶה כָּךְ וְזֶה כָּךְ, יִהְיֶה הַפְּסַק כָּךְ, הֲרֵי כְּשֶׁאָדָם יוֹדֵעַ וּמַשִּׂיג בְּשִׂכְלוֹ פְּסַק זֶה כַּהֲלָכָה הָעֲרוּכָה בְּמִשְׁנָה אוֹ גְמָרָא אוֹ פּוֹסְקִים, הֲרֵי זֶה מַשִּׂיג וְתוֹפֵס וּמַקִּיף בְּשִׂכְלוֹ רְצוֹנוֹ וְחָכְמָתוֹ שֶׁל הַקָּדוֹשׁ בָּרוּךְ הוּא, דְּלֵית מַחֲשָׁבָה תְּפִיסָא בֵּיהּ וְלֹא בִּרְצוֹנוֹ וְחָכְמָתוֹ, כִּי אִם בְּהִתְלַבְּשׁוּתָם בַּהֲלָכוֹת הָעֲרוּכוֹת לְפָנֵינוּ.

Halachah is G-d's wisdom and will. For so it arose in G-d's will that if, for example, Reuben pleads in one way and Simeon in another, the verdict should be such and such.

Now, it is possible that this particular litigation never occurred in reality. Nor is it ever destined to be presented for judgment as these precise disputes and claims. Nevertheless, G-d's will and wisdom has determined that in the event of a person pleading this way and the other litigant pleading that way, the verdict shall be such and such.

Accordingly, when we [study and] understand, and properly comprehend with our intellect the details of such a scenario in accordance with the law presented in the Mishnah, Gemara, or *poskim* [later codes], we have thereby comprehended, grasped, and encompassed with our intellect the will and wisdom of G-d!

We have effectively understood something of the One Whom no thought can grasp, and Whose will and wisdom are beyond understanding—until they are invested within the laws that have been set out for us.

TEXT 14

Butchers and Scholars

Rabbi Shneur Zalman of Liadi, *Torah Or* 94c

קַצָּב הַמִּתְעַסֵּק בְּנִתּוּחַ אֵבְרֵי הַבְּהֵמָה לִנְתָחִים וּבִבְנֵי מֵעַיִם וְכוּ' הוּא קַצָּב. אַךְ הַמִּתְעַסֵּק לֵידַע כָּל פְּרָטֵי הֲלָכוֹת הַתְּלוּיִין בְּאֵבְרֵי הַבְּהֵמָה לְהַבְדִּיל בֵּין טְרֵפָה לִכְשֵׁרָה . . . מִתְגַּלֶּה וּמִתְבָּרֵר רָצוֹן הָעֶלְיוֹן וְחָכְמָתוֹ יִתְבָּרֵךְ.

A butcher who chops an animal's limbs into pieces and processes its innards is nothing more than a butcher. By contrast, someone who occupies themself with understanding the specific details of Jewish law associated with the limbs of the animal, laws that facilitate the ability to distinguish between an animal that is kosher for consumption and one that is disqualified (*terefah*) . . . that person is revealing and clarifying the Divine will and wisdom!

KEY POINTS

1. The Talmud has influenced every facet of Jewish culture. Its study has been, and remains, a source of joy for Jewish communities worldwide. One historian suggested that the Talmud is responsible for the Jews having survived their long exile.

2. The Talmud is primarily a record of Halachah, Jewish law, which covers every facet of Jewish life, thereby allowing Jews to connect with G-d in whatever they are doing.

3. Although the Written Torah is the source of Jewish law, the vast majority of Jewish law is not explicitly recorded in it. G-d taught these laws orally to Moses when He gave us the entirety of the Torah at Mount Sinai.

4. In addition to laws received by Moses directly from G-d, the Oral Law contains laws that were derived by the sages from the Torah's text as well as laws legislated by the sages over the generations.

5. The famous Jewish devotion to learning is rooted in the tremendous spiritual significance attributed to Torah study—to the extent that it is considered one of the three pillars on which the world stands. Although most Jews are not lawyers or judges, the study of Talmud—Jewish law—occupies a large portion of traditional Jewish study.

6 Jews view the study of law as a mode of religious worship because the laws are the will and wisdom of G-d. When we absorb a Torah law with our minds, we are bonding with a sliver of the Divine mind.

7 When we study a Torah law on a given subject, we bring the Divine wisdom contained in that law into contact with that subject. And since Jewish law's scope is so broad that it encompasses every facet of our lives, studying Halachah brings holiness into every facet of our lives.

Continue learning at
myjli.com/talmud

The Philosophical Perspective

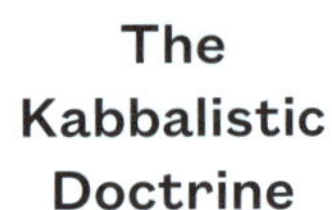

The Kabbalistic Doctrine

The Utilitarian Approach

The Chasidic Insight

The Midrashic Parable

The Philosophical Perspective

True law is right reason in agreement with nature; it is of universal application, unchanging and everlasting. It summons to duty by its commands, and averts from wrongdoing by its prohibitions. . . . It is a sin to try to alter this law, nor is it allowable to attempt to repeal any part of it, and it is impossible to abolish it entirely. We cannot be freed from its obligations by senate or people, and we need not look outside ourselves for an expounder or interpreter of it. And there will not be different laws at Rome and at Athens, or different laws now and in the future, but one eternal and unchangeable law will be valid for all nations and all times.

Cicero (*De re publica*, Book III, section 22)

SUMMARY

This perspective is often called the "natural law theory." It posits that morality is intrinsic to human nature. The laws that people and societies create to promote good actions and prohibit bad actions derive from our inherent sense of right and wrong.

The Utilitarian Approach

When mankind increased in number, craft, and ambition, it became necessary to entertain conceptions of more permanent dominion; and to appropriate to individuals not the immediate use only, but the very substance of the thing to be used. Otherwise innumerable tumults must have arisen, and the good order of the world been continually broken and disturbed, while a variety of persons were striving to get the first occupation of the same thing, or disputing which of them had actually gained it. As human life also grew more and more refined, abundance of conveniences were devised to render it more easy, commodious, and agreeable; as, habitations for shelter and safety, and raiment for warmth and decency. But no man would be at the trouble to provide either, so long as he had only an usufructuary property in them, which was to cease the instant that he quitted possession; if, as soon as he walked out of his tent, or pulled off his garment, the next stranger who came by would have a right to inhabit the one, and to wear the other.

William Blackstone (*Commentaries on the Laws of England*, vol. 2, ch. 1)

SUMMARY

Laws are created simply for practical reasons. For example, if there were no laws governing ownership and forbidding theft, people would be fighting all the time, and no one would bother to build a house or sew a garment if anyone could just come and take it from them.

The Midrashic Parable

Architects who build palaces do not do so on their own; they have scrolls and notebooks with which they consult on how to place the rooms, where to set the doors, etc. So, too, G-d looked into the Torah and created the world.

Midrash, Bereshit Rabah 1:1

SUMMARY

Laws are legislated by the Torah, defining how the Creator desires life on earth to be lived. Indeed, the laws of life preceded life itself: first there was the law, embodying the Creator's vision; then came Creation, formed to optimally reflect and implement that vision.

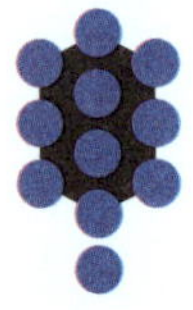

The Kabbalistic Doctrine

The soul of a righteous person has 248 limbs, and each limb has many sparks. . . . This is why the righteous cherish their possessions, as these have been bestowed on them from Above. For if this object were not critical [for the person's mission in life] it would not have been given to them by G-d.

The Arizal, Rabbi Yitzchak Luria (*Likutei Torah*, Vayishlach)

SUMMARY

The law's function is not just to create legal relationships—for example, to decree that object B belongs to person A—but also to reflect and safeguard deep-seated spiritual truths. Every existence, including inanimate objects, possesses a "soul," a spark of Divine potential. When an object is owned by particular person, this means that this person has been uniquely entrusted by G-d to develop and "elevate" that spiritual potential, which is in fact a spark of the person's own soul.

The Chasidic Insight

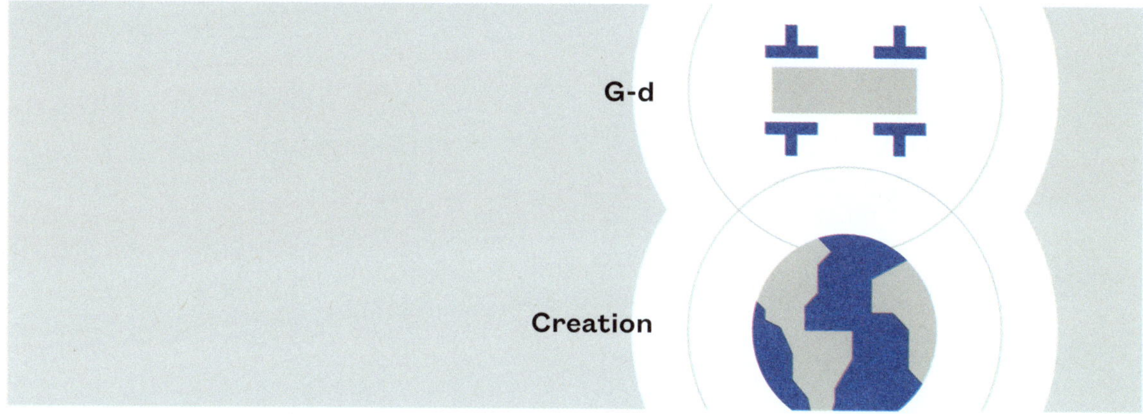

Halachah (Torah law) is G-d's wisdom and will. For so it arose in G-d's will that if, for example, Reuben pleads in one way and Simeon in another, the verdict should be thus and thus. Now, it is possible that this particular litigation never occurred in reality. Nor is it ever destined to be presented for judgment as these precise disputes and claims. Nevertheless, G-d's will and wisdom have determined that in the event of a person pleading this way and the other litigant pleading that way, the verdict shall be such and such. Accordingly, when we [study and] understand, and properly comprehend with our intellect the details of such a scenario in accordance with the law presented in the Mishnah, Gemara, or poskim *(later codes), we have thereby comprehended, grasped, and encompassed with our intellect the will and wisdom of G-d! We have effectively understood something of the One . . . Whom no thought can grasp, and Whose will and wisdom are beyond understanding—until they are invested within the laws that have been set out for us.*

Rabbi Shneur Zalman of Liadi (*Tanya, Likutei Amarim*, ch. 5)

SUMMARY

G-d is infinite and perfect, yet He desired to create and enter into a relationship with a finite and imperfect world. So G-d took His infinite, suprarational wisdom and will and invested it within the humanly comprehensible and implementable laws of the Torah. When we study and fulfill these laws, we incorporate their Divine essence as the stuff and substance of our lives.

LESSON 2

THE MISHNAH

The origins, authors, and contents of Judaism's first legal code

See how Jewish law shifted from oral tradition to written code, and encounter the Mishnah's precise style, tight structure, and tolerance for debate—and its spiritual significance in Jewish life.

THE EXODUS AND THE BABYLONIAN EXILE OF ISRAEL
Alex Levin, oil on canvas, Jerusalem, 2016

I. COMMITTING THE ORAL TORAH TO WRITING

Moses recorded the Torah with ink on parchment but he did not record *all* of the Torah; he transmitted the majority of its details orally. This oral tradition ("Oral Torah") continued to be passed faithfully through the ages by word of mouth, from sage to sage and from teacher to student. Today's study addresses the cause, purpose, and process of the oral tradition's eventual recording in written format.

The oral order of transmission was abruptly upended due to historical crises inflicted on the Jewish people through brutal and systematic Roman persecution. As a result of the upheavals, disputes in matters of Jewish law (Halachah) proliferated, threatening the very survival of the oral tradition. At that point, Rabbi Yehudah the Prince composed the Mishnah to preserve the Oral Torah for posterity.

THE LAST DAYS OF RABBI BEN EZRA
Alfred Aaron Wolmark, oil on canvas, Krakow, Poland, 1905 (Ben Uri Gallery and Museum, London)

TEXT 1

Written and Oral Boundaries

Talmud, Gitin 60b

דְּבָרִים שֶׁבִּכְתָב אִי אַתָּה רַשַּׁאי לְאוֹמְרָן עַל פֶּה,
דְּבָרִים שֶׁבְּעַל פֶּה אִי אַתָּה רַשַּׁאי לְאוֹמְרָן בִּכְתָב.

Material that was conveyed as a text may not be recited orally [without a script], and material that was conveyed orally may not be recorded as text.

BABYLONIAN TALMUD

A literary work of monumental proportions that draws upon the legal, spiritual, intellectual, ethical, and historical traditions of Judaism. The 37 tractates of the Babylonian Talmud contain the teachings of the Jewish sages from the period after the destruction of the 2nd Temple through the 5th century CE. It has served as the primary vehicle for the transmission of the Oral Law and the education of Jews over the centuries; it is the entry point for all subsequent legal, ethical, and theological Jewish scholarship.

KEY TERM 2.1

HEBREW TERM	תַּנָּא (תַּנָּאִים)
TRANSLITERATION	*tanna* (plural: *tanna'im*)
PRONUNCIATION	TAH-nah (plural: tah-NAH-eem)
LITERAL MEANING	**repeater, teacher**
MEANING	a sage whose teachings are recorded in the Mishnah

TEXT 2

Clearly Anonymous

Rabbi Sherira Ga'on, *Igeret DeRabbi Sherira Ga'on*

וְהָכֵי הַוְיָא מִילְּתָא דְרִאשׁוֹנִים לֹא אִתְיַדְעוּ שְׁמָהָתְהוֹן אֶלָּא [שְׁמוֹתָן] שֶׁל נְשִׂיאִים וְשֶׁל אֲבוֹת בָּתֵּי דִּין בִּלְבַד מִשּׁוּם דְּלָא הֲוָה מַחְלוֹקֶת בֵּינֵיהוֹן אֶלָּא כָּל טַעֲמֵי דְּאוֹרַיְיתָא הֲווּ יַדְעִין לְהוֹן יְדִיעָה בְּרוּרָה.

The ancient Torah scholars did not publish the names of the authors of particular Torah teachings—with the exception of the names of a head or deputy of the Sanhedrin—because among them there was no controversy; they had clarity of knowledge regarding all Torah concepts.

RABBI SHERIRA GA'ON
C. 906–1006

Rabbi and Halachic authority. Rabbi Sherira was born in Babylon into a prestigious scholarly family and in 968 was appointed head of the yeshiva in Pumbedita, a position known as the "Ga'on." As Ga'on, Rabbi Sherira served as the leading Halachic authority in the Jewish world, penning many responsa to communities ranging from Spain in the west to India in the east. He is best known for *Igeret DeRabbi Sherira Ga'on*, in which he explains how the Talmud was formulated and surveys Jewish history until his time.

THE SANHEDRIM IN SESSION
Engraving (artist unknown) from *The Pictorial History of the World*, James Dabney McCabe. (Philadelphia, PA, Chicago, IL, St. Louis, MO, and Dayton, OH: The National Publishing Co., 1877)

TEXT 3

Resolving Doubt

Maimonides, *Mishneh Torah*, Laws of Rebels 1:4

כְּשֶׁהָיָה בֵּית דִּין הַגָּדוֹל קַיָּם לֹא הָיְתָה מַחֲלֹקֶת בְּיִשְׂרָאֵל. אֶלָּא כָּל דִּין שֶׁנּוֹלַד בּוֹ סָפֵק לְאֶחָד מִיִּשְׂרָאֵל שׁוֹאֵל לְבֵית דִּין שֶׁבְּעִירוֹ.

אִם יָדְעוּ אָמְרוּ לוֹ. אִם לָאו הֲרֵי הַשּׁוֹאֵל עִם אוֹתוֹ בֵּית דִּין אוֹ עִם שְׁלוּחָיו עוֹלִין לִירוּשָׁלַיִם וְשׁוֹאֲלִין לְבֵית דִּין שֶׁבְּהַר הַבַּיִת.

אִם יָדְעוּ אָמְרוּ לוֹ. אִם לָאו הַכֹּל בָּאִין לְבֵית דִּין שֶׁעַל פֶּתַח הָעֲזָרָה.

אִם יָדְעוּ אָמְרוּ לָהֶן, וְאִם לָאו הַכֹּל בָּאִין לְלִשְׁכַּת הַגָּזִית לְבֵית דִּין הַגָּדוֹל וְשׁוֹאֲלִין.

אִם הָיָה הַדָּבָר שֶׁנּוֹלַד בּוֹ הַסָּפֵק לַכֹּל יָדוּעַ אֵצֶל בֵּית דִּין הַגָּדוֹל . . . אוֹמְרִים מִיָּד.

אִם לֹא הָיָה הַדָּבָר בָּרוּר אֵצֶל בֵּית דִּין הַגָּדוֹל דָּנִין בּוֹ בִּשְׁעָתָן וְנוֹשְׂאִין וְנוֹתְנִין בַּדָּבָר עַד שֶׁיַּסְכִּימוּ כֻּלָּן. אוֹ יַעַמְדוּ לְמִנְיָן וְיֵלְכוּ אַחַר הָרֹב וְיֹאמְרוּ לְכָל הַשּׁוֹאֲלִים כָּךְ הֲלָכָה.

As long as the Supreme Sanhedrin functioned, there were never prolonged differences of opinion among the Jewish people. Rather, any Jewish individual who developed a doubt regarding any law would simply inquire of the Jewish court of their city.

RABBI MOSHE BEN MAIMON (MAIMONIDES, RAMBAM) 1135–1204

Halachist, philosopher, author, and physician. Maimonides was born in Córdoba, Spain. After the conquest of Córdoba by the Almohads, he fled Spain and eventually settled in Cairo, Egypt. There, he became the leader of the Jewish community and served as court physician to the vizier of Egypt. He is most noted for authoring the *Mishneh Torah*, an encyclopedic arrangement of Jewish law; and for his philosophical work, *Guide for the Perplexed*. His rulings on Jewish law are integral to the formation of Halachic consensus.

If that local court was aware of the solution, it would inform that individual. If not, both the questioner and that court—or its agents—would ascend to Jerusalem and pose the dilemma to the [greater] court that held session on the Temple Mount.

If that court knew the answer, it would supply it. If not, the entire group would proceed together to the [higher] court that held session at the entrance to the Temple courtyard.

If it knew the solution, it would supply it. If not, they would all proceed to the Chamber of Hewn Stone, in which the Supreme Sanhedrin held court, and pose the dilemma to the Sanhedrin.

If the resolution of this matter—that was unresolved by all the previous courts—was known to the Supreme Sanhedrin . . . they would provide the decision immediately.

If the matter was unclear to the Supreme Sanhedrin, its members would deliberate on the spot, debating back and forth among themselves, until they reached a uniform decision. If they were unable to reach a consensus decision, a vote would be held and the majority position would be adopted. The Sanhedrin would then inform the entire assemblage that had posed the dilemma: "This is the Halachah."

TEXT 4

Fish out of Water

Talmud, Berachot 61b

אָמַר לוֹ: אֶמְשׁוֹל לְךָ מָשָׁל, לְמָה הַדָּבָר דּוֹמֶה – לְשׁוּעָל שֶׁהָיָה מְהַלֵּךְ עַל גַּב הַנָּהָר, וְרָאָה דָּגִים שֶׁהָיוּ מִתְקַבְּצִים מִמָּקוֹם לְמָקוֹם.

אָמַר לָהֶם: מִפְּנֵי מָה אַתֶּם בּוֹרְחִים?

אָמְרוּ לוֹ: מִפְּנֵי רְשָׁתוֹת שֶׁמְּבִיאִין עָלֵינוּ בְּנֵי אָדָם.

אָמַר לָהֶם: רְצוֹנְכֶם שֶׁתַּעֲלוּ לַיַּבָּשָׁה, וְנָדוּר אֲנִי וְאַתֶּם, כְּשֵׁם שֶׁדָּרוּ אֲבוֹתַי עִם אֲבוֹתֵיכֶם?

אָמְרוּ לוֹ: אַתָּה הוּא שֶׁאוֹמְרִים עָלֶיךָ פִּקֵּחַ שֶׁבַּחַיּוֹת?! לֹא פִּקֵּחַ אַתָּה, אֶלָּא טִפֵּשׁ אַתָּה! וּמָה בִּמְקוֹם חִיּוּתֵנוּ, אָנוּ מִתְיָרְאִין, בִּמְקוֹם מִיתָתֵנוּ – עַל אַחַת כַּמָּה וְכַמָּה.

אַף אֲנַחְנוּ עַכְשָׁיו שֶׁאָנוּ יוֹשְׁבִים וְעוֹסְקִים בַּתּוֹרָה, שֶׁכָּתוּב בָּהּ: "כִּי הוּא חַיֶּיךָ וְאֹרֶךְ יָמֶיךָ", כָּךְ, אִם אָנוּ הוֹלְכִים וּמְבַטְּלִים מִמֶּנָּה – עַל אַחַת כַּמָּה וְכַמָּה.

Rabbi Akiva said: Let me relate a parable. To what is this phenomenon compared? To a fox that strolls along a river and notices that fish have gathered and are repeatedly racing from one side of the river to the other.

The fox inquires, "What are you fleeing?"

The fish reply, "We're fleeing from nets that humans are casting for us!"

Suggests the fox, "Would you like to ascend to dry land to escape the nets? We can live together up here, just as my ancestors resided with your ancestors!"

The fish retorted, "Aren't you the creature they describe as the cleverest animal? You are not clever—you are a fool! If we are afraid for our survival while we are in the water—our natural habitat that sustains our very life—then in a habitat that causes our death we would be all the more certain of dying!"

The same is true of us Jews: We are actively engaged in studying the Torah that is described as "your life and your length of days" (DEUTERONOMY 30:20), and nevertheless, we fear for our lives. If we were to go ahead and desist from its study, we would have far greater grounds to fear for our survival!

YEARNING FOR THE SOURCE
Yossi Rosenstein, acrylic on canvas, Israel, 2020

FIGURE 2.1

The Family of the Princes

NAME	DEATH	ACHIEVEMENTS
HILLEL THE GREAT	C. 10 CE	Led the Jewish recovery from the Herodian massacres Founded *Beit Hillel*, the rabbinic school whose views are accepted as Halachah
SHIMON BEN HILLEL	Unknown	(Little is known about him)
RABBAN GAMLIEL, THE ELDER	C. 50	Led the Jewish people through the era of Roman procurator governance
RABBAN SHIMON BEN GAMLIEL, THE MARTYRED	C. 70	Murdered by the Romans during the revolt that led to the Temple's destruction
RABBAN GAMLIEL OF YAVNEH	C. 120	Led the recovery following the Temple's destruction
RABBAN SHIMON BEN GAMLIEL [THE SECOND]	C. 170	Led the recovery from the Hadrianic persecutions
RABBI YEHUDAH THE PRINCE ("REBBI")	C. 200	Organized the writing of the Mishnah

TEXT 5

The Great Teacher

Maimonides, Mishnah, introduction

וְהָיָה יָחִיד בְּדוֹרוֹ וְאֶחָד בִּזְמַנּוֹ אִישׁ שֶׁנִּמְצְאוּ בּוֹ כָּל הַחֲמוּדוֹת וְהַמִּדּוֹת הַטּוֹבוֹת עַד שֶׁזָּכָה בָּהֶם אֵצֶל אַנְשֵׁי דוֹרוֹ לִקְרוֹתוֹ רַבֵּינוּ הַקָּדוֹשׁ וּשְׁמוֹ יְהוּדָה.

וְהָיָה בְּחָכְמָה וּבְמַעֲלָה בְּתַכְלִיתָם כְּמוֹ שֶׁאָמְרוּ (גִּיטִּין נט, א) מִימוֹת מֹשֶׁה רַבֵּינוּ וְעַד רַבִּי לֹא רָאִינוּ תּוֹרָה וּגְדוּלָּה בְּמָקוֹם אֶחָד.

וְהָיָה בְּתַכְלִית הַחֲסִידוּת וְהָעֲנָוָה וְהַרְחָקַת הַתַּעֲנוּגִים . . .

וְהָיָה צַח לָשׁוֹן וּמוּפְלָג מִכָּל הָאָדָם בִּלְשׁוֹן הַקֹּדֶשׁ עַד שֶׁהַחֲכָמִים עֲלֵיהֶם הַשָּׁלוֹם הָיוּ לוֹמְדִים פֵּירוּשׁ מָה שֶׁנִּשְׁתַּבֵּשׁ עֲלֵיהֶם מֵאוֹתִיּוֹת הַמִּקְרָא מִדִּבְרֵי עֲבָדָיו וּמְשָׁרְתָיו.

He was unique in his generation, singular in his era, filled with all of the pleasant and desirable good character traits, to the extent that he earned the great merit whereby all the people of his own generation referred to him reverently: Rabbeinu Hakadosh, "our holy teacher." His name was Yehudah.

He was entirely complete in wisdom and virtue. In fact, our sages stated that "We have not seen such a combination of Torah and greatness in a single individual from the days of Moshe Rabbeinu ('our teacher Moses') until Rebbi ('the teacher')" (TALMUD, GITIN 59A).

He was perfect in piety and humility, and he distanced himself from material pleasures. . . .

He was eloquent in speech, and his knowledge of the holy tongue [biblical Hebrew] was so far beyond all other people that the sages would learn the meaning of unfamiliar words in Scripture from the terms used in casual conversation by Rabbi Yehudah's personal servants and attendants!

FIGURE 2.2

Reasons for Composing the Mishnah

PROBLEM	CAUSE	SOLUTION
Increased Halachic disputes	Inability to consult and reach consensus due to relentless persecution and increasing dispersion	Take advantage of a relatively peaceful window of time to reach consensus and record the Mishnah
Greater risk of inaccuracies	Students with increasingly limited bandwidth for studying and memorizing Halachah; reduced communication between centers of study	Compose a uniform Halachic compendium for all Torah institutions to ensure accuracy
Chain of transmission on brink of severance	Increased focus on surviving persecution reducing the ability to memorize the vast data of the oral tradition	Formulate a written record of the laws

TEXT 6

Writing Motivations

Maimonides, *Mishneh Torah*, introduction

וְלָמָּה עָשָׂה רַבֵּנוּ הַקָּדוֹשׁ כָּךְ וְלֹא הִנִּיחַ הַדָּבָר כְּמוֹת שֶׁהָיָה? לְפִי שֶׁרָאָה שֶׁתַּלְמִידִים מִתְמַעֲטִין וְהוֹלְכִין וְהַצָּרוֹת מִתְחַדְּשׁוֹת וּבָאוֹת וּמַלְכוּת רוֹמִי פּוֹשֶׁטֶת בָּעוֹלָם וּמִתְגַּבֶּרֶת. וְיִשְׂרָאֵל מִתְגַּלְגְּלִין וְהוֹלְכִין לַקְּצָווֹת.

חִבֵּר חִבּוּר אֶחָד לִהְיוֹת בְּיַד כֻּלָּם כְּדֵי שֶׁיִּלְמְדוּהוּ בִּמְהֵרָה וְלֹא יִשָּׁכַח.

Why did Rabbeinu Hakadosh make [such a radical move] instead of perpetuating the status quo? He saw that serious Torah students were consistently dwindling in number, that fresh calamities were constantly striking the Jewish people, that the oppressive Roman Empire was spreading throughout the world and becoming ever more powerful, and that the Jewish people were forced to wander far apart and disperse to the furthest ends of civilization.

He therefore composed a single compendium that would be available to everyone, so that the laws could be studied quickly and not be forgotten.

FIGURE 2.3

The *Tanna'im*

	APPROXIMATE YEARS	NOTED *TANNA'IM*	HISTORICAL EVENTS
HILLEL AND SHAMAI	40 BCE–10 CE	• Hillel • Shamai	• Roman takeover of the Holy Land • Rule of Herod
STUDENTS OF HILLEL AND SHAMAI	10 CE–70 CE	• R. Yochanan ben Zakai • R. Gamliel Hazaken • R. Shimon ben Gamliel • R. Yishma'el *Kohen Gadol*	• Era of Roman procurators • The First Jewish War • Destruction of the Temple
GENERATION OF YAVNEH	70 CE–120 CE	• R. Gamliel (the Second) • R. Yehoshua • R. Eliezer • R. Yose HaGelili	• Flavian dynasty ends • Rule of Trajan • Hadrian becomes emperor
GENERATION OF THE BAR KOCHBA REVOLT	120 CE–140 CE	• R. Akiva • R. Tarfon • R. Yishma'el	• Bar Kochba Revolt • Period of *shemad* (extreme religious persecution)
RABBI AKIVA'S STUDENTS	140 CE–165 CE	• R. Me'ir • R. Yehudah • R. Shimon • R. Yose	• Post-Hadrian recovery
THE COMPILERS OF THE MISHNAH	165 CE–220 CE	• R. Yehudah Hanasi ("the Prince") • R. Elazar ben Shimon • R. Natan	• Benign reigns of Marcus Aurelius and Commodus

II. THE MISHNAH

The Mishnah is a meticulously written compilation of the Oral Torah's laws, organized into six volumes, referred to as "the six orders of the Mishnah" (*Shishah Sidrei Mishnah*). These orders encompass a broad range of Jewish laws, reflecting the breadth of daily and religious Jewish life.

The first page of Tractate Berachot in the Kaufmann Mishnah, the oldest complete manuscript of the Mishnah. Copied on parchment in the tenth or eleventh century, the origins of this rare manuscript are not conclusively known. (David Kaufmann Collection of Medieval Hebrew Manuscripts, Hungarian Academy of Sciences Library, Budapest)

KEY TERM 2.2

HEBREW TERM	מִשְׁנָה
TRANSLITERATION	***Mishnah***
PRONUNCIATION	MISH-nah
LITERAL MEANING	**review, teaching**
MEANING	the text that serves as the initial official record of the laws of the Torah's oral tradition

FIGURE 2.4

Mishnah Units

ORDERS	6
TRACTATES	63
CHAPTERS	Approx. 525
***MISHNAYOT* (MISHNAHS)**	Approx. 4,200
WORDS	Approx. 200,000

FIGURE 2.5

The Six Orders

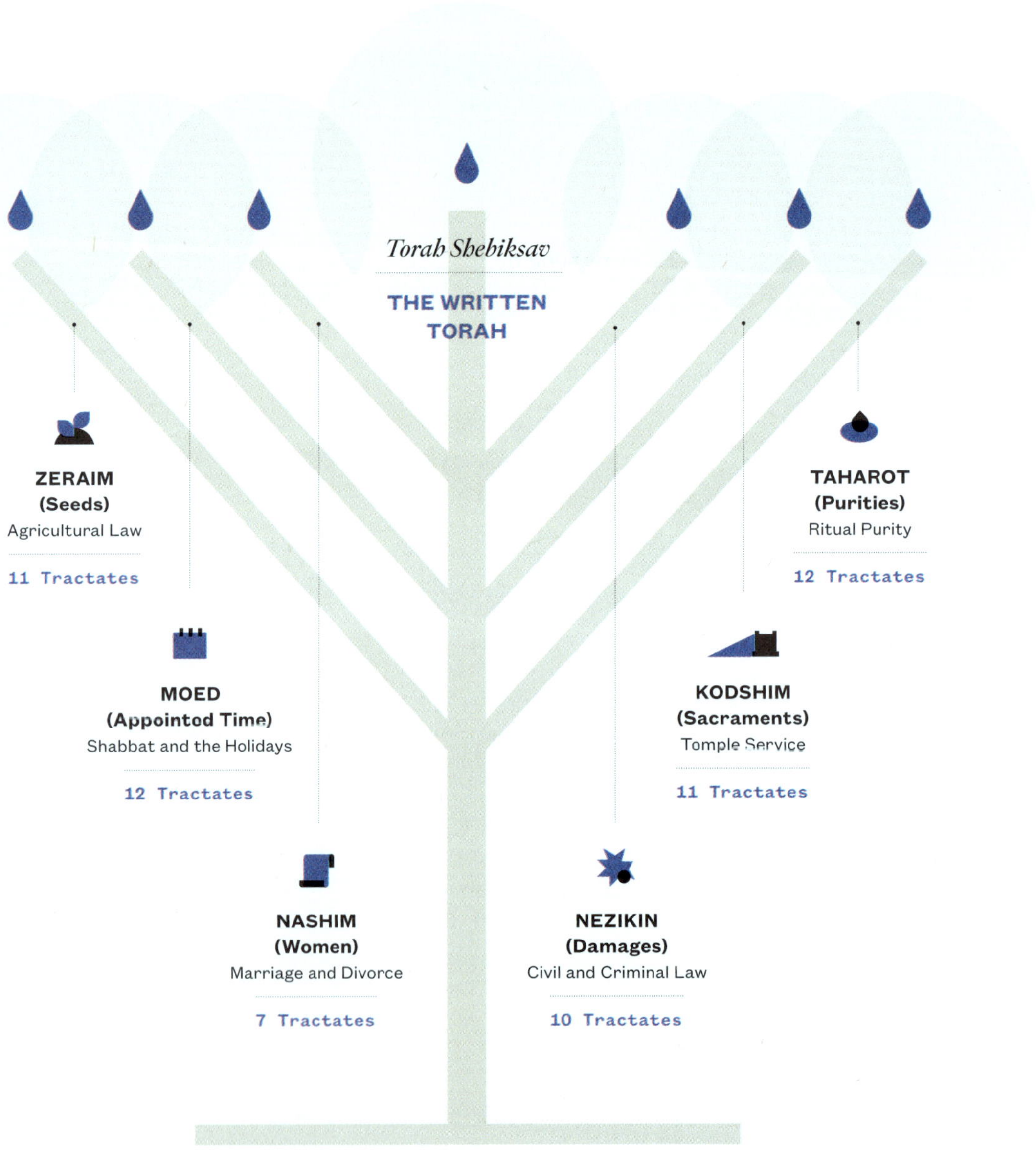

Torah Shebiksav

THE WRITTEN TORAH

ZERAIM
(Seeds)
Agricultural Law
11 Tractates

MOED
(Appointed Time)
Shabbat and the Holidays
12 Tractates

NASHIM
(Women)
Marriage and Divorce
7 Tractates

NEZIKIN
(Damages)
Civil and Criminal Law
10 Tractates

KODSHIM
(Sacraments)
Temple Service
11 Tractates

TAHAROT
(Purities)
Ritual Purity
12 Tractates

EXERCISE 2.1

Consult the above graphic for the titles of each of the Mishnah's six major divisions. Then review the following list of twelve random topics of Jewish law and record the name of the order of the Mishnah to which you best imagine each topic belongs.

1	Laws forbidding the use of the fruit of a tree during its first three years	
2	Laws governing the delivery of a bill of divorce via an agent	
3	A list of the psalms sung by the Levites during the Holy Temple's daily service	
4	Laws concerning the Red Heifer	
5	Laws concerning the Passover *seder*	
6	Laws concerning the obligation to return lost property to its owner	
7	Laws governing the portions of the Torah to be read on Shabbat and holidays	
8	Laws of vows	
9	Laws governing interactions between Jews and idolaters	
10	A discussion on the identity of the books of Scripture to be considered part of the Tanach	
11	Laws regarding the prohibition of mixing meat and milk	
12	Laws of the daily prayers	

III. A TASTE OF MISHNAH

Designed as a compact memory triggering device, the Mishnah was composed in concise and precise language. As a result, each nuance of the text is deeply meaningful. It always means more than it says, based on an assumption of prior Torah knowledge. It also includes multiple Halachic views, providing depth of understanding.

JEWISH MEDICAL ETHICS
Mark Podwal, ink on paper, New York, 1999

TEXT 7

Passover Laws

Mishnah, Pesachim 10:1–2

עַרְבֵי פְסָחִים סָמוּךְ לַמִּנְחָה, לֹא יֹאכַל אָדָם עַד שֶׁתֶּחְשַׁךְ.

וַאֲפִילוּ עָנִי שֶׁבְּיִשְׂרָאֵל לֹא יֹאכַל עַד שֶׁיָּסֵב.

וְלֹא יִפְחֲתוּ לוֹ מֵאַרְבַּע כּוֹסוֹת שֶׁל יַיִן, וַאֲפִילוּ מִן הַתַּמְחוּי.

מָזְגוּ לוֹ כוֹס רִאשׁוֹן, בֵּית שַׁמַּאי אוֹמְרִים, מְבָרֵךְ עַל הַיּוֹם, וְאַחַר כָּךְ מְבָרֵךְ עַל הַיַּיִן. וּבֵית הִלֵּל אוֹמְרִים, מְבָרֵךְ עַל הַיַּיִן, וְאַחַר כָּךְ מְבָרֵךְ עַל הַיּוֹם.

We must refrain from eating on the eve of Passover, from close to the time for reciting the Minchah prayers until after darkness has fallen.

Even the most destitute person in the Jewish nation should not eat, unless he is reclining.

He should not be provided with less than four cups of wine, even if he is being supplied by the public food bank.

When they pour him his first cup of wine, according to *Beit Shamai*, he should first recite the blessing over the festival and then the blessing over the wine. According to *Beit Hillel*, he should first recite the blessing over the wine and then the blessing over the festival.

MISHNAH

The first authoritative work of Jewish law that was codified in writing. The Mishnah contains the oral traditions that were passed down from teacher to student; it supplements, clarifies, and systematizes the commandments of the Torah. Due to the continual persecution of the Jewish people, it became increasingly difficult to guarantee that these traditions would not be forgotten. Rabbi Yehudah Hanasi therefore redacted the Mishnah at the end of the 2nd century. It serves as the foundation for the Talmud.

FIGURE 2.6

The *Haggadah*

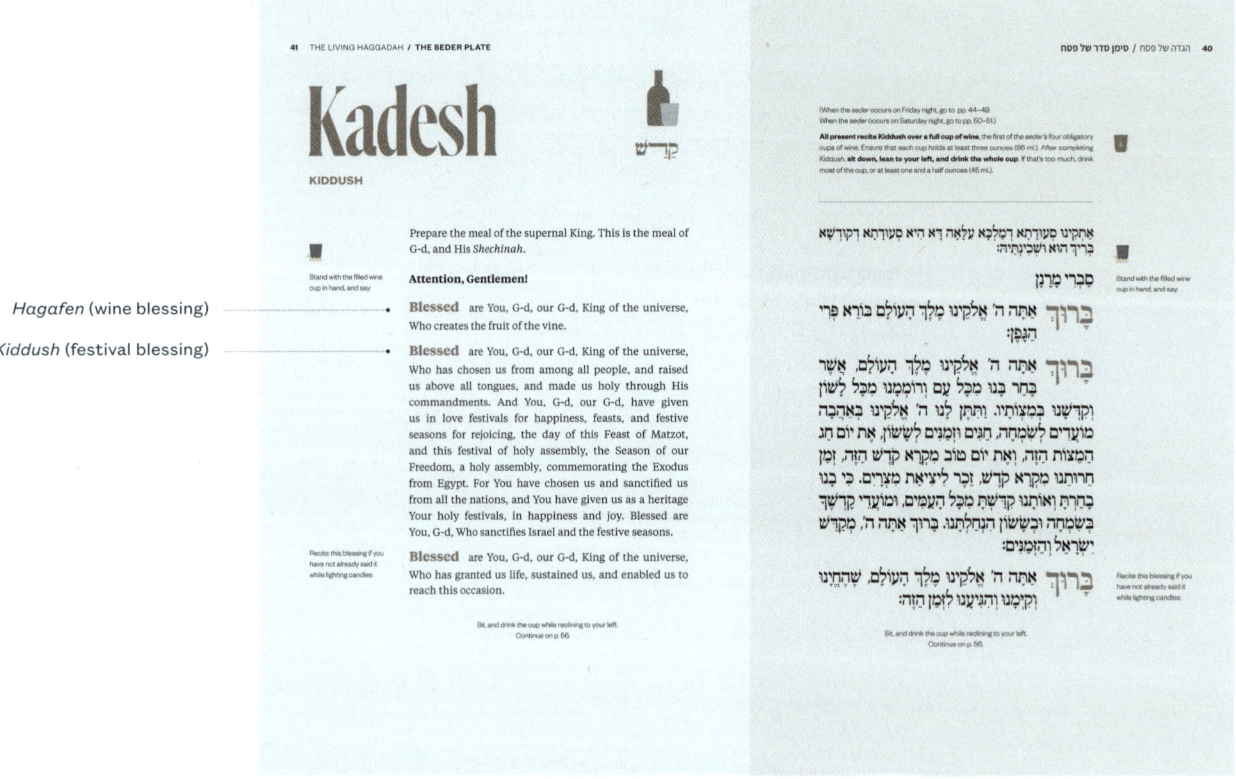

41 THE LIVING HAGGADAH / **THE SEDER PLATE**

Kadesh

קדש

KIDDUSH

Stand with the filled wine cup in hand, and say:

Prepare the meal of the supernal King. This is the meal of G-d, and His *Shechinah*.

Attention, Gentlemen!

Blessed are You, G-d, our G-d, King of the universe, Who creates the fruit of the vine.

Blessed are You, G-d, our G-d, King of the universe, Who has chosen us from among all people, and raised us above all tongues, and made us holy through His commandments. And You, G-d, our G-d, have given us in love festivals for happiness, feasts, and festive seasons for rejoicing, the day of this Feast of Matzot, and this festival of holy assembly, the Season of our Freedom, a holy assembly, commemorating the Exodus from Egypt. For You have chosen us and sanctified us from all the nations, and You have given us as a heritage Your holy festivals, in happiness and joy. Blessed are You, G-d, Who sanctifies Israel and the festive seasons.

Recite this blessing if you have not already said it while lighting candles:

Blessed are You, G-d, our G-d, King of the universe, Who has granted us life, sustained us, and enabled us to reach this occasion.

Sit, and drink the cup while reclining to your left.
Continue on p. 56.

40 הגדה של פסח / **סימן סדר של פסח**

(When the *seder* occurs on Friday night, go to pp. 44–49.
When the *seder* occurs on Saturday night, go to pp. 50–51.)

All present recite Kiddush over a full cup of wine, the first of the *seder's* four obligatory cups of wine. Ensure that each cup holds at least three ounces (86 ml.). After completing Kiddush, **sit down, lean to your left, and drink the whole cup**. If that's too much, drink most of the cup, or at least one and a half ounces (45 ml.).

Stand with the filled wine cup in hand, and say:

אתקינו סעודתא דמלכא עלאה דא היא סעודתא דקודשא בריך הוא ושכינתיה:

סברי מרנן

ברוך אתה ה׳ אלקינו מלך העולם בורא פרי הגפן:

ברוך אתה ה׳ אלקינו מלך העולם, אשר בחר בנו מכל עם ורוממנו מכל לשון וקדשנו במצותיו. ותתן לנו ה׳ אלקינו באהבה מועדים לשמחה, חגים וזמנים לששון, את יום חג המצות הזה, ואת יום טוב מקרא קדש הזה, זמן חרותנו מקרא קדש, זכר ליציאת מצרים. כי בנו בחרת ואותנו קדשת מכל העמים, ומועדי קדשך בשמחה ובששון הנחלתנו. ברוך אתה ה׳, מקדש ישראל והזמנים:

Recite this blessing if you have not already said it while lighting candles:

ברוך אתה ה׳ אלקינו מלך העולם, שהחינו וקימנו והגיענו לזמן הזה:

Sit, and drink the cup while reclining to your left.
Continue on p. 56.

FIGURE 2.7

Sample Mishnah Analysis

MISHNAH'S DIRECTIVES	INSIGHT	PRINCIPLE
Even the most destitute person in the Jewish nation **should not eat** [on Passover eve], **unless** he is reclining.	This discussion of the laws governing the *seder* meal fails to mention the basic obligation to eat the *seder* meal.	The Mishnah assumes its reader has prior knowledge of basic Torah laws.
Even the most **destitute** person in the Jewish nation should not eat [on Passover eve], unless he is **reclining**. He should not be provided with less than **four cups** of wine [for Passover eve], even if he is being supplied by a **public food bank**.	Four distinct laws are conveyed using only seventeen Hebrew words.	The Mishnah is extremely concise.
We must refrain from eating **on the eve of Passover**, from close to the time . . .	Emphasizing that this rule applies to the eve of Passover simultaneously informs us, by way of deduction, that the same rule does not apply to the eves of Shabbat and the two other annual festivals.	The Mishnah is highly selective in its wording.
We must refrain from eating on the eve of Passover . . . **until after darkness has fallen**.	The additional clause—"until after darkness has fallen"—informs us, by way of implication, that the Passover *seder* meal must begin after dark.	The Mishnah contains no superfluous phrases.
When they pour him his first cup of wine, according to ***Beit Shamai***, he should recite the blessing over the festival and then the blessing over the wine. According to ***Beit Hillel***, he should recite the blessing over the wine and then the blessing over the festival.	The Mishnah does not restrict itself to the view (of *Beit Hillel*) that has been cemented as the final law. It includes the opposing view that is not accepted as law (*Beit Shamai*).	The Mishnah will include multiple opinions on a single matter of law.

IV. THE MISHNAH AND THE SOUL

Beyond supplying the basic how-tos of Judaism, our sages viewed the Oral Torah, as it is preserved in the Mishnah, as the true basis of the covenant between G-d and the Jewish people. Studying the Mishnah serves to strengthen one's soul and deepen the connection with G-d.

TWO TALMUDISTS
Frantisek Reichental, oil on canvas, 1932. (Slovak National Gallery, Bratislava)

TEXT 8

The Crux of the Covenant

Talmud, Gitin 60b

אָמַר רַבִּי יוֹחָנָן: לֹא כָּרַת הַקָדוֹשׁ בָּרוּךְ הוּא בְּרִית עִם יִשְׂרָאֵל, אֶלָּא בִּשְׁבִיל דְבָרִים שֶׁבְּעַל פֶּה - שֶׁנֶאֱמַר: "כִּי עַל פִּי הַדְּבָרִים הָאֵלֶּה כָּרַתִּי אִתְּךָ בְּרִית וְאֶת יִשְׂרָאֵל" (שְׁמוֹת לד, כז).

Rabbi Yochanan taught: G-d made a covenant with the Jewish people only for the sake of the Torah materials that were transmitted orally [*be'al peh*]. It is therefore stated, "For on the basis [*al pi*] of these matters I have made a covenant with you and with Israel" (EXODUS 34:27).

SUKKOT MEMORIES
Gila Balsam

TEXT 9

Oral Unity

Rabbi Yehudah Loew, *Tiferet Yisrael*, ch. 68

וּלְכָךְ מִצַּד הַתּוֹרָה שֶׁבְּעַל פֶּה, שֶׁהִיא עִם הָאָדָם,
יֵשׁ לַתּוֹרָה חִבּוּר לְיִשְׂרָאֵל . . . כַּאֲשֶׁר הַתּוֹרָה עִם הָאָדָם,
וְלֹא עַל הַקְּלָף, שֶׁאָז לֹא הָיָה כָּאן חִבּוּר עִם הָאָדָם.

The *Torah Shebe'al Peh*—the oral tradition—exists through human engagement, thereby bonding the Torah with the Jewish people. . . . Had the Torah been confined exclusively to parchment it would lack this human bond.

RABBI YEHUDAH LOEW (MAHARAL OF PRAGUE) 1525–1609

Talmudist and philosopher. Maharal rose to prominence as leader of the famed Jewish community of Prague. He is the author of more than a dozen works of original philosophic thought, including *Tiferet Yisrael* and *Netzach Yisrael*. He also authored *Gur Aryeh,* a supercommentary to Rashi's biblical commentary; and a commentary on the nonlegal passages of the Talmud. He is buried in the Old Jewish Cemetery of Prague.

FIGURE 2.8

Mishnah–*Neshamah*

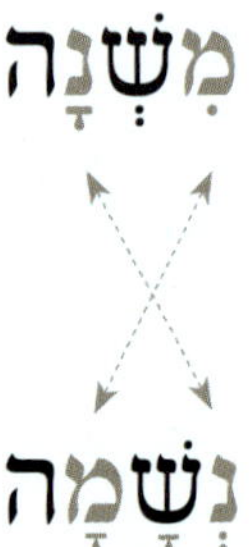

KEY POINTS

1. The oral tradition was initially preserved orally to ensure precise transmission, active engagement by students, and exclusivity to the Jewish people.

2. Disputes in Halachah began with Hillel and Shamai, due to the Sanhedrin's diminishing ability to resolve questions definitively.

3. Roman persecutions led to the proliferation of Halachic disputes and the potential loss of the Oral Torah. This necessitated its preservation in written form.

4. Rabbi Yehudah the Prince compiled the Mishnah during a peaceful period, documenting the Oral Torah to safeguard it for future generations.

5. The Mishnah was meticulously composed and organized into six orders: Zera'im, Mo'ed, Nashim, Nezikin, Kodashim, and Taharot. These cover broad categories of Jewish law.

6. The Mishnah's brevity facilitates efficient memorization and study: each of its statements conveys multiple laws or principles.

7. Every word in the Mishnah is chosen for precision and clarity, and it often implies additional rules or exceptions.

8 Although the Mishnah was composed in part to develop Halachic consensus, the authors felt compelled to include multiple opinions on many Halachic questions.

9 The study of Mishnah, whose letters are identical to those of the word *neshamah*—soul, strengthens the soul in life and in death because it is fundamental to the covenant between G-d and the Jewish people.

Continue learning at
myjli.com/talmud

Today, we tackled an original Talmudic text—a selection of Mishnah.
Here is how this section we covered appears in a contemporary printed edition of the Mishnah.

פרק י א עַרְבֵי פְסָחִים סָמוּךְ לַמִּנְחָה, **לֹא** יֹאכַל אָדָם עַד שֶׁתֶּחְשַׁךְ [ב]. וַאֲפִלּוּ עָנִי [ג] שֶׁבְּיִשְׂרָאֵל לֹא יֹאכַל עַד שֶׁיָּסֵב. וְלֹא יִפְחֲתוּ לוֹ מֵאַרְבָּעָה כוֹסוֹת שֶׁל יַיִן, וַאֲפִלּוּ מִן הַתַּמְחוּי [ד]:

ב מָזְגוּ [ה] לוֹ כוֹס רִאשׁוֹן, **בֵּית שַׁמַּאי** אוֹמְרִים, מְבָרֵךְ עַל הַיּוֹם, וְאַחַר כָּךְ מְבָרֵךְ עַל הַיַּיִן. וּבֵית הִלֵּל אוֹמְרִים, מְבָרֵךְ עַל הַיַּיִן, וְאַחַר כָּךְ מְבָרֵךְ עַל הַיּוֹם:

ג הֵבִיאוּ לְפָנָיו, מְטַבֵּל בַּחֲזֶרֶת,

רבינו עובדיה מברטנורא

פֶּרֶק י א עַרְבֵי פְּסָחִים סָמוּךְ לַמִּנְחָה. קֹדֶם לַמִּנְחָה מְעַט כְּמוֹ חֲצִי שָׁעָה, בִּתְחִלַּת שָׁעָה עֲשִׂירִית [א], דְּתָמִיד קָרֵב בְּתֵשַׁע וּמֶחֱצָה וְהוּא זְמַן הַמִּנְחָה, וְקֹדֶם לַמִּנְחָה חֲצִי שָׁעָה הֲוֵי בִּתְחִלַּת שָׁעָה עֲשִׂירִית: **לֹא יֹאכַל אָדָם.** כְּדֵי שֶׁיֹּאכַל מַצָּה לְתֵאָבוֹן מִשּׁוּם הִדּוּר מִצְוָה. וְלֶחֶם פְּשִׁיטָא דְּלָא מָצֵי אָכִיל, דְּחָמֵץ אָסוּר מִשֵּׁשׁ שָׁעוֹת וּלְמַעְלָה. וּמַצָּה נָמֵי הָא אַמְרִינַן בִּירוּשַׁלְמִי הָאוֹכֵל מַצָּה בְּעֶרֶב פֶּסַח כְּבָא עַל אֲרוּסָתוֹ בְּבֵית חָמִיו. וְלֹא נִצְרְכָה אֶלָּא לִשְׁאָר אֳכָלִין שֶׁלֹּא יְמַלֵּא כְּרֵסוֹ מֵהֶן: **עַד שֶׁיָּסֵב.** בְּמִטָּה וְעַל הַשֻּׁלְחָן כְּדֶרֶךְ בְּנֵי חוֹרִין: **וְלֹא יִפְחֲתוּ לוֹ.** גַּבָּאֵי צְדָקָה הַמְפַרְנְסִים אֶת הָעֲנִיִּים: **וַאֲפִלּוּ הוּא מִתְפַּרְנֵס מִן הַתַּמְחוּי.** דְּהַיְנוּ עָנִי שֶׁבַּעֲנִיִּים דִּתְנַן בְּמַסֶּכֶת פֵּאָה מִי שֶׁיֵּשׁ לוֹ מְזוֹן שְׁתֵּי סְעוּדוֹת לֹא יִטֹּל מִן הַתַּמְחוּי: **מֵאַרְבָּעָה כוֹסוֹת.** כְּנֶגֶד אַרְבַּע לְשׁוֹנוֹת שֶׁל גְּאֻלָּה שֶׁיֵּשׁ בְּפָרָשַׁת וָאֵרָא, וְהוֹצֵאתִי, וְהִצַּלְתִּי, וְגָאַלְתִּי, וְלָקַחְתִּי: **ב מְבָרֵךְ עַל הַיּוֹם.** בַּתְּחִלָּה קִדּוּשׁ הַיּוֹם וְאַחַר כָּךְ בּוֹרֵא פְּרִי הַגָּפֶן, שֶׁתְּחִלָּה קָדַשׁ הַיּוֹם וְאַחַר כָּךְ בָּא הַיַּיִן, וּכְשֵׁם שֶׁקָּדַם לַכְּנִיסָה כָּךְ קֹדֶם לַבְּרָכָה: **מְבָרֵךְ עַל הַיַּיִן.** תְּחִלָּה, וְהוּא הַדִּין לִמְקַדֵּשׁ עַל הַפַּת. שֶׁהַיַּיִן אוֹ הַפַּת גּוֹרְמִים לְקִדּוּשׁ הַיּוֹם, שֶׁאִם אֵין לוֹ יַיִן אוֹ פַּת לֹא יְקַדֵּשׁ: **ג הֵבִיאוּ לְפָנָיו.** הַיְּרָקוֹת. כְּדֵי שֶׁיַּכִּיר תִּינוֹק וְיִשְׁאַל, לְפִי שֶׁאֵין דֶּרֶךְ לְהָבִיא יְרָקוֹת קֹדֶם סְעוּדָה: **מְטַבֵּל בַּחֲזֶרֶת.** לָאו דַּוְקָא חֲזֶרֶת, דְּטִבּוּל רִאשׁוֹן זֶה הֲוֵי בִּשְׁאָר יְרָקוֹת, אֶלָּא אִם אֵין לוֹ שְׁאָר יְרָקוֹת מְטַבֵּל בַּחֲזֶרֶת בִּמְקוֹם שְׁאָר יְרָקוֹת. וּלְשׁוֹן מְטַבֵּל אוֹכֵל, וּלְפִי שֶׁכָּל אֲכִילָתָן עַל יְדֵי טִבּוּל הָיְתָה, קָרֵי לַאֲכִילָה

עיקר תוספות יו"ט

הכא משום דר"י לטעמיה דס"ל בפ"ח מ"ז דאין שוחטין את הפסח על היחיד הלכך מעיקרא לאמנויי אחרים בהדיה קאי וכאחד מבני חבורה דמי ולדינא הלכה כמשניות אלו אף דפסקינן כרבי יוסי דלעיל. ועתוי"ט: [בז] אם שלי. וכמו כן יאמר השני לחבירו. הר"מ: פרק י: [א] מנחה קטנה היא דלא כמ"כ דפ"ק דשבת. דהכא טעמא משום הידור מצוה וסגי בהכי: [ב] עד שתחשך. דאז זמן אכילת מצה כדתניא בתוספתא. הפסח ומצה ומרור מצותן משתחשך. וטעמא משום דכתיב ואכלו את הבשר בלילה הזה ואינך איתקשו לפסח. תוספ': [ג] ואפילו עני. דס"ד דהסיבת עני לאו חשיבה הסיבה דאין לו על מה להסב. וי"מ דאדלעיל קאי עד שתחשך ואפילו עני כו' פירש שלא אכל כמה ימים לא יאכל עד שתחשך: [ד] מן התמחוי. גמרא פשיטא לא נצרכה אלא אפילו לר"ע דאמר עשה שבתך חול ואל תצטרך לבריות. הכא משום פרסומי ניסא מודה: [ה] מזגו. ושתו ביין מסכתי תרגומו ואשתו

Map of the Talmud

ORDER 1

Zera'im—"Seeds"

The daily prayers; agricultural laws

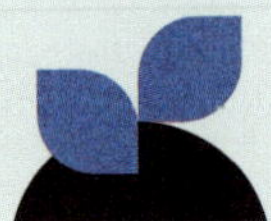

BERACHOT *"Blessings"*

Reading of the Shema; daily prayers; blessings on food

9 64 68

+ Mealtime etiquette; the life of King David; the meaning of dreams

PE'AH *"Sides"*

Agricultural leavings for the poor; charity

8 37

+ Laws and practices of Torah study; prohibitions against gossip and slander

DEMAI *"Mixtures"*

Produce whose tithed status is in doubt

7 34

KILAYIM *"Hybrids"*

Forbidden hybrids in planting, breeding animals, and garment making

9 44

SHEVIIT *"Seventh Year"*

Laws of the Sabbatical and Jubilee years

10 31

TERUMOT *"Upliftings"*

Portion of produce that is consecrated and given to the *Kohanim*

11 59

MAASROT *"Tithes"*

Tithes of the produce given to the Levites and the poor

5 26

MAASER SHENI *"Second Tithe"*

Portions of the land's produce that were eaten in Jerusalem

5 33

CHALAH *"Loaf"*

Portion of the dough that is consecrated and given to the *Kohanim*

4 28

ORLAH *"Stoppage"*

Laws governing the first three years' produce of fruit trees

3 20

BIKURIM *"First Fruits"*

First fruits of the year's harvest, which were brought to the Holy Temple in Jerusalem

3 13

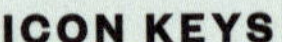

ICON KEYS

Mishnah (chapters)

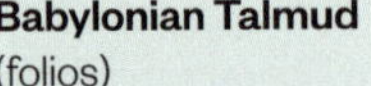

Babylonian Talmud (folios)

Jerusalem Talmud (folios)

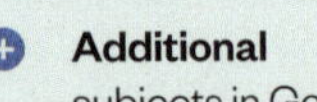

Additional subjects in Gemara

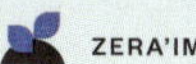 ZERA'IM 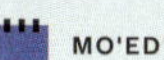 MO'ED  NASHIM  NEZIKIN  KODASHIM  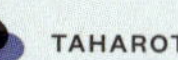 TAHAROT

ORDER 2

Mo'ed—"Appointed Times"

Shabbat and the festivals; the Jewish calendar

SHABBAT

Laws of Shabbat observance

24 157 92

+ The festival of Chanukah; account of the Giving of the Torah at Mount Sinai; laws of circumcision

EIRUVIN

Continuation of the laws of Shabbat, focusing primarily on the *eiruv* mechanisms that permit carrying objects and traveling in specially designated spaces

10 105 65

+ Tips and pointers on the study and acquisition of knowledge

PESACHIM *"Passovers"*

Observances of the festival of Passover

10 121 71

+ Proper speech; guidelines in following the local custom; Kiddush and Havdalah

SHEKALIM

The annual half-shekel coin contributed by each Jew toward the service in the Holy Temple; rules pertaining to the daily management of the Holy Temple

8 33

YOMA *"The Day"*

Observances of Yom Kippur; repentance

8 88 42

SUKKAH

Observances of the festival of Sukkot

5 56 26

BEITZAH *"Egg"*

Laws pertaining to the prohibition of work on the festivals; laws of *muktzeh* (objects that should not be handled on Shabbat and the festivals)

5 40 22

ROSH HASHANAH *"Head of the Year"*

Setting of the Jewish calendar; observances of Rosh Hashanah

4 35 22

TAANIT *"Fasting"*

Observances of the fast days; prayers for rain; notable dates and events in Jewish history

4 31 26

+ Narratives on the lives of the sages

MEGILAH *"Scroll"*

Observances of Purim; laws pertaining to the synagogue, the synagogue service, and the public Torah readings

4 32 34

+ The story of Purim; expositions on the Book of Esther

MO'ED KATAN *"Minor Festival"*

Laws of the "intermediate days" of the festivals; laws of mourning for the dead

3 29 19

CHAGIGAH *"Festival Offering"*

The three annual pilgrimages to the Holy Temple in Jerusalem

3 27 22

+ Mystical secrets of the Creation cosmology

ORDER 3

Nashim—“Women”

Marriage and divorce

YEVAMOT *“Levirates”*

Laws of *yibum* (levirate marriage) and *chalitzah*; the *arayot* (forbidden incestuous relations)

16 122 85

- Conversion to Judaism

KETUVOT *“Marriage Contracts”*

The financial and marital obligations of a husband to his wife

13 112 72

- Legal contracts, veracity of testimony in court, and numerous other topics; this tractate is often called “the minor Talmud” due to the multitude of legal subjects it touches on

NEDARIM *“Vows”*

Laws governing personal vows and pledges

11 91 40

- Circumcision; the mitzvah of visiting the sick

NAZIR *“The Nazirite”*

Laws of the “Nazirite” who takes a vow not to drink wine, cut their hair, or become ritually impure through contact with the dead

9 66 47

- The different levels of ritual impurity

SOTAH *“Wayward Wife”*

Laws of the *sotah* (a woman suspected of adultery); the priestly blessing and other prayers; laws of warfare; the procedure for an unsolved murder (*eglah arufah*)

9 49 47

- Divine reward and retribution; accounts of the Egyptian exile, the Exodus, and the Israelites’ entry into the Promised Land; the story of Samson; expositions on Job; descriptions of the eve of the messianic era

GITIN *“Writs of Divorce”*

Laws of divorce; *shelichut* (legal agency) ; various rabbinic ordinances instituted for the common good

9 90 54

- Events surrounding the destruction of Jerusalem and the Holy Temple

KIDUSHIN *“Consecration”*

Laws of marriage; laws pertaining to purchases and acquisitions; the differing obligations of men and women regarding various *mitzvot*

4 82 48

- The mitzvah to honor one’s parents; paternal obligations toward their children

ICON KEYS

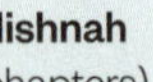
Mishnah (chapters)

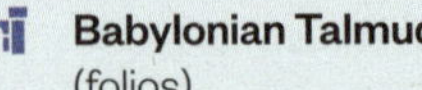
Babylonian Talmud (folios)

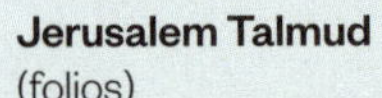
Jerusalem Talmud (folios)

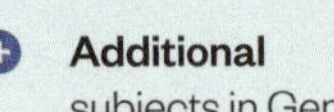
Additional subjects in Gemara

ZERA'IM MO'ED NASHIM NEZIKIN KODASHIM TAHAROT

ORDER 4

Nezikin—“Damages”

Civil and criminal law

BAVA KAMA *“First Gate”**

A person's responsibility for damages caused by their person or property; theft and robbery

 10 119  44

BAVA METZI'A *“Middle Gate”**

Determining the ownership of disputed property; the obligation to return a lost object; responsibilities of a bailee; loans; usury, exchange rates, and fraud; employment and leasing

 10  119  37

BAVA BATRA *“Last Gate”**

Partnerships; neighbor law; proof of ownership; purchases and acquisitions; financial contracts and appraisals; inheritance

10 176 34

+ Intangible damages; municipal levies and taxes; the collection and distribution of charity; composition of the Tanach; the Rabbah bar bar Chanah legends

SANHEDRIN *“High Court”*

Structure of the criminal justice system; judicial procedures; capital punishment; kidnapping and murder; self-defense; treason; government

11 113  57

+ Fundamental beliefs of Judaism; prophecy; principles of morality; the preservation of life; the seven Noahide laws; warfare; burial; the messianic era and the World to Come

MAKOT *“Lashings”*

Corporal punishment; the penalties for unintentional killing and false testimony

 3  24  9

SHEVU'OT *“Oaths”*

Oaths and vows

 8 49  44

+ Honesty and truth-telling

EDUYOT *“Testimonies”*

Record of a variety of legal traditions and disputations

8

AVODAH ZARAH *“Alien Worship”*

Idolatry; relations with non-Jews

5 76 37

+ *Agadot* (non-Halachic teachings) on various events in Jewish history; the methodologies of Torah study; the responsibility not to be the cause of another person's transgression

AVOT *“Fathers”*

Ethics and character

5

HORAYOT *“Rulings”*

Mistaken rulings issued by the court

3  14  19

* These three tractates were originally part of one tractate called *Nezikin* (“Damages”), which was divided into three parts due to its size

ORDER 5

Kodashim—"Sacraments"

The Temple service; the kosher dietary laws

ZEVACHIM *"Sacrifices"*

Laws pertaining to the animal sacrifices brought in the Holy Temple in Jerusalem

14 120

The principles of Halachic exposition

MENACHOT *"Offerings"*

The grain, wine, and oil offerings brought in the Holy Temple

13 110

Tzitzit and *tefilin*

CHULIN *"Non-Sacred Foods"*

The kosher dietary laws

12 142

BECHOROT *"Firstborns"*

Redemption of the firstborn; the firstborn animals and the animal tithes that was offered in the Holy Temple

9 61

ARACHIN *"Estimations"*

Property pledged to the Holy Temple

9 34

The Levite musicians in the Holy Temple; the prohibition of various types of negative speech (*lashon hara*)

TEMURAH *"Exchange"*

Temple offerings that got mixed with other animals, or were disqualified for other reasons

7 34

KERITOT *"Cutting Off"*

The *chatat* and *asham* offerings brought in atonement for various transgressions

6 28

The formula for the *ketoret* (incense) offered daily in the Holy Temple

ME'ILAH *"Betrayal"*

Penalties for the unauthorized use of Temple property

6 22

TAMID *"Constant"*

The daily service in the Holy Temple

7 8

MIDOT *"Measurements"*

Detailed description of the physical structure of the Holy Temple in Jerusalem

5

KINIM *"Nests"*

Laws dealing with various types of bird offerings that got mixed up with each other

3

ICON KEYS

 **Mishnah** (chapters)

 **Babylonian Talmud** (folios)

 **Jerusalem Talmud** (folios)

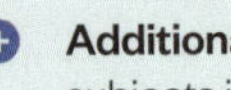 **Additional** subjects in Gemara

ORDER 6

Taharot—"Purities"

Laws of ritual purity

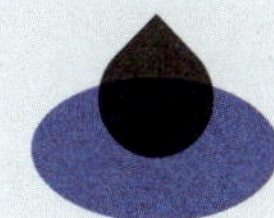

KELIM *"Vessels"*
The different types of ritual purity and impurity, and the status of various vessels regarding their susceptibility to contamination

30

OHALOT *"Canopies"*
Ritual impurity acquired through contact with a dead body

18

NEGA'IM *"Afflictions"*
Laws of *tzaraat* ("leprosy") that afflicts a person, clothes, or home

14

PARAH *"Heifer"*
Laws of the "red heifer"

12

TAHAROT *"Purities"*
Laws of ritual purity and impurity

10

MIKVA'OT *"Pools"*
Laws of the *mikveh* (ritually cleansing pool of water)

10

NIDAH *"Menstruant"*
Laws pertaining to the prohibition of marital relations during menstruation, and the state of ritual impurity it engenders

10  73  13

Conception, pregnancy, and birth; the soul's descent into the physical world

MACHSHIRIN *"Preparation"*
The manner in which the "seven liquids" make foods susceptible to ritual contamination

6

ZAVIM *"Emissions"*
Ritual impurity engendered by bodily emissions

5

TEVUL YOM *"Daytime Immersion"*
Ritual status of one who has immersed in a *mikveh* but must wait until sunset to be fully purified

4

YADAYIM *"Hands"*
Ritual washing of the hands; disputations between the Pharisees and the Sadducees

4

UKTZIN *"Stems"*
The status of various components and containers of foods in regard ritual impurity; the rewards of the righteous in the World to Come

3

ORDER 7

The "Minor Tractates"

The Minor Tractates are Baraitot ("external teachings"), i.e., Mishnaic-era teachings not included in the Mishnah

AVOT DERABBI NATAN
"Rabbi Nathan's 'Fathers'"
An expansion of the Mishnaic tractate *Avot* ("Ethics of the Fathers")

CHAPTERS: 41

SOFRIM *"Scribes"*
The writing of a Torah scroll; the annual Torah reading cycle

CHAPTERS: 21

SEMACHOT *"Happy Occasions"*
Burial and mourning

CHAPTERS: 14

KALAH *"Bride"*
Marriage and marital relations

CHAPTERS: 1

KALAH RABATI *"Greater Bride"*
Modesty and etiquette in various areas of everyday life

CHAPTERS: 10

DERECH ERETZ RABAH
"Greater Everyday Behavior"
Proper behavior in various areas of everyday life

CHAPTERS: 11

DERECH ERETZ ZUTA
"Minor Everyday Behavior"
Proper behavior for a Torah scholar; the value of peace

CHAPTERS: 11

GERIM *"Converts"*
Conversion to Judaism; the status of a non-Jewish "resident-sojourner"

CHAPTERS: 4

KUTIM *"Cuthites"*
Laws governing relations between Jews and Cuthites (Samaritans)

CHAPTERS: 2

AVADIM *"Servants"*
Laws of the indentured servant

CHAPTERS: 3

SEFER TORAH *"Torah Scroll"*
The writing and format of a Torah scroll

CHAPTERS: 5

TEFILIN *"Phylacteries"*
Laws of *tefilin*

CHAPTERS: 1

TZITZIT *"Fringes"*
Laws of *tzitzit*

CHAPTERS: 1

MEZUZAH *"Doorpost"*
Laws of *mezuzah*

CHAPTERS: 2

The Chain of Tradition

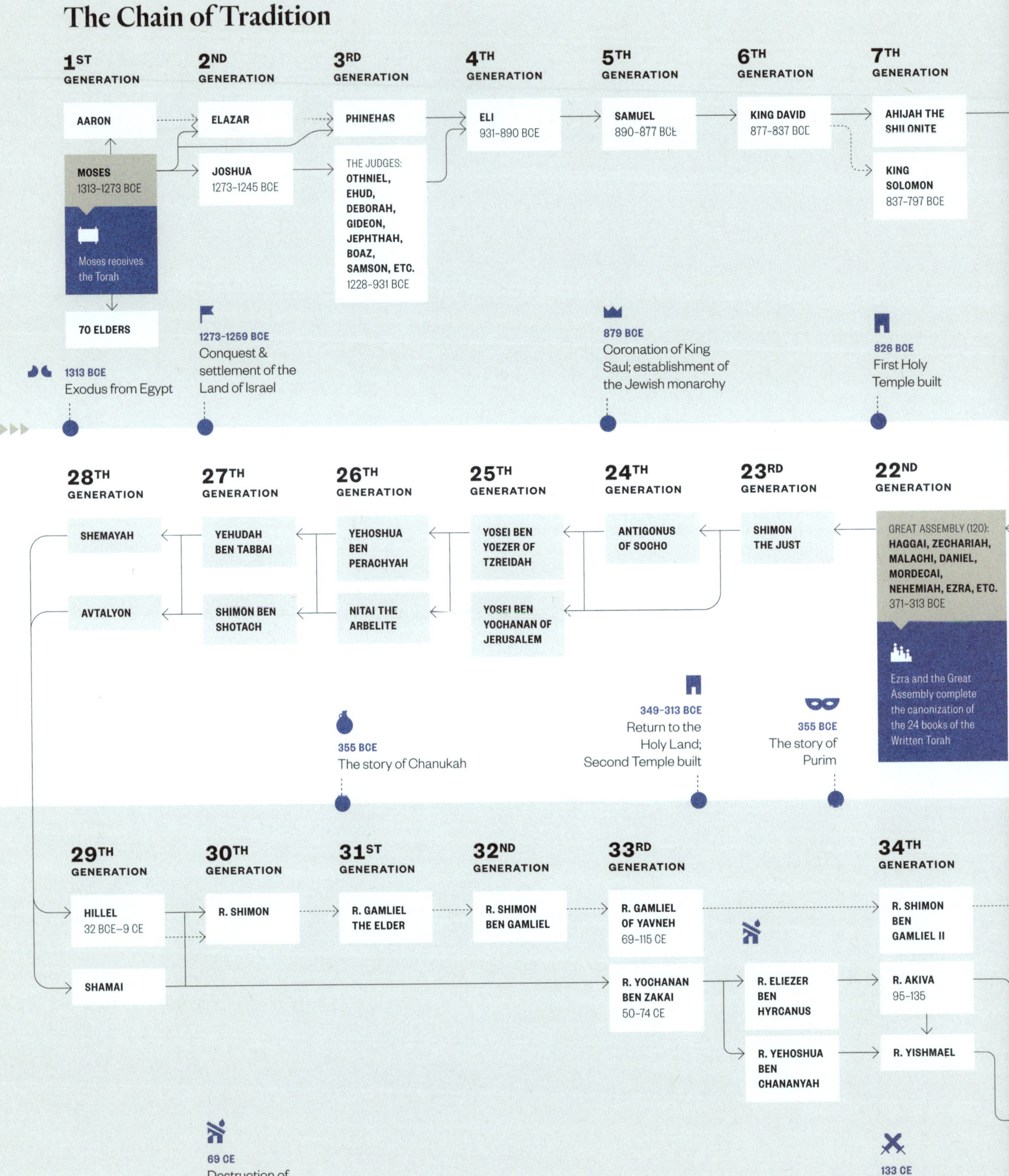

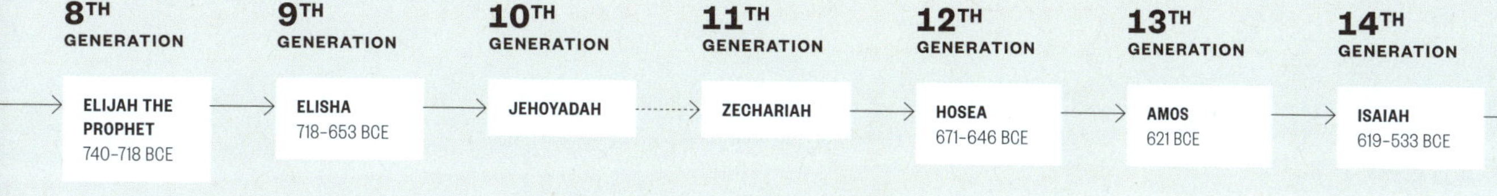
8TH GENERATION
ELIJAH THE PROPHET 740-718 BCE
9TH GENERATION
ELISHA 718-653 BCE
10TH GENERATION
JEHOYADAH
11TH GENERATION
ZECHARIAH
12TH GENERATION
HOSEA 671-646 BCE
13TH GENERATION
AMOS 621 BCE
14TH GENERATION
ISAIAH 619-533 BCE

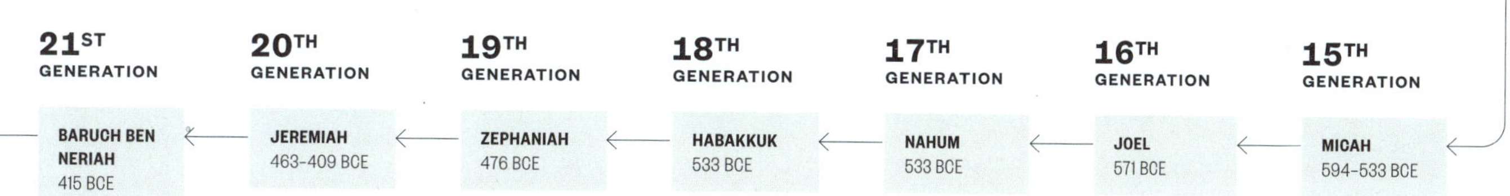
21ST GENERATION
BARUCH BEN NERIAH 415 BCE
20TH GENERATION
JEREMIAH 463-409 BCE
19TH GENERATION
ZEPHANIAH 476 BCE
18TH GENERATION
HABAKKUK 533 BCE
17TH GENERATION
NAHUM 533 BCE
16TH GENERATION
JOEL 571 BCE
15TH GENERATION
MICAH 594-533 BCE

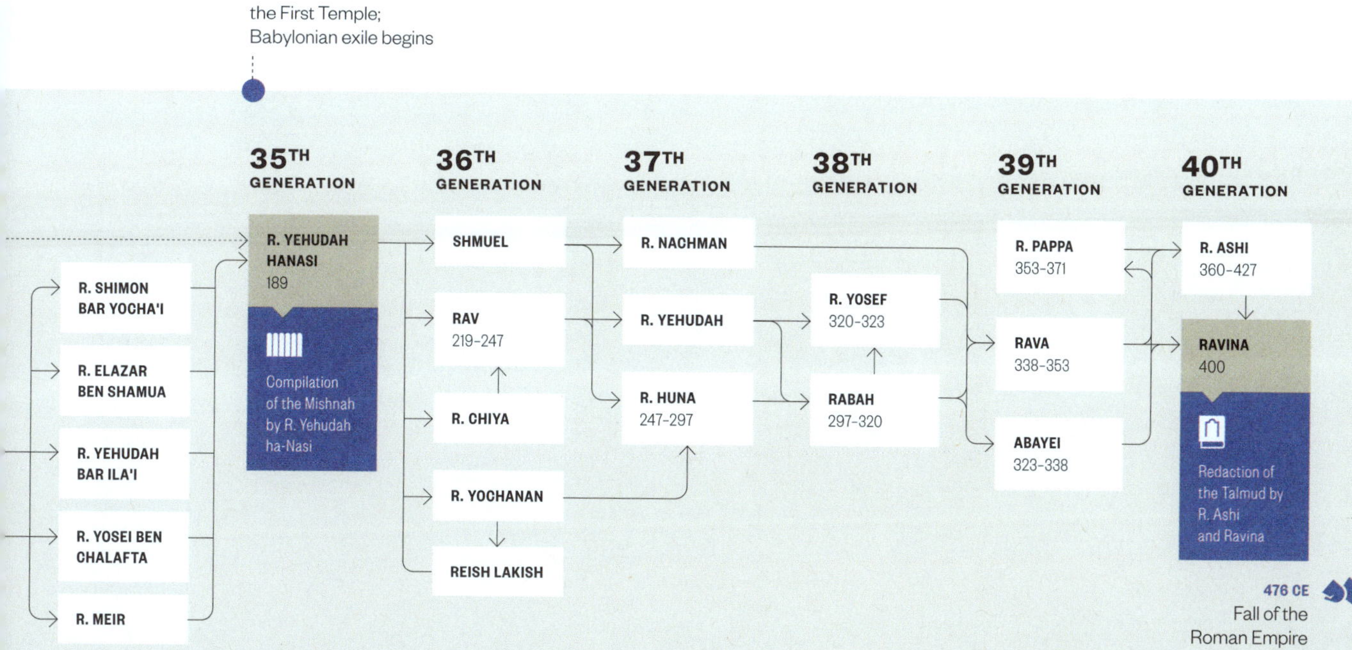
423 BCE
Destruction of the First Temple; Babylonian exile begins
35TH GENERATION
R. YEHUDAH HANASI 189
Compilation of the Mishnah by R. Yehudah ha-Nasi
R. SHIMON BAR YOCHA'I
R. ELAZAR BEN SHAMUA
R. YEHUDAH BAR ILA'I
R. YOSEI BEN CHALAFTA
R. MEIR
36TH GENERATION
SHMUEL
RAV 219-247
R. CHIYA
R. YOCHANAN
REISH LAKISH
37TH GENERATION
R. NACHMAN
R. YEHUDAH
R. HUNA 247-297
38TH GENERATION
R. YOSEF 320-323
RABAH 297-320
39TH GENERATION
R. PAPPA 353-371
RAVA 338-353
ABAYEI 323-338
40TH GENERATION
R. ASHI 360-427
RAVINA 400
Redaction of the Talmud by R. Ashi and Ravina
476 CE
Fall of the Roman Empire

APPENDIX

TEXT 10

Disputed Origins

Talmud, Sanhedrin 88b

תַּנְיָא, אָמַר רַבִּי יוֹסֵי: מִתְּחִילָּה לֹא הָיוּ מַרְבִּין מַחֲלוֹקֶת בְּיִשְׂרָאֵל . . . מִשֶּׁרַבּוּ תַּלְמִידֵי שַׁמַּאי וְהִלֵּל שֶׁלֹּא שִׁמְּשׁוּ כָּל צָרְכָּן רָבוּ מַחְלוֹקֶת בְּיִשְׂרָאֵל וְנַעֲשֵׂית תּוֹרָה כִּשְׁתֵּי תוֹרוֹת.

Rabbi Yose taught, “Initially, no one propagated Halachic disputes among the Jewish people. . . . But when the number of students of Shamai and Hillel who had not served a sufficient apprenticeship with their teachers proliferated, disputes proliferated among the Jewish people, until the Torah appeared fractured into two.”

TEXT 11

Decreasing Diligence

Maimonides, Mishnah, introduction

כָּל ב' אֲנָשִׁים בִּהְיוֹתָם שָׁוִים בְּשֵׂכֶל וּבְעִיּוּן וּבִידִיעַת הָעִיקָּרִים שֶׁיּוֹצִיאוּ מֵהֶם הַסְּבָרוֹת לֹא תִּפּוֹל בֵּינֵיהֶם מַחְלוֹקֶת בִּסְבָרָתָם בְּשׁוּם פָּנִים . . .

אֲבָל כַּאֲשֶׁר רָפְתָה שְׁקִידַת הַתַּלְמִידִים עַל הַחָכְמָה וְנֶחְלְשָׁה סְבָרָתָם נֶגֶד סְבָרַת הִלֵּל וְשַׁמַּאי, וּבָם נָפְלָה מַחְלוֹקֶת בֵּינֵיהֶם בְּעִיּוּן עַל דְּבָרִים רַבִּים, שֶׁסְּבָרַת כָּל אֶחָד וְאֶחָד מֵהֶם הָיְתָה לְפִי שִׂכְלוֹ וּמָה שֶׁיֵּשׁ בְּיָדוֹ מִן הָעִיקָּרִים.

When two people are of equal intelligence and analytical ability, and they are equally fluent in the principles from which the theories are derived, no dispute will ever arise between them in their analyses. . . .

However, when students became less diligent in their pursuit of wisdom, and their analytical abilities declined in comparison to that of their teachers, Hillel and Shamai, disputes arose among them in their individual analysis of numerous topics. Each student's analysis reflected his personal degree of intelligence and the degree to which he understood the underlying principles.

TEXT 12

Disputes from Sinai

Rabbi Yisrael Baal Shem Tov, *Keter Shem Tov* 2:320

מֹשֶׁה קִיבֵּל תּוֹרָה מִסִּינַי.
מֹשֶׁה רָאשֵׁי תֵּיבוֹת, מַחְלֹקֶת שַׁמַּאי הִלֵּל.

פֵּירוּשׁ, שֶׁלֹּא תֹּאמַר מֵחֲמַת תַּלְמִידֵי שַׁמַּאי וְהִלֵּל
שֶׁלֹּא שִׁמְּשׁוּ כָּל צָרְכָּן, מֵחֲמַת זֶה רָבְתָה מַחְלוֹקֶת.
כִּי אִם מַחְלֹקֶת זֶה קִיבֵּל מֹשֶׁה מִסִּינַי.

כִּי הִלֵּל מִיְּמִין מֹשֶׁה, עַל כֵּן הוּא מִצַּד הַחֶסֶד,
עַל כֵּן בֵּית הִלֵּל תָּמִיד לְקוּלָא. שַׁמַּאי מִשְּׂמֹאל
מֹשֶׁה, עַל כֵּן בֵּית שַׁמַּאי הֵם תָּמִיד לְחוּמְרָא.

Our sages state that "Moses received the Torah from [Mount] Sinai" (MISHNAH, AVOT 1:1). Moses's name [in Hebrew: Moshe, **משה**, *m-sh-h*] forms the acronym of the phrase ***m**achloket* **Sh**amai **H**illel—"the disputes of Shamai and Hillel."

This informs us that we should not lay the blame for the proliferation of Halachic disputes on the fact that the students of Shamai and Hillel were insufficiently trained. Rather, these very same disputes were received by Moses at [Mount] Sinai.

Hillel's spiritual source is to Moses's right, the side of kindness; consequently, the School of Hillel is always more lenient. Shamai's spiritual source is to Moses's left [which is associated with severity]; consequently, the School of Shamai is always stricter.

RABBI YISRAEL BAAL SHEM TOV (BESHT) 1698–1760

Founder of the Chasidic movement. Born in Slutsk, Belarus, the Baal Shem Tov was orphaned as a child. He served as a teacher's assistant and clay digger before founding the Chasidic movement and revolutionizing the Jewish world with his emphasis on prayer, joy, and love for every Jew, regardless of their level of Torah knowledge.

DECRYPTING THE MISHNAH

How the sages studied, debated, and understood the Mishnah

Discover the tools, methods, and principles the sages employed in the centuries-long effort to unpack the Mishnah's full practical implications.

THE TALMUDISTS
Max Weber, oil on canvas, New York, 1934

I. GEMARA

After previously exploring the Mishnah, the present lesson focuses on the Gemara, a vastly larger text that serves as the Mishnah's essential companion. Taken together, the Mishnah and the Gemara form "the Talmud."

The Mishnah is a collection of laws; the Gemara is not. Rather, the Gemara records the painstaking efforts of the post-Mishnaic era of sages, known collectively as the *amora'im*, to fathom and explain the laws recorded in the Mishnah.

Today's study begins with an examination of the Gemara's method of analyzing the Mishnah.

THE PHILOSOPHERS
Seymour Rosenthal, lithograph, New York, c. 1980

KEY TERM 3.1

HEBREW TERM	אָמוֹרָא/ים
TRANSLITERATION	*amora (plural: amora'im)*
PRONUNCIATION	ah-MOH-rah (plural: ah-MOH-rah-eem)
LITERAL MEANING	**speaker(s)**
MEANING	the sages whose teachings are recorded in the Gemara

FIGURE 3.1

The Components of the Talmud

NAME	LITERAL MEANING	REFERS TO
TALMUD	Study	The combination of Mishnah and Gemara
MISHNAH	Material to be reviewed	The original code of the Oral Law; compiled in the late 2nd–early 3rd century
GEMARA	Material to be learned	The text that records the interpretation and analysis of the Mishnah. In common usage, it also refers to the "editor's voice" within the Gemara text. (Therefore, if a question or answer is presented anonymously, Talmudic students will describe it as "the Gemara asks" or "the Gemara explains," etc.)
SHAS	An acronym of ***Sh****ishah* ***S****edarim*, "six orders."	A common alternative title for the Talmud (due to the Mishnah's division into six orders).

TEXT 1

Passover Laws

Mishnah, Pesachim 10:1–2

עַרְבֵי פְסָחִים סָמוּךְ לַמִּנְחָה, לֹא יֹאכַל אָדָם עַד שֶׁתֶּחְשַׁךְ.

וַאֲפִילוּ עָנִי שֶׁבְּיִשְׂרָאֵל לֹא יֹאכַל עַד שֶׁיָּסֵב.

וְלֹא יִפְחֲתוּ לוֹ מֵאַרְבַּע כּוֹסוֹת שֶׁל יַיִן, וַאֲפִילוּ מִן הַתַּמְחוּי.

מָזְגוּ לוֹ כּוֹס רִאשׁוֹן, בֵּית שַׁמַּאי אוֹמְרִים, מְבָרֵךְ עַל הַיּוֹם, וְאַחַר כָּךְ מְבָרֵךְ עַל הַיַּיִן. וּבֵית הִלֵּל אוֹמְרִים, מְבָרֵךְ עַל הַיַּיִן, וְאַחַר כָּךְ מְבָרֵךְ עַל הַיּוֹם.

One must refrain from eating on the eve of Passover, from close to the time for reciting the Minchah prayers until after darkness has fallen.

Even the most destitute person in the Jewish nation should not eat unless he is reclining.

He should not be provided with less than four cups of wine, even if he is being supplied by the public food bank.

When they pour him his first cup of wine, according to Beit Shamai, he should first recite the blessing over the festival and then the blessing over the wine. According to Beit Hillel, he should first recite the blessing over the wine and then the blessing over the festival.

MISHNAH

The first authoritative work of Jewish law that was codified in writing. The Mishnah contains the oral traditions that were passed down from teacher to student; it supplements, clarifies, and systematizes the commandments of the Torah. Due to the continual persecution of the Jewish people, it became increasingly difficult to guarantee that these traditions would not be forgotten. Rabbi Yehudah Hanasi therefore redacted the Mishnah at the end of the 2nd century. It serves as the foundation for the Talmud.

EXERCISE 3.1

Examine the five laws in this chart. Pick at least two of the laws and generate your own probing questions.

LAW	QUESTION
On Passover eve, we avoid eating from Minchah time until nightfall.	
At the *seder*, we eat while reclining.	
At the *seder*, we drink four cups of wine.	
Public food banks must provide poor people with four cups of wine.	
Beit Hillel teaches that when reciting Kiddush, the wine blessing is recited before the festival blessing. Beit Shamai insists on the reverse.	

FIGURE 3.2

The Gemara's Treatment of the Mishnah

Checks for contradictions	*Four* cups of wine contradicts the principle of not doing things in pairs.
Examines nuances in terminology	"Eve of *Passover*" implies exclusivity; the rule does not extend to the eves of the other holidays.
Checks the necessity of each detail	Providing the needy with wine for Passover appears to be an obvious obligation; the Gemara demonstrates that it is not.
Clarifies the scope of its laws	"Eat while reclining" suggests that reclining is essential while eating at any point during the *seder*. The Gemara clarifies that reclining is required only for the consumption of the matzah, sacrificial lamb, and wine.
Explores reasons for its laws and for varying opinions	The Gemara probes the opposing views of Beit Shamai and Beit Hillel regarding Kiddush.

II. THE BARAITA-MISHNAH RELATIONSHIP

The compilers of the Mishnah were highly selective: Not all of the available material was included. Valuable teachings of the *tanna'im* that were omitted are referred to as *Baraitot* (plural form of the singular term *Baraita*)—*external teachings*, i.e., excluded material.

Such texts were an invaluable resource for the generations of *amora'im* who worked to interpret the Mishnah, due to the additional context and perspectives they offer.

Regarding the above sample Mishnah, for example, the Gemara leans on a Baraita for assistance in analyzing the Mishnaic debate between Beit Shamai and Beit Hillel regarding the order of the Kiddush blessings on Passover eve.

SHABBAT KIDDUSH CUP, WINE, FLOWERS
Rhonda Roth, watercolor on paper, USA, 2023

KEY TERM 3.2

HEBREW TERM	בְּרַיְיתָא
TRANSLITERATION	*Baraita (plural: Baraitot)*
PRONUNCIATION	Ba-RYE-ta (plural: Ba-rye-TOT)
LITERAL MEANING	**external material**
MEANING	teachings of the sages of the Mishnaic period that were excluded from the body of the Mishnah

TEXT 2

Baraita Usage

Rabbi Sherira Ga'on, *Igeret DeRabbi Sherira Ga'on*

וְרַבָּנָן אֵימוֹרָאֵי דְבָתַר רֶבִּי הֲווּ צְרִיכִין טוּבָא לְהָלֵין בְּרַיְיתָא דְמִינְהוֹן מִינְפְּקָן כָּל מִילֵי עֲמִיקְתָּא דְאַמֵירָן בְּמַתְנִיתָן בְּלִישְׁנָא קַיְיטָא וּבְרִמְזֵי וּבִכְלָלֵי וְיוֹצְאִין מֵהֶן עֲנָפִים וְחִידוּשִׁין וְתוֹלָדוֹת.

The *amora'im* who came after Rebbi [Yehudah Hanasi] had much need for these *Baraitot*. The *Baraitot* helped them extract many profound ideas that were recorded in the Mishnah in extremely succinct language, captured in hints and broad statements. Using these *Baraitot*, the *amora'im* were able to extrapolate, develop fresh insight, and extract secondary derivations from the Mishnah's laws.

RABBI SHERIRA GA'ON
C. 906–1006

Rabbi and Halachic authority. Rabbi Sherira was born in Babylon into a prestigious scholarly family and in 968 was appointed head of the yeshiva in Pumbedita, a position known as the "Ga'on." As Ga'on, Rabbi Sherira served as the leading Halachic authority in the Jewish world, penning many responsa to communities ranging from Spain in the west to India in the east. He is best known for *Igeret DeRabbi Sherira Ga'on*, in which he explains how the Talmud was formulated and surveys Jewish history until his time.

FIGURE 3.3

Introductory Terminology

The phrase that introduces a Mishnah	**תְּנַן—We taught**
Phrases that introduce a Baraita	**תַּנְיָא ,תָּנָא—It was Taught** **תָּנוּ רַבָּנָן—Our rabbis taught**

MOTIFS WITH JEWISH MEN
Lennart Rosensohn, oil on canvas, Sweden, 1975

FIGURE 3.4

Reprise of Text 1

Mishnah, Pesachim 10:1–2

עַרְבֵי פְסָחִים סָמוּךְ לַמִּנְחָה, לֹא יֹאכַל אָדָם עַד שֶׁתֶּחְשַׁךְ.

וַאֲפִילוּ עָנִי שֶׁבְּיִשְׂרָאֵל לֹא יֹאכַל עַד שֶׁיָּסֵב.

וְלֹא יִפְחֲתוּ לוֹ מֵאַרְבַּע כּוֹסוֹת שֶׁל יַיִן, וַאֲפִילוּ מִן הַתַּמְחוּי.

מָזְגוּ לוֹ כוֹס רִאשׁוֹן, בֵּית שַׁמַּאי אוֹמְרִים, מְבָרֵךְ עַל הַיּוֹם, וְאַחַר כָּךְ מְבָרֵךְ עַל הַיַּיִן. וּבֵית הִלֵּל אוֹמְרִים, מְבָרֵךְ עַל הַיַּיִן, וְאַחַר כָּךְ מְבָרֵךְ עַל הַיּוֹם.

One must refrain from eating on the eve of Passover, from close to the time for reciting the Minchah prayers until after darkness has fallen.

Even the most destitute person in the Jewish nation should not eat unless he is reclining.

He should not be provided with less than four cups of wine, even if he is being supplied by the public food bank.

When they pour him his first cup of wine, according to Beit Shamai, he should first recite the blessing over the festival and then the blessing over the wine. According to Beit Hillel, he should first recite the blessing over the wine and then the blessing over the festival.

FIGURE 3.5

The *Seder* Night *Kiddush*

Kadesh

קדש

KIDDUSH

Stand with the filled wine cup in hand, and say:

Prepare the meal of the supernal King. This is the meal of G-d, and His *Shechinah*.

Attention, Gentlemen!

Hagafen (wine blessing)

Blessed are You, G-d, our G-d, King of the universe, Who creates the fruit of the vine.

Kiddush (festival blessing)

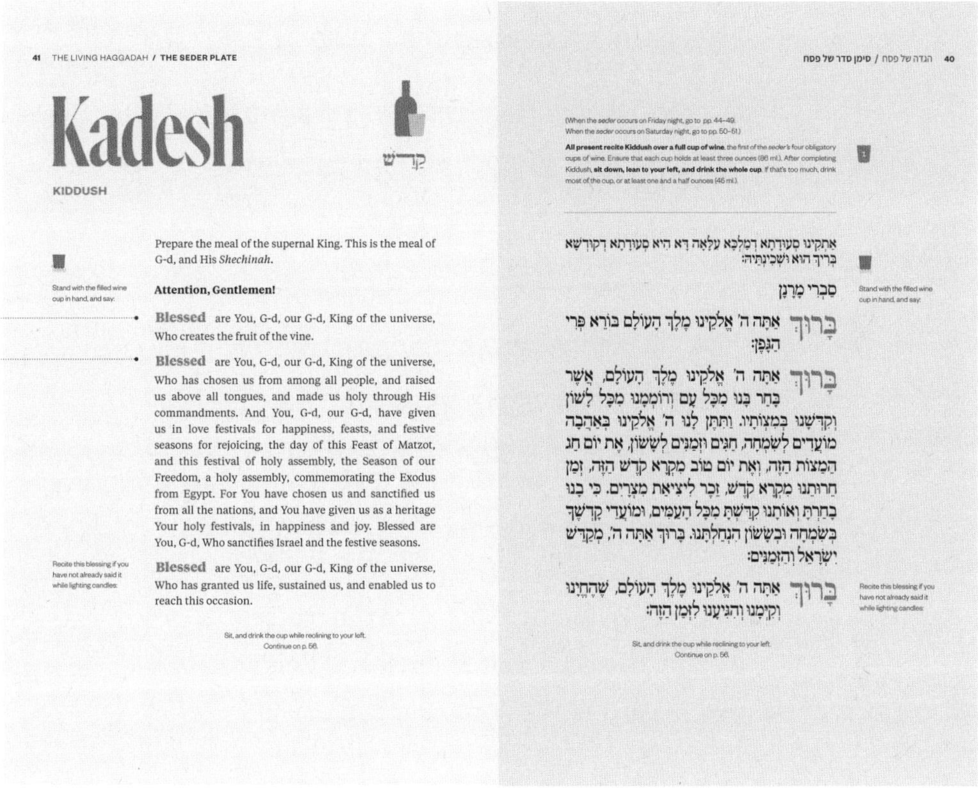

Blessed are You, G-d, our G-d, King of the universe, Who has chosen us from among all people, and raised us above all tongues, and made us holy through His commandments. And You, G-d, our G-d, have given us in love festivals for happiness, feasts, and festive seasons for rejoicing, the day of this Feast of Matzot, and this festival of holy assembly, the Season of our Freedom, a holy assembly, commemorating the Exodus from Egypt. For You have chosen us and sanctified us from all the nations, and You have given us as a heritage Your holy festivals, in happiness and joy. Blessed are You, G-d, Who sanctifies Israel and the festive seasons.

Recite this blessing if you have not already said it while lighting candles:

Blessed are You, G-d, our G-d, King of the universe, Who has granted us life, sustained us, and enabled us to reach this occasion.

Sit, and drink the cup while reclining to your left.
Continue on p. 56.

(When the *seder* occurs on Friday night, go to pp. 44–49.
When the *seder* occurs on Saturday night, go to pp. 50–51.)

All present recite Kiddush over a full cup of wine, the first of the *seder's* four obligatory cups of wine. Ensure that each cup holds at least three ounces (86 ml.). After completing Kiddush, **sit down, lean to your left, and drink the whole cup**. If that's too much, drink most of the cup, or at least one and a half ounces (46 ml.).

Stand with the filled wine cup in hand, and say:

אתקינו סעודתא דמלכא עלאה דא היא סעודתא דקודשא בריך הוא ושכינתיה:

סברי מרנן

ברוך אתה ה׳ אלקינו מלך העולם בורא פרי הגפן:

ברוך אתה ה׳ אלקינו מלך העולם, אשר בחר בנו מכל עם ורוממנו מכל לשון וקדשנו במצותיו. ותתן לנו ה׳ אלקינו באהבה מועדים לשמחה, חגים וזמנים לששון, את יום חג המצות הזה, ואת יום טוב מקרא קדש הזה, זמן חרותנו מקרא קדש, זכר ליציאת מצרים. כי בנו בחרת ואותנו קדשת מכל העמים, ומועדי קדשך בשמחה ובששון הנחלתנו. ברוך אתה ה׳, מקדש ישראל והזמנים:

Recite this blessing if you have not already said it while lighting candles:

ברוך אתה ה׳ אלקינו מלך העולם, שהחינו וקימנו והגיענו לזמן הזה:

Sit, and drink the cup while reclining to your left.
Continue on p. 56.

TEXT 3

Blessing Order

Talmud, Pesachim 114a

תָּנוּ רַבָּנָן, דְּבָרִים שֶׁבֵּין בֵּית שַׁמַּאי וּבֵית הִלֵּל בִּסְעוּדָה.

בֵּית שַׁמַּאי אוֹמְרִים, מְבָרֵךְ עַל הַיּוֹם וְאַחַר כָּךְ מְבָרֵךְ עַל הַיַּיִן. מִפְּנֵי שֶׁהַיּוֹם גּוֹרֵם לַיַּיִן שֶׁיָּבֹא, וּכְבָר קִידֵּשׁ הַיּוֹם וַעֲדַיִין יַיִן לֹא בָּא.

וּבֵית הִלֵּל אוֹמְרִים, מְבָרֵךְ עַל הַיַּיִן וְאַחַר כָּךְ מְבָרֵךְ עַל הַיּוֹם. מִפְּנֵי שֶׁהַיַּיִן גּוֹרֵם לַקִּידּוּשׁ שֶׁתֵּאָמֵר. דָּבָר אַחֵר, בִּרְכַּת הַיַּיִן תְּדִירָה וּבִרְכַּת הַיּוֹם אֵינָהּ תְּדִירָה, תָּדִיר וְשֶׁאֵינוֹ תָּדִיר תָּדִיר קוֹדֵם.

וְהִילְכְתָא כְּדִבְרֵי בֵּית הִלֵּל.

Our rabbis taught: These are the matters of dispute between Beit Shamai and Beit Hillel with regard to the *Halachot* of a meal:

Beit Shamai says: When reciting Kiddush over wine, one recites a blessing over the sanctification of the day and thereafter recites a blessing over the wine, because (a) the day causes the wine to come before the meal. Furthermore, (b) the day has already been sanctified and the wine has not yet arrived.

Beit Hillel says: One recites the blessing over the wine and thereafter recites a blessing over the day because (a) the wine causes Kiddush to be recited. Alternatively, (b) the blessing

BABYLONIAN TALMUD

A literary work of monumental proportions that draws upon the legal, spiritual, intellectual, ethical, and historical traditions of Judaism. The 37 tractates of the Babylonian Talmud contain the teachings of the Jewish sages from the period after the destruction of the 2nd Temple through the 5th century CE. It has served as the primary vehicle for the transmission of the Oral Law and the education of Jews over the centuries; it is the entry point for all subsequent legal, ethical, and theological Jewish scholarship.

over wine is recited frequently and the blessing over the day is not recited frequently, and there is a general principle: when a frequent practice and an infrequent practice coincide, the frequent practice takes precedence over the infrequent practice.

The Halachah is in accordance with the statement of Beit Hillel.

EXERCISE 3.2

1. **Review the above Baraita (Text 3) with a study partner, and in your own words, fill in the first and second arguments for each school of thought:**

	FIRST ARGUMENT	SECOND ARGUMENT
BEIT SHAMAI		
BEIT HILLEL		

2. **Now select one of these arguments and make a compelling case for it:**

III. A TALMUDIC *SUGYA*

The following section presents a sample Talmudic discussion (*sugya*). Each such discussion addresses another particular issue that arises from the text of the Mishnah.

The selected *sugya* questions the application of the Mishnaic statement regarding eating prior to the formal meal on the eve of Passover. The discussion centers on whether the prohibition is exclusive to the eve of Passover or is inclusive of the eves of Shabbat and the other two annual festivals. The Gemara considers different opinions and evidence that lead it to a final conclusion. The Gemara's analysis and reasoning are demonstrated step-by-step.

MATZOH MOON
Mark Podwal, ink on paper, New York, 1991

KEY TERM 3.3

HEBREW TERM	**סוּגְיָא**
TRANSLITERATION	*sugya*
PRONUNCIATION	SOOG-ya
LITERAL MEANING	**path or walk**
MEANING	a Talmudic discussion

FIGURE 3.6

Reprise of Text 1

Mishnah, Pesachim 10:1–2

עַרְבֵי פְסָחִים סָמוּךְ לַמִּנְחָה, לֹא יֹאכַל אָדָם עַד שֶׁתֶּחְשַׁךְ.

וַאֲפִילוּ עָנִי שֶׁבְּיִשְׂרָאֵל לֹא יֹאכַל עַד שֶׁיָּסֵב.

וְלֹא יִפְחֲתוּ לוֹ מֵאַרְבַּע כּוֹסוֹת שֶׁל יַיִן, וַאֲפִילוּ מִן הַתַּמְחוּי.

מָזְגוּ לוֹ כּוֹס רִאשׁוֹן, בֵּית שַׁמַּאי אוֹמְרִים, מְבָרֵךְ עַל הַיּוֹם, וְאַחַר כָּךְ מְבָרֵךְ עַל הַיַּיִן. וּבֵית הִלֵּל אוֹמְרִים, מְבָרֵךְ עַל הַיַּיִן, וְאַחַר כָּךְ מְבָרֵךְ עַל הַיּוֹם.

One must refrain from eating on the eve of Passover, from close to the time for reciting the Minchah prayers until after darkness has fallen.

Even the most destitute person in the Jewish nation should not eat unless he is reclining.

He should not be provided with less than four cups of wine, even if he is being supplied by the public food bank.

When they pour him his first cup of wine, according to Beit Shamai, he should first recite the blessing over the festival and then the blessing over the wine. According to Beit Hillel, he should first recite the blessing over the wine and then the blessing over the festival.

KEY TERM 3.4

HEBREW TERM	דִיוּק
TRANSLITERATION	***diyuk***
PRONUNCIATION	dee-YOOK
LITERAL MEANING	**precision**
MEANING	a precise examination of a textual nuance

CUP OF REDEMPTION
Chanie Chanin, oil on canvas, New York, 2024

TEXT 4

Mishnah Precision

Rabbi Adin Even-Israel (Steinsaltz), *The Talmud, the Steinsaltz Edition: A Reference Guide* (New York: Random House, 1989), p. 6

Every word of the Mishnah . . . was precisely weighed and measured . . . hence even the most far-reaching conclusions may be drawn not only from the wording of the Mishnah but also from the way it uses language; from expressions that the Mishnah could have used but did not use, and from the order in which things are mentioned. All these elements comprise the basis for the characteristic Talmudic study called *diyuk*—"precision."

RABBI ADIN EVEN-ISRAEL STEINSALTZ 1937–2020

Talmudist, author, and philosopher. Rabbi Steinsaltz is considered one of the foremost Jewish thinkers of the 20th century. A resident of Jerusalem, Rabbi Steinsaltz was the founder of the Israel Institute for Talmudic Publications, a society dedicated to the translation and elucidation of the Talmud, and he authored numerous works about the Talmud and Jewish mysticism. Praised by *Time* magazine as a "once-in-a-millennium scholar," he was awarded the Israel Prize for his contributions to Jewish study.

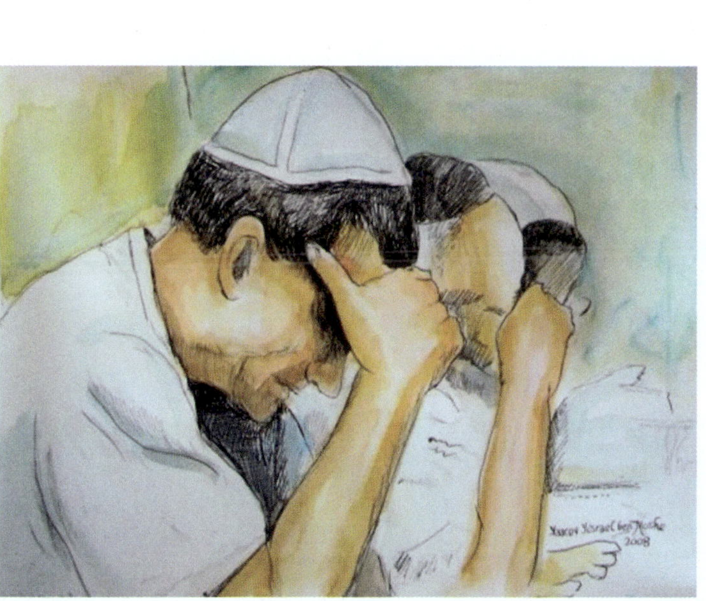

SILENT DEVOTION
Jeff Sterling (Yakov Yisrael ben Moshe), watercolor and India ink on paper, Fort Lauderdale, FL, 2008

TEXT 5

The Problem

Talmud, Pesachim 99b

מַאי אִירְיָא עַרְבֵי פְסָחִים, אֲפִילוּ עַרְבֵי שַׁבָּתוֹת וְיָמִים טוֹבִים נַמִי.

דְתַנְיָא, לֹא יֹאכַל אָדָם בְּעַרְבֵי שַׁבָּתוֹת וְיָמִים טוֹבִים מִן הַמִנְחָה וּלְמַעְלָה כְּדֵי שֶׁיִכָּנֵס לְשַׁבָּת כְּשֶׁהוּא תַּאֲוָה, דִבְרֵי רַבִּי יְהוּדָה. רַבִּי יוֹסֵי אוֹמֵר, אוֹכֵל וְהוֹלֵךְ עַד שֶׁתֶּחְשַׁךְ.

Why does it specify "the eve of *Passover*"? Even the eve of Shabbat and [other] festivals also [trigger this prohibition]! For we learned in a Baraita:

"One should not eat on the eves of Shabbat or festivals from the time of Minchah and onward so that one enters Shabbat [or the festivals] with an appetite. This is the opinion of Rabbi Yehudah. [Conversely,] Rabbi Yose says that one may continue eating until it grows dark."

EXERCISE 3.3

Fill in the chart based on the Gemara's understanding at this point in the discussion.

MAY ONE EAT A MEAL?			
	According to Rabbi Yehudah	. . . on the eve of Passover?	
		. . . on the eves of Shabbat / other festivals?	
	According to Rabbi Yose	. . . on the eve of Passover?	
		. . . on the eves of Shabbat / other festivals?	

TEXT 6

Rav Huna's Answer

Talmud, Pesachim 99b

אָמַר רַב הוּנָא, לָא צְרִיכָא אֶלָּא לְרַבִּי יוֹסֵי. דְּאָמַר, אוֹכֵל וְהוֹלֵךְ עַד שֶׁתֶּחְשַׁךְ, הָנֵי מִילֵּי בְּעַרְבֵי שַׁבָּתוֹת וְיָמִים טוֹבִים, אֲבָל בְּעֶרֶב הַפֶּסַח, מִשּׁוּם חִיּוּבָא דְּמַצָּה מוֹדֶה.

Rav Huna said: This [distinction between Passover and Shabbat or the other festivals] is necessary for Rabbi Yose, who said, "One may continue eating until it grows dark." That will apply to the eve of Shabbat and other festivals, but on the eve of Passover, he will concede [that it is prohibited] due to the obligation to eat matzah.

EXERCISE 3.4

Fill in the chart based on the Gemara's understanding at this point in the discussion.

MAY ONE EAT A MEAL?			
	According to Rabbi Yehudah	. . . on the eve of Passover?	
		. . . on the eves of Shabbat / other festivals?	
	According to Rabbi Yose	. . . on the eve of Passover?	
		. . . on the eves of Shabbat / other festivals?	

TEXT 7

Rav Pappa's Answer

Talmud, Pesachim 99b

רַב פָּפָּא אָמַר, אֲפִילּוּ תֵּימָא רַבִּי יְהוּדָה. הָתָם בְּעַרְבֵי שַׁבָּתוֹת
וְיָמִים טוֹבִים מִן הַמִּנְחָה וּלְמַעְלָה הוּא דְּאָסִיר, סָמוּךְ לְמִנְחָה
שָׁרֵי. אֲבָל בְּעֶרֶב הַפֶּסַח, אֲפִילּוּ סָמוּךְ לַמִּנְחָה נַמִּי אָסוּר.

Rav Pappa said: We can explain the Mishnah in a way that conforms with Rabbi Yehudah's view:

[The distinction between Passover and other occasions is that] there, in the case of the eve of Shabbat and other festivals, the prohibition is in force from the time of Minchah and onward. However, in *proximity* to the time of Minchah [eating is still] permitted.

Conversely, on the eve of Passover, the prohibition comes into force even during the time that is *proximate* to Minchah [shortly prior to Minchah].

EXERCISE 3.5

Fill in the chart based on the Gemara's understanding at this point in the discussion.

MAY ONE EAT A MEAL?			
	According to Rabbi Yehudah	. . . on the eve of Passover?	
		. . . on the eves of Shabbat / other festivals?	
	According to Rabbi Yose	. . . on the eve of Passover?	
		. . . on the eves of Shabbat / other festivals?	

TEXT 8

The Second Baraita

Talmud, Pesachim 99b

וּבְעֶרֶב שַׁבָּת סָמוּךְ לַמִּנְחָה שָׁרֵי?

וְהָתַנְיָא, לֹא יֹאכַל אָדָם בְּעֶרֶב שַׁבָּת וְיָמִים טוֹבִים מִתֵּשַׁע
שָׁעוֹת וּלְמַעְלָה, כְּדֵי שֶׁיִּכָּנֵס לַשַּׁבָּת כְּשֶׁהוּא תַּאֲוֶה, דִּבְרֵי
רַבִּי יְהוּדָה. רַבִּי יוֹסֵי אוֹמֵר, אוֹכֵל וְהוֹלֵךְ עַד שֶׁתֶּחְשַׁךְ.

But is it the case that on the eve of Shabbat, [eating] is permitted in proximity to the time for Minchah? Surely we learned [the contrary] in a Baraita:

"One may not eat on the eve of Shabbat or festivals, from the ninth hour and onward, so that they enter Shabbat with an appetite. That is the opinion of Rabbi Yehudah. [However,] Rabbi Yose maintains that one may continue eating until it grows dark."

EXERCISE 3.6

Fill in the chart based on the Gemara's understanding at this point in the discussion.

MAY ONE EAT A MEAL?			
	According to Rabbi Yehudah	. . . on the eve of Passover?	
		. . . on the eves of Shabbat / other festivals?	
	According to Rabbi Yose	. . . on the eve of Passover?	
		. . . on the eves of Shabbat / other festivals?	

TEXT 9

Mar Zutra's Challenge

Talmud, Pesachim 99b–100a

אָמַר מַר זוּטְרָא, מַאן לֵימָא לָן דִּמְתָּרַצְתָּא הִיא? דִּילְמָא מְשַׁבַּשְׁתָּא הִיא.

Mar Zutra said: Who can tell us whether [this Baraita] is accurate? Perhaps it is erroneous?

EXERCISE 3.7

Fill in the chart based on the Gemara's understanding at this point in the discussion.

MAY ONE EAT A MEAL?			
	According to Rabbi Yehudah	. . . on the eve of Passover?	
		. . . on the eves of Shabbat / other festivals?	
	According to Rabbi Yose	. . . on the eve of Passover?	
		. . . on the eves of Shabbat / other festivals?	

TEXT 10

Mareimar's Statement

Talmud, Pesachim 100a

אָמַר לֵיהּ מַרֵימַר, וְאִיתֵימָא רַב יֵימַר, אֲנָא
אִיקְלְעִי לְפִירְקֵיהּ דְרַב פִּנְחָס בְּרֵיהּ דְרַב אַמִי,
וְקָם תַּנָא וְתָנֵי קַמֵיהּ וְקִיבְּלָה מִינֵיהּ.

אִי הָכִי קַשְׁיָא. אֶלָא מְחַוַּורְתָּא כִּדְרַב הוּנָא.

Mareimar (some claim that it was Rav Yeimar) responded, "I visited the public lecture of Rav Pinchas, son of Rav Ami; there, a reciter arose and recited [this same Baraita] in the presence of [Rav Pinchas]—and he accepted it!"

If so, we indeed have a difficulty [with Rav Pappa's suggestion]. Rav Huna's answer is therefore more plausible.

EXERCISE 3.8

Fill in the chart based on the Gemara's understanding at this point in the discussion.

MAY ONE EAT A MEAL?			
	According to Rabbi Yehudah	. . . on the eve of Passover?	
		. . . on the eves of Shabbat / other festivals?	
	According to Rabbi Yose	. . . on the eve of Passover?	
		. . . on the eves of Shabbat / other festivals?	

FIGURE 3.7

The Talmud's Back-and-Forth

Whom does the Mishnah Follow?

	RABBI YEHUDAH	NOBODY	RABBI YOSE
THE PROBLEM		The Mishnah seems to say that Passover is different from Shabbat and the other holidays. This doesn't accord with R. Yose or R. Yehudah.	
RAV HUNA'S ANSWER			R. Yose makes a distinction between Passover and the other days. He agrees with there being a prohibition for Passover.
RAV PAPPA'S ANSWER	R. Yehudah distinguishes between Passover and the other days - the prohibition starts earlier on Passover.		
THE SECOND BARAITA			The prohibition for all days starts at the same time as for Passover, so R. Pappa's distinction doesn't hold up and we must assume R. Huna's interpretation is correct.
MAR ZUTRA'S CHALLENGE	The text of the 2nd Baraita might be corrupt. R. Pappa's interpretation might hold up.		
MAREIMAR'S STATEMENT			The 2nd baraita was taught at R. Pinchas' Lecture, so R. Pappa's distinction doesn't hold up and we must assume that R. Huna's interpretation is correct.

IV. HALACHIC DIVERSITY

The next section explores the concept of Halachic diversity. Certain Halachic opinions are not accepted as the final law, but they are nevertheless considered "the Words of the Living G-d." This means that they are valid expressions of the Divine Will embodied in Jewish law—albeit not the *final* law.

This concept is illustrated by the dispute regarding the biblical obligation to destroy any unleavened food (*chametz*) prior to the onset of Passover. Although there is only a single final decision on the matter, the diverse views provide guidance for personal and spiritual growth.

L'EXAMEN DU LEVAIN
(INSPECTION OF THE LEAVEN)
Bernard Picart, engraving, Amsterdam, 1723

TEXT 11

"Words of the Living G-d"

Talmud, Eruvin 13b

שָׁלֹשׁ שָׁנִים נֶחְלְקוּ בֵּית שַׁמַּאי וּבֵית הִלֵּל. הַלָּלוּ אוֹמְרִים הֲלָכָה כְּמוֹתֵנוּ, וְהַלָּלוּ אוֹמְרִים הֲלָכָה כְּמוֹתֵנוּ.

יָצְאָה בַּת קוֹל וְאָמְרָה, אֵלּוּ וָאֵלּוּ דִּבְרֵי אֱלֹקִים חַיִּים הֵן, וַהֲלָכָה כְּבֵית הִלֵּל.

For three years, Beit Shamai and Beit Hillel argued. These claimed, "The Halachah is in accordance with us," while these claimed, "The Halachah is in accordance with us."

Then a Heavenly voice emerged and declared, "These and these are [both] the Words of the Living G-d. And the Halachah is in accordance with Beit Hillel."

TEXT 12

Destruction Methods

Mishnah, Pesachim 2:1

רַבִּי יְהוּדָה אוֹמֵר, אֵין בִּעוּר חָמֵץ אֶלָּא שְׂרֵפָה. וַחֲכָמִים אוֹמְרִים, אַף מְפָרֵר וְזוֹרֶה לָרוּחַ אוֹ מַטִּיל לַיָּם.

Rabbi Yehudah said that the destruction of *chametz* can be accomplished only through burning. However, the sages said that we may also crumble it and cast it into the wind or drop it into the sea.

TEXT 13

Substance and Form

Rabbi Yosef Rosen, *Tzafnat Paane'ach Al HaTorah*, Vayikra 26:6

וְאָזִיל לְשִׁיטָתוֹ דְאֵין בִּיעוּר חָמֵץ אֶלָא שְׂרֵיפָה.
רָצָה לוֹמַר, דְצָרִיךְ שֶׁלֹא תְּהֵא הַכַּמוּת . . .

אֲבָל רַבִּי שִׁמְעוֹן סְבִירָא לֵיהּ דְהַשְׁבָּתָה
הַוֵי גַם כֵּן בִּיטוּל אֵיכוּת הַדָבָר.

Rabbi Yehudah's view—that the destruction of *chametz* can be accomplished only through *burning*—is intended to emphasize that the destruction must involve the obliteration of the food's very *substance*.

Conversely, Rabbi Shimon's view is that merely destroying the food's *quality* constitutes a valid "destruction."

RABBI YOSEF ROSEN (ROGATCHOVER GA'ON) 1858–1936

One of the prominent Talmudic scholars of the early 20th century. Born in Rogachev, Belarus, to a Chasidic family, his unusual capabilities were recognized at a young age. At 13 he was brought to Slutsk to study with Rabbi Yosef Ber Soloveitchik. He remained there for a full year, studying primarily with the rabbi's son, the legendary Chaim Soloveitchik. Later, he moved on to Shklov, where he studied with Rabbi Moshe Yehoshua Leib Diskin. After a period in Warsaw, the home city of his wife, he assumed the rabbinate of the Chasidic community in Dvinsk, Latvia. His works, titled *Tzafnat Paane'ach*, are famed for both their depth and difficulty.

TALMUDIC HOUSE IN ANCIENT QATSRIN
Shmuel Mushnick, acrylic on canvas, Jerusalem, Israel, 2014

KEY POINTS

1. The Gemara is the essential companion to the Mishnah. It is not a collection of laws but a documentation of the *amora'im*'s efforts to understand and expound upon the Mishnah.

2. The Gemara engages deeply with the Mishnah, posing critical questions regarding its laws, to uncover deeper understandings of the Halachic ideas.

3. *Baraitot* are critical resources for the *amora'im*'s efforts to interpret the Mishnah. These texts provide essential context, explanations, and additional perspectives that help clarify, expand, and deepen the understanding of the Mishnah.

4. In Talmudic study, the precision (*diyuk*) of the Mishnaic text is of great importance. Students are taught to carefully consider the exact wording of the Mishnah and to explore the implications of every word choice.

5. Significant effort is invested in resolving even seemingly minor points of ritual law, fueled by the realization that each Halachah is an opportunity to connect with G-d. The detailed study reflects a deep engagement with the Divine Will.

6 The *sugya* in tractate Pesachim explores the prohibition against eating prior to the Passover *seder* to determine whether a similar prohibition extends to the eves of Shabbat and other festivals.

7 Halachic views that are not accepted as final law are nevertheless considered "the Words of the Living G-d"—legitimate expressions of the Divine Will that contribute to a richer understanding of Jewish law.

8 Alternative but nonbinding Halachic views provide valuable guidance for personal and spiritual growth. For example, a dispute regarding the destruction of *chametz* prior to Passover reflects the question of how to deal with negative elements in our lives.

Continue learning at
myjli.com/talmud

Today, we tackled an original Talmudic text—a selection of Gemara.
Here is how this section we covered appears in a classic printed edition of the Talmud.

צט: ערבי פסחים פרק עשירי פסחים

ערב פסחים סמוך למנחה לא יאכל
אדם עד שתחשך אפילו
עני שבישראל לא יאכל עד שיסב ולא
יפחתו לו מארבע כוסות של יין ואפילו מן
התמחוי: **גמ'** מאי איריא ערבי פסחים אפי'
ערבי שבתות וימים טובים נמי דתניא לא
יאכל אדם בערבי שבתות וימים טובים מן
המנחה ולמעלה כדי שיכנס לשבת כשהוא
תאוה דברי רבי יהודה רבי יוסי אומר אוכל
והולך עד שתחשך אמר רב הונא לא צריכא
אלא לר' יוסי דאמר אוכל והולך עד שתחשך
הני מילי בערבי שבתות וימים טובים אבל
בערב הפסח משום חיובא דמצה מודה רב
פפא אמר אפילו תימא רבי יהודה התם
בערבי שבתות וימים טובים מן המנחה
ולמעלה הוא דאסיר סמוך למנחה שרי אבל
בערב הפסח אפילו סמוך למנחה נמי
אסור ובערב שבת סמוך למנחה שרי
והתניא לא יאכל אדם בערב שבת וימים
טובים מתשע שעות ולמעלה כדי שיכנס
לשבת כשהוא תאוה דברי רבי יהודה
רבי יוסי אומר אוכל והולך עד שתחשך
אמר מר זוטרא מאן לימא לן דמתרצתא היא
דילמא

דילמא משבשתא היא א"ל מרימר ואיתימא רב ייסא אנא איקלעי לפירקיה דרב פנחס בריה דרב אמי וקם תנא ותני קמיה וקיבלה מיניה אי הכי קשיא אלא מחוורתא כדרב הונא ולרב הונא מי ניחא והאמר רבי ירמיה א"ר יוחנן ואיתימא א"ר אבהו א"ר יוסי בר רבי חנינא הלכה כר' יהודה בערב הפסח והלכה כר' יוסי בע"ש הלכה כר' יהודה בערב הפסח מכלל דפליג רבי יוסי בתרוייהו לא הלכה מכלל דפליגי בהפסקה דתניא מפסיקין לשבתות דברי רבי יהודה רבי יוסי אומר אין מפסיקין ומעשה ברשב"ג [ורבי יהודה] ורבי יוסי שהיו מסובין בעכו וקדש עליהם היום א"ל רשב"ג לרבי יוסי ברבי רצונך נפסיק וניחוש לדברי יהודה חבירנו אמר לו בכל יום ויום אתה מחבב דברי לפני רבי יהודה ועכשיו אתה מחבב דברי רבי יהודה בפני הגם לכבוש את המלכה עמי בבית א"ל א"כ לא נפסיק שמא יראו התלמידים ויקבעו הלכה לדורות אמרו לא זזו משם עד שקבעו הלכה כר' יוסי: אמר רב יהודה אמר שמואל אין הלכה לא כר' יהודה ולא כר' יוסי אלא פורס מפה ומקדש איני והא אמר רב תחליפא בר אבדימי אמר שמואל כשם שמפסיקין לקידוש
כך

רשב"ם

משבשתא היא. והכי איבעי ליה למיתני מט' שעות ומחצה ואילך: **וקא תנא קמיה.** לכך מתניתא הכי מט' שעות ולמעלה אלמא מתרצתא היא: **אלא מחוורתא כרב הונא.** ומן המנחה דקתני מתניתא קמייתא סמוך למנחה קאמר: **הלכה מכלל דפליגי להפסקה.** הא דא"ר ירמיה הלכ' כר' יהודה בערב הפסח למשמע דפליג נמי רבי יוסי בערב הפסח להפסקה הוא דפליג דאם התחיל לאכול אף בערב הפסח אינו מפסיק אבל להתחיל מודה ר' יוסי לאסור ומתניתין בהתחלה כרבי יוסי איצטריך דקמשמע לן דמודה רבי יוסי בערב הפסח דאין מתחילין: **דפליג.** דבהפסקה נמי פליגי: **אין הלכה כרבי יהודה.** דאמר מפסיקין דמשמע עקירת שולחן: **ולא כרבי יוסי.** דאמר אין מפסיקין כלל: **אלא פורס מפה.** על השולחן ומקדש היום וחוזר ואוכל:
כך

רשב"ם

דילמא משבשתא היא. דה"ל למיתני מט' שעות ומחצה ולמעלה א"כ מן המנחה ולמעלה כדתניא בהאי קמייתא: **אמר מרימר.** לאו משבשתא היא: **אלא קשיא.** הך ברייתא בתרייתא דקתני מט' ולמעלה אלמא סמוך למנחה נמי קאסר רבי יהודה בערבי שבתות ויו"ט וליכא לאוקומי השתא מתניתין כרבי יהודה דמאי שנא ערבי פסחים דנקט בהו סמוך למנחה טפי מערבי שבתות ויו"ט: **אלא מחוורתא כרב הונא.** דלרבי יוסי איצטריך ומן המנחה דקתני הך ברייתא סמוך למנחה קאמר: **מכלל דפליג רבי יוסי בתרוייהו.** אפי' בערב הפסח והיכי מוקי למתני' כר' יוסי: **מכלל דפליגי להפסקה.** הא דא"ר ירמיה הלכה כרבי יהודה בערב הפסח למשמע דפליג נמי רבי יוסי בע"פ להפסקה הוא דפליג דאי התחיל לאכול אף בע"פ אינו מפסיק אבל להתחיל מודי ר' יוסי לאסור ומתני' בהתחלה ולר' יוסי איצטריך דקמ"ל דמודי ר' יוסי בערב הפסח דאין מתחילין: **דפליג.** דבהפסקה נמי פליגי: **מפסיקין לשבתות.** אם התחיל סעודתו בהיתר קודם המנחה והיה אוכל והולך עד שתחשך (א) אפי' לר' יהודה מפסיק סעודתו מיד כשיחשיך ומקדש היום: **וקדש עליהן.** שהחשיך: ה"ג בתוספתא דברכות **אמר לו רבן גמליאל לר' יוסי כו' רצונך שנפסיק וניחוש לדברי יהודה חבירנו אמר לו בכל יום אתה מחבב דברי לפני יהודה ועכשיו אתה מחבב דברי יהודה בפני הגם לכבוש את המלכה עמי בבית אמר לו א"כ לא נפסיק שמא יראו כו': ברבי.** כך קראו רשב"ג לר' יוסי בר חלפתא כלומר גדול הדור: **הגם לכבוש.** כלומ' בפני אתה מביישני: **אמר לו רשב"ג א"כ לא נפסיק כו'.** משמעינן מהכא דבערבי פסחים אסור לאכול מסוף ט' שעות ולמעלה כפשט מתני' אבל בערבי שבתות ויו"ט מותר לאכול מן המנחה ולמעלה דהא סתם לן תנא דמתני' כרבי יוסי מדנקט ערבי פסחים מכלל דבשאר י"ט שרי וקי"ל נמי (עירובין דף מו:) הלכה כר' יוסי מחבירו דר' יוסי אפי' להתחיל ולאכול אחר ט' שרי בהדיה לקמן [ע"ב] בשמעתין דאמר אלא הא דתניא ושוין שמתחילין לימא לאו בע"פ הא פליג ר' יהודה ומיהו לענין הפסקה אין הלכה כר' יוסי בערבי פסחים אלא כר' יהודה שאם התחיל לאכול קודם ט' אפי' הכי מפסיק עד שתחשיכה צריך לעקור את השולחן מיד כשיחשיך ולחזור לשם פסח ובשבתות ובי"ט לא יפסיק אלא פורס מפה ומקדש ואח"כ גומר סעודתו: **ולא כר' יהודה.** דאמר מפסיקין דמשמע עקירת שולחן: **ולא כר' יוסי.** דאמר א"ל להפסיק כלל אלא יגמור סעודתו אפי' משחשיכה ויברכו בהמ"ז ואח"כ מביא לו כוס שני לקידוש היום כדתניא לקמן בשמעתין אלא פורס מפה על המאכל כדין כל שבתות השנה שהביאו לחם על השולחן קודם קידוש [illegible] וחוזר ואוכל וגומר סעודתו. ונראה בעיני דס"ל לשמואל דהלכה כרבי יוסי דקתני בברייתא שקבעו הלכה כמותו אלא שבא להחמיר על עצמו קצת שלא יגמור סעודתו ויקדש אח"כ אלא יקדש תחלה ואח"כ יגמור סעודתו דלהא"ה שמואל דאמר' כמאן דהא ברייתא דקתני פורס מפה ומקדש לא קאי אהפסקה אכילה כלל אלא בבא לקדש עתה ולאכול בשבת בתחלה מיירי:
כך

תוספות

דילמא משבשתא היא. וברייתא קמייתא דקתני מן המנחה ולמעלה היא עיקר משום דלדידיה אתיא מתני' ככולי עלמא[א]:

ה"ג **והאמר ר' ירמיה א"ר יוחנן ואיתימא רבי אבהו א"ר יוסי בר ר' חנינא.** ולא גרס רבי יוחנן א"ר אבהו דרבי אבהו תלמידיה דר' יוחנן הוה:

מכלל דפליגי בהפסקה כדתניא. לא גרס דתניא דהא בברייתא לא פליגי בהפסקה דפסח אלא כדתניא גרס ומייתי כי היכי דפליגי בהפסקה דשבת הכי קים ליה דפליגי נמי בהפסקה דפסח ומורי רבינו יחיאל אמר דגרס דתניא ודייק מדקאמר ר' יוסי אין מפסיקין והיינו אפילו בערב הפסח דאין מתחילין דבע"ש שרי רבי יוסי אפי' להתחיל[ב] עוד נראה דאמר לקמן (ד' קב.) בני חבורה שהיו מסובין וקדש כו' וקתני פלוגתא דר' יהודה ורבי יוסי והתם סתמא קתני וקידש בין שבת בין פסח:

מפסיקין לשבתות. פי' בעקירת שולחן כדמוכח בסמוך והיינו שמברך ברכת המזון כדתניא לקמן (שם:) ראשון אומר עליו ברכת המזון והיו רגילין לסלק השולחן לפני ברכת המזון כדאמר בפרק [כילד מברכין] (ברכות דף מב.) סילק אסור מלאכול ולכך קאמר בסמוך[ג] דבעי לר' יהודה עקירת שולחן ולספרים דגרסי לקמן ראשון אומר עליו קידוש היום ושני ברכת המזון היו עוקרין את השולחן לפני קידוש כדי להפסיק אלא שהקידוש עושה קודם לפי שאסור לשתות כוס של ברכת המזון בלא קידוש דע"כ עקירת שולחן אינו בין קידוש לברכת המזון מדקאמר פורס מפה ומקדש ופריסת המפה היא במקום עקירת שולחן לרבי יהודה:

רבי יוסי אומר אין מפסיקין. וגומר כל הסעודה ומברך ברכת המזון ואח"כ מקדש כדמוכח בברייתא דלקמן (דף קב.) משמע דאין צריך לעשות סעודה[ד] לשם שבת[ה] דאי צריך מה לו להמתין יפסיק מיד וא"ת ואיך יעשו קידוש בלא סעודה הלא אין קידוש אלא במקום סעודה וי"ל דחשיב קידוש במקום סעודה כיון שמיד אחר הסעודה עושה קידוש ואותה סעודה עולה לו לסעודת שבת כדמוכח בתוספתא דקתני במילתיה דרבי יוסי ומזכיר של שבת בברכת המזון ומיהו קשה לר' יוסי איך יעשו ד' כוסות כיון שלא יקדשו אלא אחר ברכת המזון ולא יעשו סעודה אחרת וי"ל דיעשו ד' כוסות שלא כסדר הרגילין לעשות כוס ברכת המזון תחלה ואחריו כוס של קידוש וירקות ואחריו כוס שלישי למה נשתנה ואחריו מרור ועל כוס רביעי הלל: **אין מפסיקין.** בהתחילו בהיתר איירי דבהתחילו באיסור מודה ר' יוסי דמפסיקין ולרבי יהודה נמי דמפסיקין היינו כשכבר קידש היום כדמוכח בעובדא דמייתי דקתני וקידש עליהן היום אבל הגיע שעת מנחה אין מפסיקין והלכה כרבי יוסי ובערבי שבתות וי"ט אפי' להתחיל שרי כר' יוסי דרבי יהודה ור' יוסי הלכה כר' יוסי כדמוכח בעירובין (דף מו:) ובערבי פסחים אסור להתחיל ואם התחיל אפי' בהיתר מפסיקין בברכת המזון דהא פסקינן כר' יהודה ומורי רבינו יחיאל אומר מדפסיק כר' יוסי בהפסקה בההוא עובדא מכלל דלכתחלה לא קי"ל כוותיה ועוד כתב בה"ג דבע"ש אין להתחיל לאכול מן המנחה ולמעלה דאפי' ר' יוסי לא קאמר אלא דלא יפסיק אבל לאתחולי לא[ו] וע"כ ה"פ דלא קי"ל כרבי יוסי אלא להפסקה אבל לא להתחיל[ז]: **שהיו** מסובין והתחילו בהיתר שהרי רבי יהודה היה שם. ה"ג בתוספתא אמר לו א"כ לא נפסיק וה"פ א"כ כיון שמחית[ח] לא נפסיק שמא יראו התלמידים: **אלא** פורס מפה ומקדש. פי' רשב"ם דאית ליה לשמואל דהלכה כר' יוסי אלא שבא להחמיר על דבריו שלא לגמור סעודה קודם קידוש דאי לא תימא הכי שמואל דאמר כמאן דברייתא דקתני פורס מפה ומקדש לא מיירי בהפסקת אכילה אלא בבא להתחיל לאכול ובחנם דחק דשמואל סבר כחכמים דהכי איתא בירושלמי רב יהודה בשם שמואל זו דברי ר' יהודה ור' יוסי אבל חכמים אומרים פורס מפה ומקדש וצריך לדקדק כמאן הלכה דאע"ג דאמר ר' יוחנן לעיל הלכה כר' יוסי ובמי שהוליאוהו (שם ד' מו:) משמע דהלכה כר' יוחנן לגבי שמואל איכא חד לישנא דלא א"ר יוחנן ורב נמי סבר לקמן (ד' קה.) כשמואל וקאמר שבת קובעת נפשה ואע"ג דבכל סופרים הלך אחר המיקל היינו דוקא בשוין כדאמר בפ"ק דמסכת ע"ג (ד' ז.):
כך

עין משפט נר מצוה

ו א מיי' פכ"ט מהלכות שבת הלכה יב סמג עשין כט טוש"ע או"ח סימן רעא סעיף ד:

רבינו חננאל

ושקלינן וטרינן ואוקמה רב הונא למתני' כרבי יוסי, ובערב הפסח משום חיובא דמצה אסיר למיכל מן המנחה ולמעלה, ומודה ליה לרבי יהודה בערב הפסח. והא **דאמר** ר' יוחנן **הלכה כרבי יהודה בערב הפסח והלכה כרבי יוסי בערבי שבתות ובערבי ימים טובים.** אוקימנה להפסקה, דתניא מפסיקין לשבת, ועוקרין את השלחן ומקדשין ומברכין ברכת המזון. דברי רבי יהודה. רבי יוסי אומר אין מפסיקין, אלא גומרין סעודתן ומברכין ברכת המזון ואחר כך מקדשין. ומעשה ברבן גמליאל ור' יוסי ור' יהודה שהיו מסובין בעכו וכו' עד לא זזו משם עד שקבעו הלכה כרבי יוסי. **אמר** רב יהודה אמר שמואל אין הלכה לא כרבי יהודה ולא כרבי יוסי אלא פורס מפה ומקדש.

מסורת הש"ס

א) [שבת קו: וש"נ], ב) [תוספתא דברכות רפ"ה], ג) [לעיל לט:], ד) [ע"ב],

תורה אור השלם

1. וְהַמֶּלֶךְ שָׁב מִגִּנַּת הַבִּיתָן אֶל בֵּית מִשְׁתֵּה הַיַּיִן וְהָמָן נֹפֵל עַל הַמִּטָּה אֲשֶׁר אֶסְתֵּר עָלֶיהָ וַיֹּאמֶר הַמֶּלֶךְ הֲגַם לִכְבּוֹשׁ אֶת הַמַּלְכָּה עִמִּי בַּבָּיִת הַדָּבָר יָצָא מִפִּי הַמֶּלֶךְ וּפְנֵי הָמָן חָפוּ: אסתר ז ח

הגהות הב"ח

(א) רשב"ם ד"ה מפסיקין וכו' עד שתחשך לר' יהודה כצ"ל ותיבת אפילו נמחק:

גליון הש"ס

תוס' ד"ה מכלל. ודייק מדאמרינן אין מפסיקין וכו' דבע"ש שרי ר"י אפי' להתחיל. קשה לי הא ר"י אמר דאין מפסיקין אפי' אחר שתחשך דלהתחיל אסור קודם קידוש דמ"מ אין מפסיקין וצ"ע:

מוסף תוספות

א. אפי' כר' יהודה. תוס' שאנץ. ב. כל שכן דאין מפסיקין. תוס' ר"פ. ג. גבי אין הלכה לא כר' יהודה ולא כר' יוסי. תוס' שאנץ. ד. אחרת. שם. ה. ולשם פסח. שם. ו. וקשה דלכאורה משמע בשמעתין דשני מחלוקות הם, דפליגי בהתחלה ופליגי בהפסקה. תוס' ר"פ. ז. כדברי רבינו יחיאל. שם. ח. נ"א. כלומר כיון שאתה כרוס. שם.

The Three Components *of* Jewish Learning

"

A person should divide their years [of Torah learning] into three parts:

One-third in Scripture, one-third in Mishnah, and one-third in Talmud.

Talmud, Avodah Zarah 19b

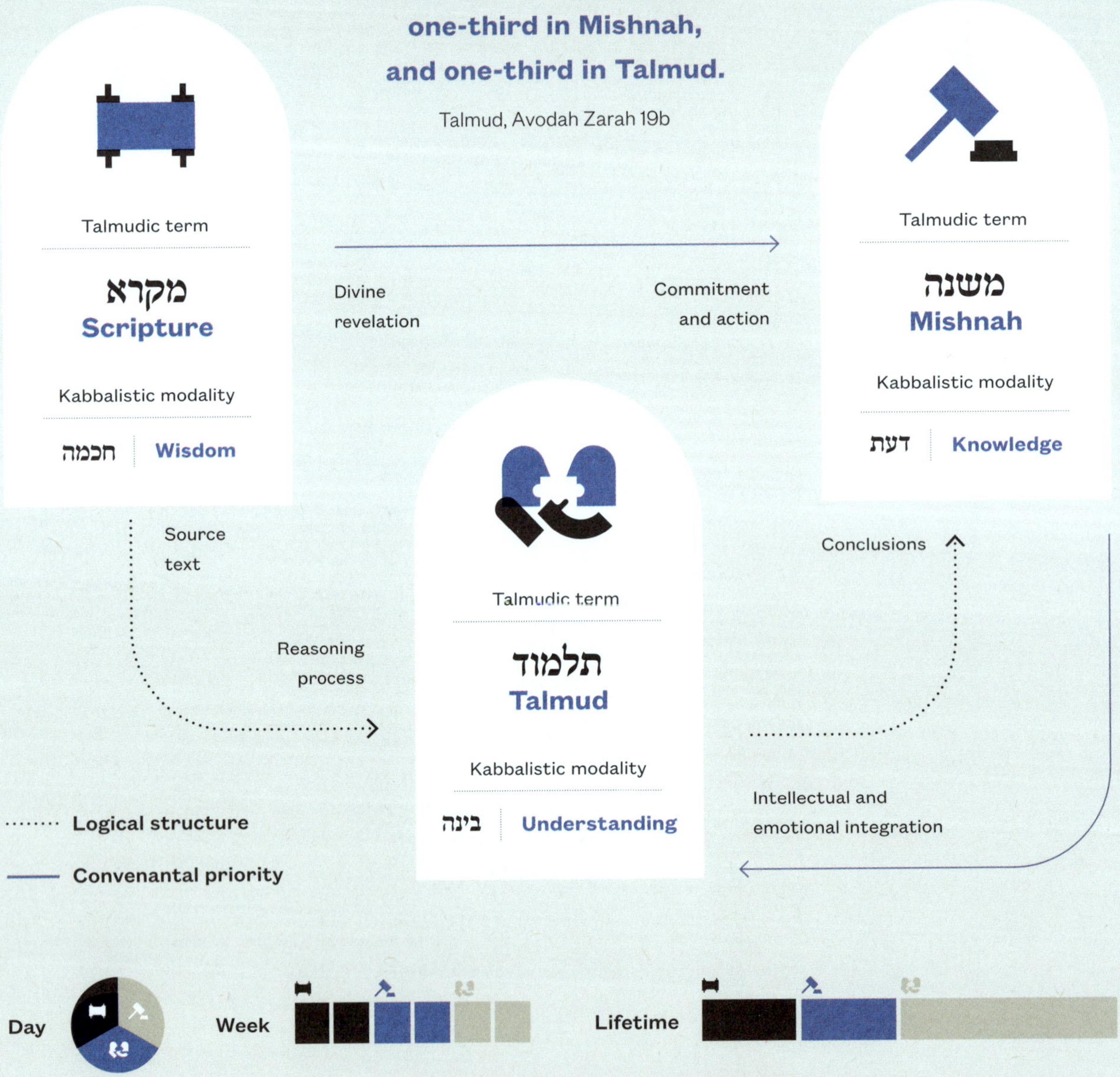

Talmudic term

מקרא
Scripture

Kabbalistic modality

חכמה | **Wisdom**

Divine revelation → Commitment and action

Talmudic term

משנה
Mishnah

Kabbalistic modality

דעת | **Knowledge**

Source text

Reasoning process

Talmudic term

תלמוד
Talmud

Kabbalistic modality

בינה | **Understanding**

Conclusions

Intellectual and emotional integration

······ **Logical structure**

—— **Convenantal priority**

Day

Week

Lifetime

Background and Explanation

The Talmud instructs: "A person should divide their years [of Torah learning] into three parts: one-third in *Scripture*, one-third in *Mishnah*, and one-third in *Talmud*."[1]

What are these three components of Torah?

Source, Process, and Conclusion

1) Scripture (*Mikra* in Hebrew) refers to the "Written Torah"—the twenty-four books of the Tanach (Jewish Bible). These include the Five Books of Moses and the books of the Prophets (*Neviim*) and the Scriptures (*Ketuvim*). The texts of the Written Torah are the "source texts" for the whole of Jewish teaching. In a broader sense, this category includes all the teachings that derive exclusively from Divine revelation (rather than human reasoning) and were handed down by tradition, such as the core teachings of Kabbalah.[2]

2) Mishnah is the Halachic component of Torah. The work commonly known as "the Mishnah" was compiled by Rabbi Yehudah Hanasi toward the end of the second century CE, and was the first written summary of Torah law. In the broader sense, "Mishnah" denotes Halachah, the final legal rulings of Torah law. The field of Halachah includes works such as Maimonides's *Mishneh Torah*, the Shulchan Aruch ("Code of Jewish Law"), and the many other works that detail the laws and customs that make up Jewish practice.

3) Talmud is actually the intermediary step between "Scripture" and "Mishnah." The field of Talmud (meaning "learning") includes the interpretations, explanations, expositions, debates, and discussions that originate from the source texts of "Scripture" and result in the Halachic rulings of "Mishnah."

Wisdom, Understanding, and Knowledge

The great Jewish mystic and philosopher Maharal writes[3] that these three areas of Torah correspond to the three intellectual faculties of **wisdom**, **understanding**, and **knowledge** (*chochmah*, *binah*, and *daat*, in Hebrew). These terms are used throughout Torah literature, and particularly in

---

1 Talmud, Avodah Zarah 19b. There is some discussion among the Halachic authorities as to how this directive is to be implemented in practice. According to Maimonides, each day's study time should be divided into three equal parts, each devoted to one of the three components, while Rashi understands this to mean that one should devote two days a week to each field of study (*Mishneh Torah*, Laws of Torah Learning 1:11; Rashi on Talmud, ad loc.). According to the Rabbi Nissim Gerondi (the "Ran"), however, this does not mean that a person should divide their time into three equal parts, but rather that each day's learning should include all three components, allocating to each the amount appropriate to the person's learning needs (cited in Ritva to Talmud, Avodah Zarah 19b). The Shulchan Aruch distinguishes between the first years of a person's Torah learning, when they should divide their time equally between the three components, and later in life, when the majority of one's learning time should be devoted to "Talmud," while allocating some time to the other two components as well (Shulchan Aruch, *Yoreh De'ah 246:4*). Rabbeinu Tam posits that the Babylonian Talmud includes elements of all three components, so a person who devotes all their learning time to studying the Talmud fulfills the obligation to learn all three (cited by Rama and Shach in *Yoreh De'ah,* ad loc.). However, most Halachic authorities rule that each day's learning should also include the study of Tanach and Halachah (see *Shulchan Aruch HaRav, Hilchot Talmud Torah 2:2*)

2 See *Likutei Sichot* 30, p. 173.

3 The Maharal of Prague, Rabbi Yehudah Loew (1520–1609), *Chidushei Agadot*, Kidushin 30a.

Kabbalah and Chasidism, to refer to the three primary intellectual faculties of the human mind. Briefly, "wisdom" (*chochmah*) is the ability to conceive ideas, "understanding" (*binah*) is the ability to analyze ideas, and "knowledge" (*daat*) is the ability to reach a conclusive decision and apply it to our lives.

Hence "Scripture"—the source texts of Torah from which all the ideas and laws of the other areas of Torah derive—is the "wisdom" component of Torah, similar to how the seed of an idea conceived by the mind's faculty of wisdom encapsulates all the details that will emerge from it. "Talmud" corresponds with "understanding," which is the ability to analyze a concept, to compare and contrast ideas, and to derive one principle from another. Finally, "Mishnah" is the parallel of "knowledge," which is the ability to apply the wisdom we conceived and the understanding we processed in the here and now of our lives.

Mishnah before Talmud?

Based on the above, the order in which the Talmud lists these three components of Torah learning seems incongruous. Shouldn't the sequence be, "Scripture, Talmud, and Mishnah"? This would describe a process in which we begin with the source text, then analyze it and deliberate its meanings, and then reach a conclusion. Instead, the Talmud tells us to divide our learning time between "Scripture, Mishnah, and Talmud," placing the conclusions *before* the reasoning process!

But this "out of order" sequence is quite intentional, as it reflects a very important truth about how Torah is learned.

Once we have imbibed the Divine revelation embodied in "Scripture," the first thing that, we need to learn is the actual laws (*Halachot*) and the guidance to life that Torah provides. It is only after that that we get into the "Talmud" mode of learning—exploring the processes by which these laws and conclusions are derived from the source texts of the Written Torah.

To use a simple analogy: Let us say that there are two people who want to learn how to lead a healthy lifestyle. The first person (let's call this "approach a") says: "I'm only going to learn the practicalities of healthy living: I'll consult with a dietitian on what to eat and what not to eat, I'll have a personal trainer instruct me in an exercise routine, and if I have any medical issues, I'll have a doctor prescribe medications and treatments. But I have no interest in studying the science behind it all, the different schools and their theories. I only need the practical instructions.

The second person takes an opposite approach (which we'll call "approach b"): "On the contrary, first I want to study the theory and the reasoning behind all these rules and instructions. I want to study the data, the proofs and counterproofs, and weigh the pros and cons behind each directive. Only after that will I be prepared to consider the conclusions that these fields of study have reached."

When it comes to Torah learning, both these approaches are wrong.

The problem with "approach b" is obvious. To become an expert in any field requires a lifetime of study; even then, a person may not reach any clear-cut conclusions on their own. The wise thing is to avail yourself of the collective wisdom of many generations of learning by thousands of individuals, by studying the conclusions they reached. After that, you can go back and explore the processes and methodologies by which these conclusions were reached in order to deepen your understanding.

But "approach a" is also not ideal. To study only the conclusions results in a shallow knowledge and, ultimately, a lackluster commitment.[4] It is only when we study the reasoning behind the conclusions that we gain a mature understanding of them, which also results in a greater appreciation and a stronger commitment.

But the *order* in which we approach Torah study is: First we study "Mishnah," the conclusions of the many generations of Torah learning that preceded us. Then we backtrack to "Talmud," to explore, deliberate, and contribute to the process by which these laws and principles are derived.

Indeed, this sequence can also be seen in the history of the documentation of the Torah. "Scripture," the Written Torah, was received from the start in written form. But the other two components—"Mishnah" and "Talmud"—are what is called the "Oral Torah," and for many centuries, it was handed down from teacher to student as an oral tradition. The first part of the Oral Torah to be documented in writing was the Mishnah, which almost entirely consists of a concise summary of Torah law rulings. The Talmud, which records the deliberations behind these laws, was only committed to writing centuries later.

"Hearing" the Torah

Thus, the Torah tells us that when Moses gathered the people of Israel at the foot of Mount Sinai in preparation to receiving the Torah, the people proclaimed, "All that G-d has spoken, we will do and we will hear."[5] The sages[6] point to this statement as the ultimate expression of our commitment to the Torah—the fact that we first said "we will do," and after that proclaimed "we will hear" and comprehend (the Hebrew word *nishma*, "we will hear," also means "we will understand"—i.e., not just do the *mitzvot* but also study and comprehend them).

It is noteworthy, however, that the people of Israel assembled at Sinai did not simply say "we will do," which, at first glance, may seem to express an even greater degree of obedience and commitment. Rather, their virtue lay in that they also said "we will hear," but placed "we will do" before "we will hear." The "we will hear" component is critical, but it must come after "we will do." First comes the commitment to do what G-d commands, but after that, a no less critical commitment to "hear"—to study and comprehend the meaning and purpose of the Divine commandments.

---

4 This is aside from the fact that if you don't know the reason behind the law, you may end up applying it in the wrong way.

5 Exodus 24:7.

6 Talmud, Shabbat 88a–b, et al.

The *Machloket*

INTRODUCTION

An axiom of the Talmudic discourse is that "the Torah is not in Heaven."[1] The Torah embodies the wisdom and will of G-d; at the same time, G-d desires the participation of the human mind as His partner in the formulation of the Torah. Thus, while the text of the Written Torah, and the methodology by which it is interpreted and expounded, were communicated by G-d to Moses at Mount Sinai, the particulars of Torah law are decided not in Heaven, but by means of study, analysis, and debate by the Torah sages of each generation.

The nature of the human mind is fractious and pluralistic. This means that two minds examining the same event or legal principle will often arrive at two different conclusions. The fact that the Torah incorporates the human mind as a full partner in its development means that the Torah embraces, and even celebrates, the phenomenon of *machlokes*—debate and disagreement between the sages. The Torah anticipates these disagreements, and decrees that the final ruling should be decided by the majority view. But the "rejected" view, while not followed in practice, is also part and parcel of the Torah. In the words of the Talmud, "these and these are both the words of the living G-d."[2]

A most fascinating component of Talmudic study is the concept of *leshitasaihu* ("according to their approach"). Often, we find the same two sages engaged in multiple debates on a variety of topics that, on the surface, appear to be unconnected. But upon closer examination, we discover that a common thread runs through these different debates, illuminating the particular *shitah*, or Torah approach, that each sage follows.

The following pages present a series of debates between two great Mishnaic sages, Rabbi Akiva and Rabbi Yishma'el, as well as the underlying approach that defines each sage's positions in these debates.[3]

---

1 Based on Deuteronomy 30:12.

2 Talmud, Eruvin 13b.

3 Rabbi Yishma'el is not explicitly mentioned as a party to Debate #5 ("To Weep or to Laugh"), but that debate describes a difference between Rabbi Akiva and many of his colleagues which fits the same pattern as the other four debates.

The Disputants

Rabbi Yishma'el

Rabbi Yishma'el ben Elisha (died ca. 130 CE) was a colleague and frequent disputant of Rabbi Akiva. Rabbi Yishma'el was a *Kohen*, a member of the priestly clan who performed the service in the Holy Temple, and a descendant of *Kohanim Gedolim* ("High Priests"; some say that he also served briefly as a *Kohen Gadol*). A leading Mishnaic sage, the Halachic Midrash *Mechilta* is based on his teachings.

Spiritual Personality:

The *Tzadik*

The *tzadik* is a perfectly righteous person whose life trajectory follows the Divine blueprint for life as spelled out in the Torah. The *tzadik's* life is characterized by a step-by-step progression to successively greater levels of perfection, achieving a perfect harmony between the natural world and Divine potential inherent within it.

The Debates

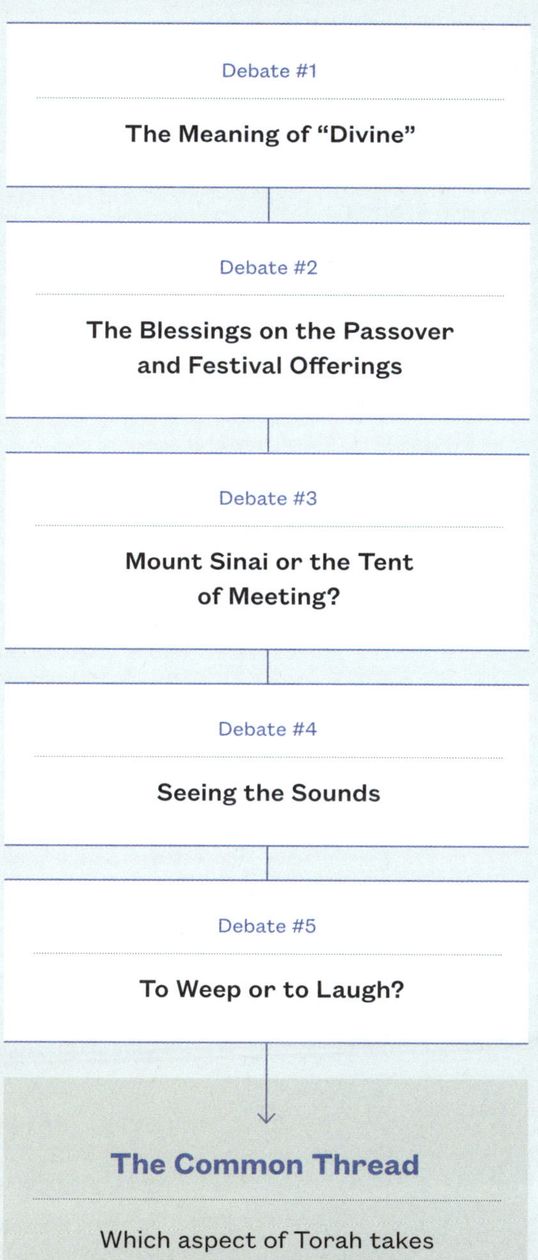

The Disputants

Rabbi Akiva

Rabbi Akiva (c. 15–135 CE) was a descendant of converts to Judaism and an illiterate shepherd until the age of 40. At the urging of his wife, Rachel, he left home to study Torah under the great sages of the day, returning after 24 years as an accomplished sage with thousands of students of his own. Toward the end of his life, Rabbi Akiva defied a Roman ban on teaching Torah publicly, and he was arrested and cruelly executed.

Spiritual Personality:

The *Baal Teshuvah*

The life of the *baal teshuvah* ("master of return") is characterized by upheaval and radical self-transformation. For the *baal teshuvah*, human nature is not something to be developed but to be superseded; the *baal teshuvah's* standards and priorities are dictated not by the natural reality but by the Divine reality.

DEBATE #1

The Meaning of "Divine"

In Exodus 22:27, the Torah commands: "Do not curse the Divine."

What is the meaning of this commandment?

Rabbi Yishma'el

It is forbidden to curse the judges of a *beit din* (court of Torah law), who are the agents of Divine justice in this world.

Rabbi Akiva

This is a prohibition to curse G-d.

The Blessings on the Passover and Festival Offerings

Mount Sinai or the Tent of Meeting?

Seeing the Sounds

To Weep or to Laugh?

The Common Thread

Which aspect of Torah takes precedence: The G-dly or the human? (see page 117)

DEBATE #2

The Meaning of "Divine"

The Blessings on the Passover and Festival Offerings

Two offerings were brought in the Holy Temple to celebrate the festival of Passover: a) the "festival offering," which was eaten as part of the festive *seder* meal; b) the "Passover offering," which was eaten at the end of the *seder* meal. Each of these offerings had a special blessing that was recited before it was eaten—i.e., "Blessed are You, G-d our G-d, who has sanctified us with His commandments, and has commanded us to eat the festival sacrifice" and "Blessed are You . . . to eat the Passover sacrifice." But what if a person recites the latter blessing—"to eat the Passover sacrifice"—first? Do they still need to recite a separate blessing for the festival offering?

Rabbi Yishma'el

Regarding the blessings made on food, the law is that once a person has said the blessing for a "primary" food, they do not need to say the blessing for a secondary food. For example, if a person recites the *Hamotzi* blessing on bread, they don't need to recite the separate blessing (*Haadamah*) for vegetables eaten in the same meal. The same applies to the blessings on the festival offerings. Once a person has said the blessing on the Passover offering, which is the more primary *mitzvah* of the night, they do not need to also recite the blessing for the festival offering.

Rabbi Akiva

Regarding the blessings we make to thank G-d for the foods He provides to us, we distinguish between primary and secondary sources of nutrition and pleasure. But the blessings recited before doing a *mitzvah* are different. *Mitzvot* are Divine commandments, and no Divine commandment can be said to be more "primary" than any other. So each *mitzvah* will always require its own blessing.

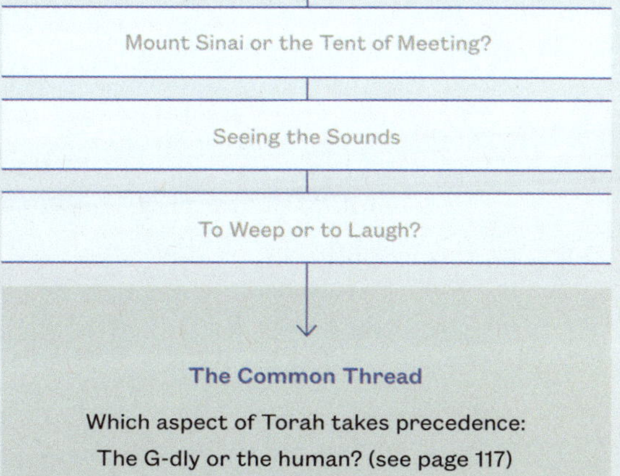

The Common Thread

Which aspect of Torah takes precedence: The G-dly or the human? (see page 117)

DEBATE #3

Rabbi Yishma'el

The general principles were given to Moses at Mount Sinai. Subsequently, the detailed laws were taught to Moses in the "Tent of Meeting" (the Tabernacle) in the course of the forty years that the Children of Israel journeyed in the wilderness.

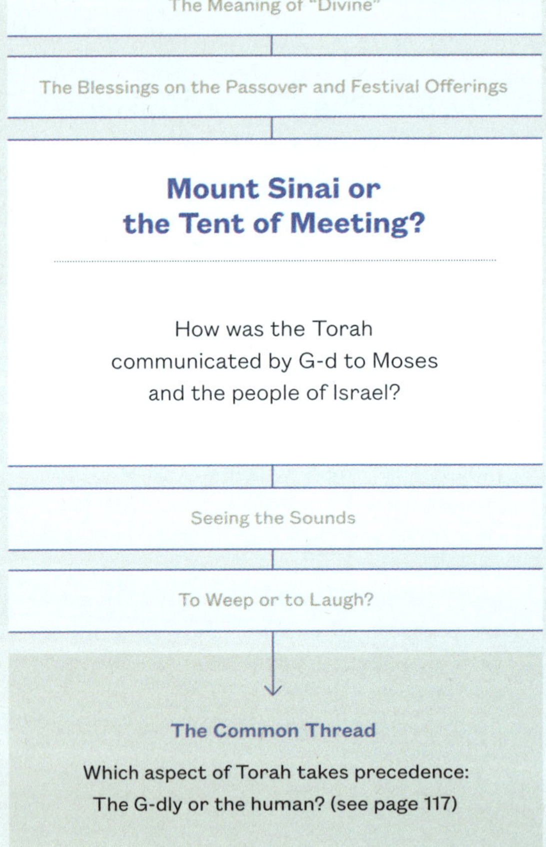

Rabbi Akiva

Both the general principles and the detailed laws were given to Moses at Mount Sinai. The distinction between "general principles" and "detailed laws" is germane to how the human mind processes knowledge. But as regards the revelation of the Divine wisdom and will, such distinctions are subsumed within the suprarational essence of the Divine communication.

DEBATE #4

The Meaning of "Divine"

The Blessings on the Passover and Festival Offerings

Mount Sinai or the Tent of Meeting?

Seeing the Sounds

The Torah describes the revelation at Mount Sinai in the following manner: "All the people saw the sounds and the flames and the mountain smoking; and the people saw and they trembled, and they stood from afar" (Exodus 20:15).

Rabbi Yishma'el

What the people actually saw were the flames and the smoke mentioned later in the verse, while the "sounds" were heard, not literally seen. The entire point of the revelation at Mount Sinai was that they should experience G-dliness within the bounds of their own natural existence. So their natural faculties functioned as they normally do: they saw the sights and they heard the sounds.

Rabbi Akiva

At Mount Sinai, the natural reality was completely overturned. Realities that are normally seen—i.e., the material world—were no more than a concept, an abstract idea that is "heard" and understood. And spiritual realities, which are usually only "heard," became real and tangible. Hence the Torah states that the people "saw the sounds"—they saw what is ordinarily heard, and they heard what is ordinarily seen.

To Weep or to Laugh?

The Common Thread

Which aspect of Torah takes precedence: The G-dly or the human? (see page 117)

DEBATE #5

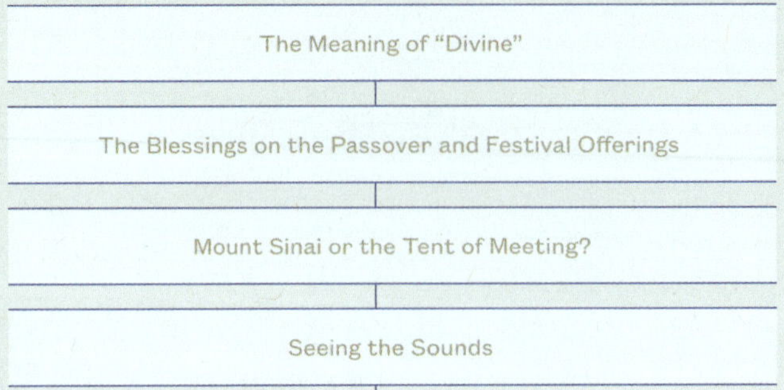

To Weep or to Laugh?

The Talmud (Makot 24b) relates the following incident:

Again it happened that Rabban Gamliel, Rabbi Elazar ben Azariah, Rabbi Yehoshua, and Rabbi Akiva went up to Jerusalem. . . . When they reached the Temple Mount, they saw a fox emerging from the place of the Holy of Holies. Rabbi Akiva's colleagues started weeping. Rabbi Akiva laughed.

Said they to him, "Why are you laughing?" Said he to them, "Why are you weeping?" Said they to him, "A place so holy that it is said of it, 'The stranger that approaches it shall die' (Numbers 1:51); now foxes traverse it, and we should not weep?"

Said he to them: "That is why I laugh . . . ! Uriah prophesied, 'Zion shall be plowed as a field; Jerusalem shall become heaps, and the Temple Mount like the high places of a forest' (Micah 3:12). And Zechariah prophesied, 'Old men and women shall yet sit in the streets of Jerusalem' (Zechariah 8:4). As long as the prophecy of Uriah had not been fulfilled, I feared that the prophecy of Zechariah may not be fulfilled. But now that Uriah's prophecy has been fulfilled, it is certain that Zechariah's prophecy will be fulfilled."

With these words they responded to him: "Akiva, you have consoled us! Akiva, you have consoled us!"

Rabbi Akiva's Colleagues

What is real to us is what we experience in the here and now. We hope and pray for the future Redemption and have complete faith that G-d will ultimately restore the Holy Temple to its former glory, but the future hasn't happened yet. Our current reality demands that we mourn and weep over the destruction and exile.

Rabbi Akiva

As Jews, we are not slaves to the conventions of the material reality. We inhabit a Divine reality that transcends the strictures of time and space. In this Divine reality, every potential is fully realized, and every future promise is joyously materialized.

The Common Thread

Which aspect of Torah takes precedence: The G-dly or the human? (see page 117)

THE COMMON THREAD

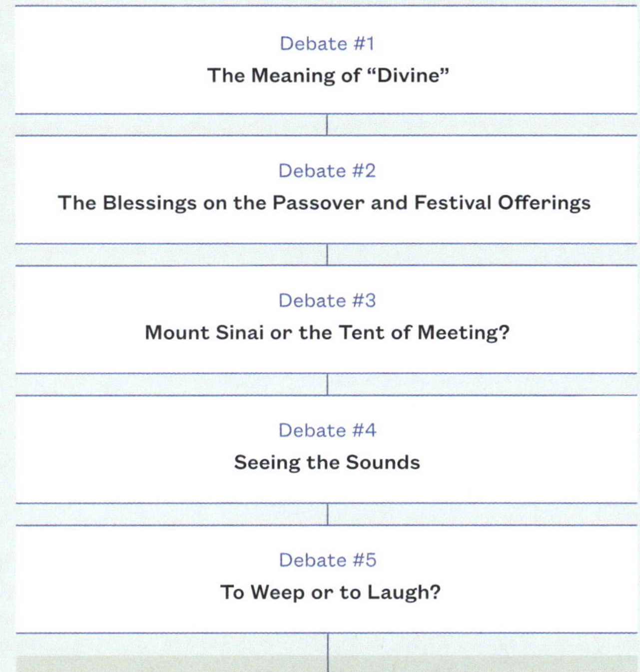

The Common Thread

The Torah is a partnership of Heaven and earth, a collaboration of Divine revelation and human reason. Thus, every law and event in Torah incorporates both elements: a G-dly essence and a human iteration; a supranatural core and pedestrian application.

While these two elements are present in every component of Torah, at times the Divine element is more pronounced, while at other times the human element is more expressed. Thus, when there are two possible ways to interpret a verse, or two possible ways to rule on a law, Rabbi Yishma'el favors the natural-human iteration, while Rabbi Akiva tends toward the supernatural-Divine exposition.

LESSON 4

TO CREATE THE TALMUD

How the sages shaped its structure and substance

Meet the pivotal sages in the Talmud's story—from Rav and Shmuel's first academies to Rav Ashi and Ravina's final text—and see how they wove in stories as well as ethical and philosophical teachings.

THE TORAH SCRIBE
Maurycy Gottlieb, oil on board, Poland, 1876. (National Museum of Wroclaw, Poland)

I. THE MAKING OF THE TALMUD

The story of the creation of the Talmud is the saga of the Diaspora community of Babylonia (Bavel). For over three hundred years, the sages of both Israel and Babylonia labored at interpreting and expounding upon the Mishnah. Eventually, the sages of Babylonia compiled all the interpretations of the Mishnah that had been offered and organized them into the text we call the Talmud, or Gemara.

KEY TERM 4.1

HEBREW TERM	בָּבֶל
TRANSLITERATION	***Bavel***
PRONUNCIATION	BAH-vell
LITERAL MEANING	**Babylonia**
MEANING	The area within the Parthian and Sassanid Empires that is north of the ancient city of Babylon. The majority of Diaspora Jews during the era of the Second Temple and the Mishnah lived in this area.

TALMUD AND MISHNA
Elena Kalman, mixed media and acrylic on paper, USA, 2022

FIGURE 4.1

Babylonia During the Talmudic Era

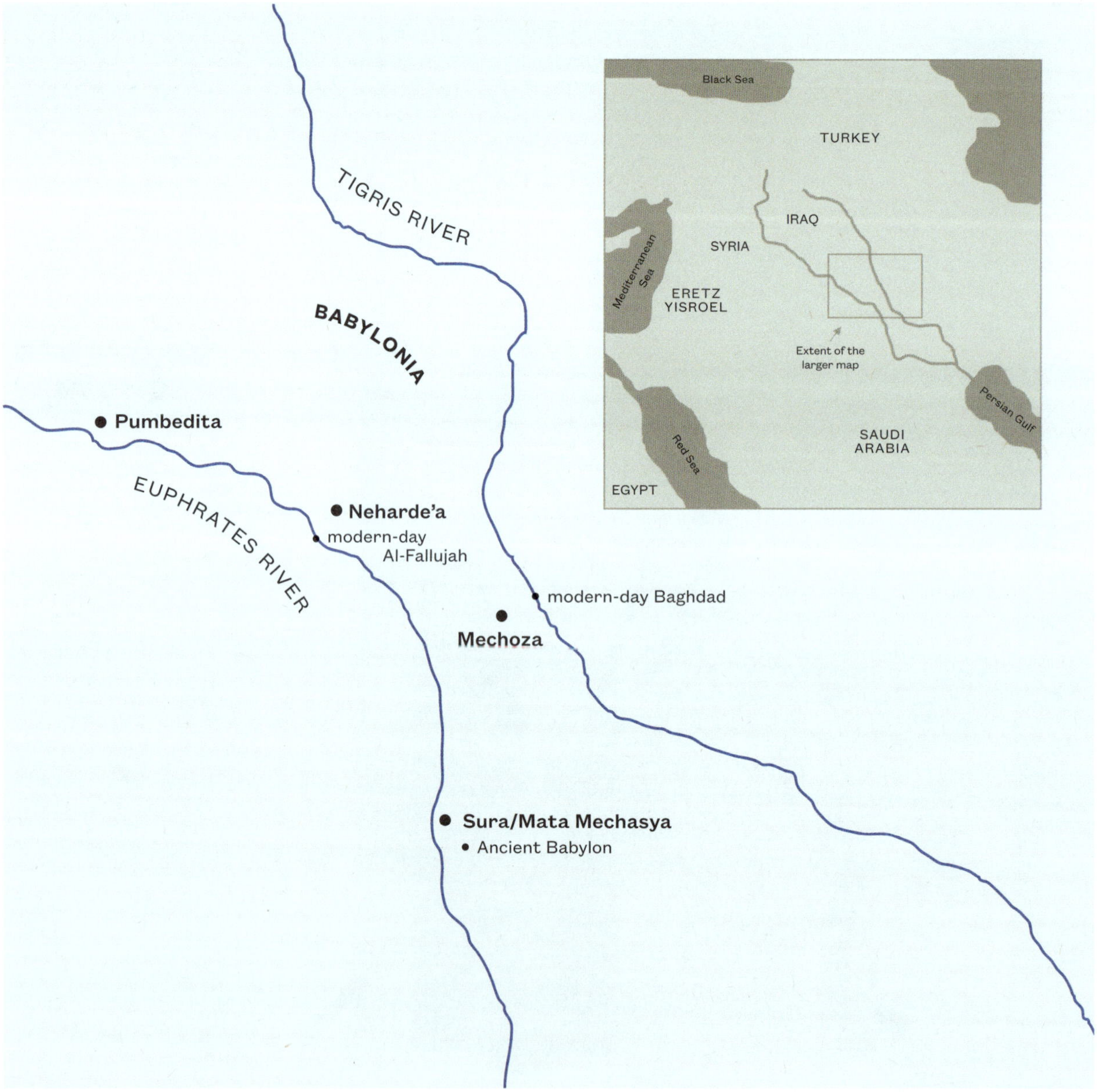

TEXT 1

Charitable Dispersion

Talmud, Pesachim, 87b

אָמַר רַבִּי אוֹשַׁעְיָא . . . צְדָקָה עָשָׂה הַקָּדוֹשׁ בָּרוּךְ הוּא בְּיִשְׂרָאֵל שֶׁפִּזְּרָן לְבֵין הָאוּמוֹת.

Rabbi Oshaya taught: . . . "The Holy One, Blessed be He, acted charitably with the people of Israel by scattering them among the nations."

BABYLONIAN TALMUD

A literary work of monumental proportions that draws upon the legal, spiritual, intellectual, ethical, and historical traditions of Judaism. The 37 tractates of the Babylonian Talmud contain the teachings of the Jewish sages from the period after the destruction of the 2nd Temple through the 5th century CE. It has served as the primary vehicle for the transmission of the Oral Law and the education of Jews over the centuries; it is the entry point for all subsequent legal, ethical, and theological Jewish scholarship.

JEWISH QUARTERS IN AMSTERDAM
Auguste Lepere, wood engraving, 1931

FIGURE 4.2

The Sages of the Talmud

CE	*Amora'im* in Israel	*Amora'im* in Babylonia	Historic Events	*Yeshivot*
200–250	R. Chanina R. Yannai R. Chiya R. Oshiya R. Yochanan (d. 279) Reish Lakish	Rav (d. 247) Shmuel (d. 254)	Sassanid Empire replaces the Parthian Empire in Babylonia (224)	Tiberias (Israel) Sura (Babylonia) Neharde'a (Babylonia)
250–300		R. Huna (d. 297) R. Yehudah (d. 299) R. Chisda (d. 309)	Sack of Neharde'a (259)	Tiberias (Israel) Sura (Babylonia) Pumbedita (Babylonia)
300–350	R. Ami R. Asi R. Yirmiyah	Rabbah (d. 323) R. Yosef (d. 325) Abaye (d. 338) Rava (d. 352)	Rome adopts Christianity	Tiberias (Israel) Caesarea (Israel) Pumbedita (Babylonia)
350–400		R. Pappa R. Nachman bar Yitzchak R. Ashi (d. 427) Ravina	Rule of Yazdegerd I in Babylonia	Pumbedita (Babylonia) Narash (Babylonia) Mata Mechasya (Babylonia)
400–450		Mar bar R. Ashi		Mata Mechasya (Babylonia)
450–500		Ravina II		Pumbedita (Babylonia)

TEXT 2

Ruling Rules

Talmud, Bechorot 49b

כָּל הֵיכָא דִפְלִיגִי רַב וּשְׁמוּאֵל, הִלְכְתָא
כְּרַב בְּאִיסוּרֵי וְכִשְׁמוּאֵל בְּדִינֵי.

In every instance of disagreement between Rav and Shmuel, the Halachah accords with Rav's opinion regarding ritual matters and with Shmuel's opinion regarding monetary matters.

TEXT 3

Rising with the Dust

Talmud, Ketubot 106a

כִּי הֲווּ קַיְימִי רַבָּנָן מִמְתִיבְתָּא דְרַב הוּנָא וְנָפְצִי
גְלִימַיְיהוּ הֲוָה סָלֵיק אַבְקָא וְכָסֵי לֵיהּ לְיוֹמָא.

וְאָמְרִי בְּמַעֲרָבָא: קָמוּ לֵיהּ מִמְתִיבְתָּא דְרַב הוּנָא בַּבְלָאָה.

After listening to lectures in the yeshiva of Rav Huna, the assembled sages would rise and dust off their cloaks. The dust would rise and block out the sun.

They would exclaim in the West [i.e., in the Land of Israel, upon seeing a large dust cloud in the distance], "They have just arisen in the academy of Rav Huna the Babylonian!"

TEXT 4

Combining Schools

Rabbi Yosef Colon, *Shu"t Maharik*, responsa 84

דְעַד אַבַּיֵי וְרָבָא לֹא הָיוּ הַתַּלְמִידִים לוֹמְדִים אֶלָא עַל פִּי קַבָּלַת רַבּוֹתֵיהֶם כְּפִי מָה שֶׁהָיוּ שׁוֹנִים לָהֶם מֵהֶם הָיוּ שׁוֹנִים עַל פִּי רַבִּי חִיָיא וְרַבִּי אוֹשַׁעְיָא וּמֵהֶם עַל פִּי מִשְׁנַת בַּר קַפָּרָא אוֹ מַתְנִיתָא דְבֵי לֵוִי אוֹ מַתְנִיתָא דְבֵי שְׁמוּאֵל וְכֵן כּוּלָם . . .

אֲבָל מֵאַבַּיֵי וְרָבָא וָאֵילַךְ לָמְדוּ כָּל הַדֵעוֹת . . . הִתְחִילָה לִלְמוֹד כָּל הַבְּרַיְיתוֹת וְיָשְׁבוּ וְתִרְצוּ אֶת כּוּלָם שֶׁלֹא יִקְשֶׁה מִזֶה עַל זֶה וּמִתּוֹךְ כָּךְ הוֹצִיאוּ כַּמָה דִינִים וְהֶעֱמִידוּ כַּמָה שְׁמוּעוֹת עַל בּוּרְיָין וְעַל אֲמִתָּתָם.

Until the period of Abaye and Rava, students studied exclusively the branches of tradition that they received from their own teachers, precisely as it was recited to them. As a result, some students only studied the tradition according to Rabbi Chiya and Rabbi Oshiya; other students studied it only according to the Mishnah of Bar Kapara; others according to the *Baraitot* of the House of Levi, or the *Baraitot* of the House of Shmuel, and so on. . . .

During the era of Abaye and Rava, and forever after, students were introduced to the method of studying all of the diverse views. . . . They studied all of the *Baraitot* and resolved and reconciled their discrepancies until they were no longer contradictory. In the course of this process, they succeeded in extracting many laws, clarifying many teachings, and uncovering their true intentions.

RABBI YOSEF COLON (MAHARIK)
C. 1420–1480

Rabbi Colon was born in France. Eventually he settled in northern Italy, where he held several important rabbinical positions. His responsa were internationally famous and widely circulated. Rabbi Ovadiah of Bartenura, the noted commentator on the Mishnah, was his student.

TEXT 5

Compiling the Talmud

Rashi, Bava Metzi'a 86a

רַב אַשִׁי וְרָבִינָא סִידְרוּ שְׁמוּעוֹת אֲמוֹרָאִין שֶׁלִּפְנֵיהֶם וְקָבְעוּ עַל סֵדֶר הַמַּסֶּכְתּוֹת כָּל אֶחָד וְאֶחָד אֵצֶל הַמִּשְׁנָה הָרְאוּיָה וְהַשְּׁנוּיָה לָהּ.

וְהִקְשׁוּ קוּשְׁיוֹת שֶׁיֵּשׁ לְהָשִׁיב וּפֵירוּקִים שֶׁרְאוּיִם לְתָרֵץ הֵם וְהָאֲמוֹרָאִים שֶׁעִמָּהֶם וְקָבְעוּ הַכֹּל בַּגְּמָרָא . . .

Rav Ashi and Ravina arranged the teachings of the *amora'im* that preceded them. They organized them according to the order of the tractates, placing each teaching next to the appropriate and relevant Mishnah.

Along with their contemporary *amora'im*, Rav Ashi and Ravina posed necessary questions and provided appropriate solutions. They established all of this in the Gemara.

RABBI SHLOMO YITZCHAKI (RASHI) 1040–1105

Most noted biblical and Talmudic commentator. Born in Troyes, France, Rashi studied in the famed *yeshivot* of Mainz and Worms. His commentaries on the Pentateuch and the Talmud, which focus on the straightforward meaning of the text, appear in virtually every edition of the Talmud and Bible.

II. REVIEW AND REVIEW

Due to the Talmud's complexity, it is not sufficient to simply read a *sugya* once, even if it is understood the first time. Review is critical to Talmud study. Students must review the texts repeatedly to ensure they properly grasp the full import and can then analyze them further.

The present section offers a review of the *sugya* analyzed in our previous lesson, which will provide an opportunity to glean fresh insights.

AT THE SYNAGOGUE
Joseph Budko, woodcut

TEXT 6

Scholarly Review

Rashi, Berachot 5a

וְאִם תַּלְמִיד חָכָם הוּא, שֶׁרָגִיל בְּמִשְׁנָתוֹ לַחֲזוֹר עַל גִּרְסָתוֹ תָּמִיד.

"If he is a Torah scholar (*talmid chacham*)": This refers to those who are consistent in their study, constantly reviewing their lessons.

HAMATMID
(THE DILIGENT STUDENT)
Brachi Brilofsky, oil on canvas, Israel, 2014

EXERCISE 4.1

The following series of exercises poses review questions regarding the Talmudic *sugya* from Pesachim 99b–110a studied in Lesson Three on pages 92-97.

The Mishnah used the phrase *arvei Pesachim*. The Gemara assumed that this meant that the prohibition against eating applied only on the eve of Passover, not on the eve of Shabbat or other festivals. Explain why that seemed to conflict with both the opinion of Rabbi Yehudah and the opinion of Rabbi Yose that appear in the Baraita.

EXERCISE 4.2

What was the solution suggested by Rav Huna? According to Rav Huna, whose opinion does the Mishnah follow?

EXERCISE 4.3

What was the solution suggested by Rav Pappa? According to Rav Pappa, whose opinion does the Mishnah follow?

EXERCISE 4.4

Mar Zutra offered a solution to rescue Rav Pappa's interpretation. What was his suggestion?

EXERCISE 4.5

How did Ameimar (or Rav Yeimar) respond to Mar Zutra's suggestion?

III. THE GEMARA'S STRUCTURE

The Gemara is structured as a compilation of multiple discussions on various Mishnahs. It is fascinating to realize that these discussions actually stretch across several centuries. In their effort to compile the Gemara, the editors took great pains to attribute each teaching to the sage that authored it, allowing us to trace the course of discussion across time.

CHAIR, BOOKS, AND A SUITCASE
Meir Pichhadze (1955-2010), oil on canvas, Israel

TEXT 7

International Conversations

Harry Freedman, *The Talmud—A Biography: Banned, Censored and Burned. The Book They Couldn't Suppress* (London, U.K.: Bloomsbury Publishing, 2014), pp. 51–52

For all its complex composition the Talmud appears to the reader to be a seamless work. It's not until we analyze it closely that we can see the joints between the layers. Although written in Babylon, the Talmud can quote the opinion of people who lived their whole lives elsewhere, yet it will [feel] as if they were standing in the same room as native Babylonians.

HARRY FREEDMAN
1950–

Author. Born in London, Harry Freedman is an author who focuses on Jewish history and culture. His books include *The Talmud: A Biography*, and *Shylock's Venice: The Remarkable History of Venice's Jews and the Ghetto*.

AT THE *BAIT MIDRASH* (STUDY HALL)
Zvi Malnovitzer, oil on canvas, Israel

TEXT 8

Accurate Attribution

Talmud, Nedarim 8b

אָמַר רַבִּי שִׁמְעוֹן בַּר זְבִיד, אָמַר רַבִּי יִצְחָק בַּר טַבְלָא, אָמַר רַבִּי חִיָּיא אֲרִיכָא דְבֵי רַבִּי אַחָא, אָמַר רַבִּי זֵירָא, אָמַר רַבִּי אֶלְעָזָר, אָמַר רַבִּי חֲנִינָא, אָמַר רַבִּי מְיָאשָׁה מִשְּׁמֵיהּ דְּרַבִּי יְהוּדָה בַּר אִילָעאִי:

מַאי דִּכְתִיב "וְזָרְחָה לָכֶם יִרְאֵי שְׁמִי [שֶׁמֶשׁ צְדָקָה וְגוֹ']" (מַלְאָכִי ג, כ).

אֵלּוּ בְּנֵי אָדָם שֶׁהֵן יְרֵאִין לְהוֹצִיא שֵׁם שָׁמַיִם לְבַטָּלָה.

Rabbi Shimon bar Zevid said that Rabbi Yitzchak bar Tavla said that Rabbi Chiya Aricha of the school of Rabbi Acha said that Rabbi Zeira said that Rabbi Elazar said that Rabbi Chanina said that Rabbi Meyashah said in the name of Rabbi Yehudah bar Elai:

What is the significance of the phrase "fear My name" in the verse, "But for you that fear My name the sun of righteousness will arise with healing in its wings" (MALACHI 3:20)?

It refers to people who are afraid to mention G-d's name in vain.

IV. THE MEANDERING GEMARA

An intriguing feature of the Gemara's structure is the manner in which it seemingly wanders from one topic to the next. A glance at the flow of the *sugya* in our previous lesson reveals that the Gemara, in just one small discussion, finds itself discussing multiple subjects far afield from the original laws on which the Mishnah was focused (the Passover *seder*).

GOLDEN RIVER
Karin Foreman, mixed media on canvas, Santa Rosa Valley, California, 2018

TEXT 9

Purposeful Digressions

Rabbi Adin Even-Israel (Steinsaltz), *Reference Guide to the Talmud* (Jerusalem: Koren Publishers, 2014), p. 7

The focus of attention may shift from subject to subject until we find ourselves far from the original starting point. However . . . it is guided by an inner connection—sometimes very subtle, but often very strong—between all the subjects discussed. This connection is never merely superficial, and the seemingly wayward digressions in fact add substance and interest to the central theme.

RABBI ADIN EVEN-ISRAEL STEINSALTZ 1937–2020

Talmudist, author, and philosopher. Rabbi Steinsaltz is considered one of the foremost Jewish thinkers of the 20th century. A resident of Jerusalem, Rabbi Steinsaltz was the founder of the Israel Institute for Talmudic Publications, a society dedicated to the translation and elucidation of the Talmud, and he authored numerous works about the Talmud and Jewish mysticism. Praised by *Time* magazine as a "once-in-a-millennium scholar," he was awarded the Israel Prize for his contributions to Jewish study.

AT THE TABLE
Artur Markowitz, oil on canvas, Poland, 1913

FIGURE 4.3

The Meandering *Sugya* River

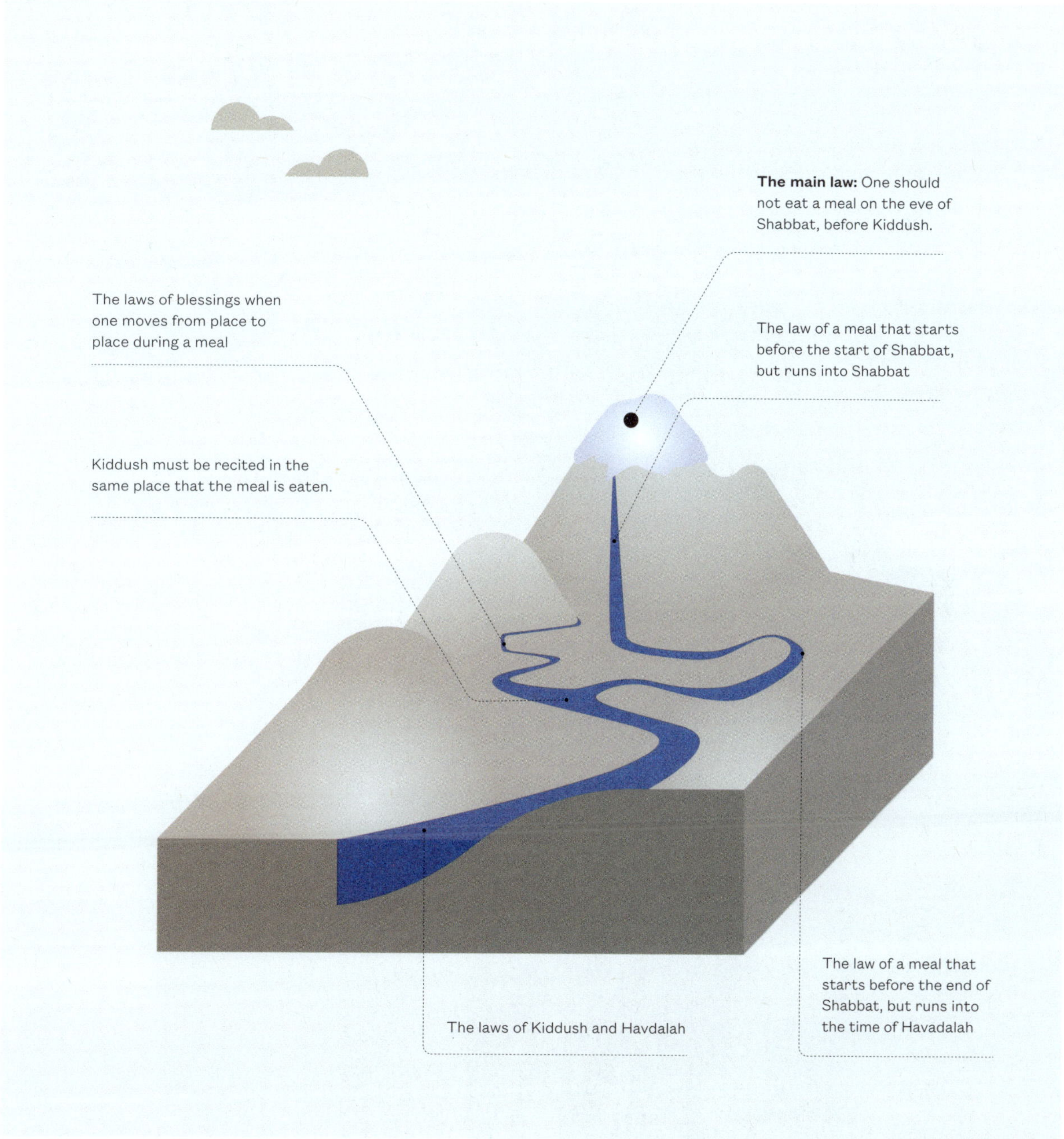

V. THE TALES AND TEACHINGS OF THE *AGADAH*

The Gemara includes a vast treasury of non-Halachic material, known as *agadata*. These teachings are quite different from the Gemara's typical Halachic discussions; they include ethical, moral, and philosophical ideas, and they also bring the sages of the Talmud to life with stories, sayings, and the like. These teachings, in particular, can sometimes appear deliberately simplistic or baffling, but in fact allude to profound mystical insights. The present section presents a sample of *agadata*.

SEFARIM **(BOOKS)**
Samuel Bak, oil on canvas, Boston, MA, 2001. (Pucker Gallery, Boston, MA)

KEY TERM 4.2

HEBREW TERM	אַגַדְתָא/אַגָדָה/אַגָדוֹת/הַגָדָה
TRANSLITERATION	*agadata/agadah/agadot/hagadah*
PRONUNCIATION	ah-GAH-dah-tah/ah-GAH-dah/ ah-ga-DOT/ha-GAH-dah
LITERAL MEANING	**that which has been related**
MEANING	The non-Halachic teachings of the sages of the Mishnah and Gemara

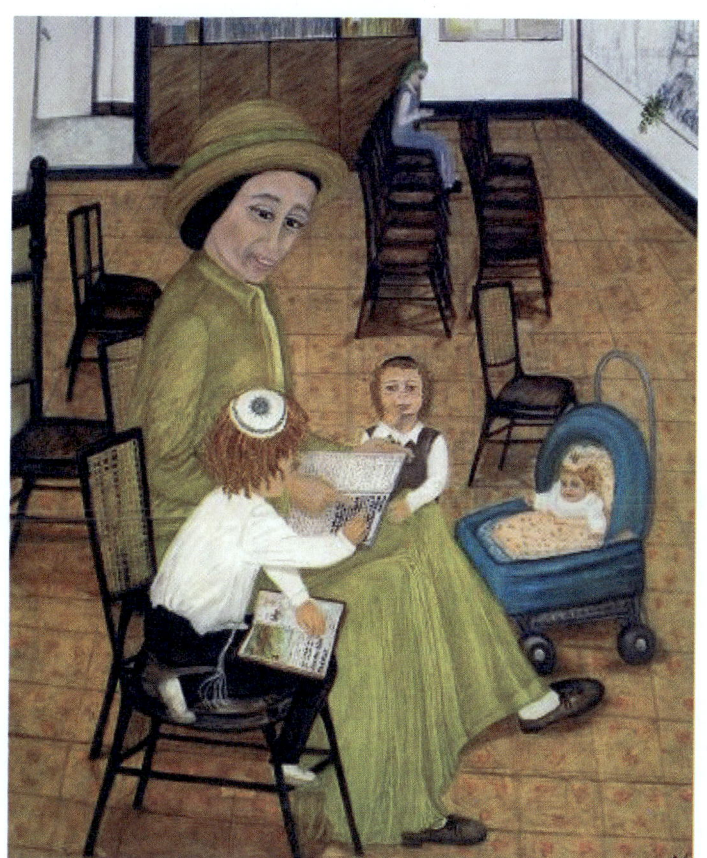

AND TALK TO YOUR CHILDREN
Socam, oil on canvas, Israel, 2009

TEXT 10

Life Advice

Talmud, Pesachim 112a

שִׁבְעָה דְבָרִים צִוָּה רַבִּי עֲקִיבָא אֶת רַבִּי יְהוֹשֻׁעַ בְּנוֹ:

בְּנִי,

אַל תֵּשֵׁב בְּגוֹבְהָהּ שֶׁל עִיר וְתִשְׁנֶה,

וְאַל תָּדוּר בְּעִיר שֶׁרָאשֶׁיהָ תַּלְמִידֵי חֲכָמִים,

וְאַל תִּכָּנֵס לְבֵיתְךָ פִּתְאוֹם, כָּל שֶׁכֵּן לְבֵית חֲבֵירְךָ,

וְאַל תִּמְנַע מִנְעָלִים מֵרַגְלֶיךָ,

הַשְׁכֵּם וֶאֱכוֹל, בַּקַּיִץ מִפְּנֵי הַחַמָּה, וּבַחוֹרֶף מִפְּנֵי הַצִּינָּה,

וַעֲשֵׂה שַׁבַּתְּךָ חוֹל וְאַל תִּצְטָרֵךְ לַבְּרִיּוֹת,

וֶהֱוֵי מִשְׁתַּדֵּל עִם אָדָם שֶׁהַשָּׁעָה מְשַׂחֶקֶת לוֹ.

Rabbi Akiva provided his son, Rabbi Yehoshua, with seven pieces of advice:

"My son:

"1) Do not sit in the busy part of a town and study;

"2) Do not dwell in a city whose leaders are Torah scholars;

"3) Do not enter your own home unannounced, and certainly not your fellow's home;

"4) Do not deprive your feet of shoes;

"5) Eat early in the day—during summer, because of the heat, and during winter, because of the cold;

"6) If need be, reduce your Shabbat meal to the basics like a weekday meal rather than accepting charity [by which to enhance the Shabbat meals];

"7) Do business with a person who is currently experiencing good fortune."

FIGURE 4.4

Agadata Sample Types

TYPE OF *AGADATA*	EXAMPLE
Teachings regarding the episodes and events described in Tanach	A Midrashic elaboration on the story of Esther
Ethical teachings and life advice offered by individual *tanna'im* and *amora'im*	Rabbi Akiva's advice to his son
Information and sagas regarding Jewish history	Details of the Roman siege of Jerusalem that led to the Temple's destruction
Stories about individual *tanna'im* and *amora'im*	An episode in which Rabbi Akiva breached the Roman ban on publicly teaching Torah, and justified it with a fox-and-fish parable
Theological and philosophical discussions	The tradition that "Every Jew has a portion in the World to Come"

TEXT 11

Deep Wisdom

Nachmanides, Shir Hashirim, introduction, chapter 2

הֵם בּוֹרוֹת עֲמֻקִּים שֶׁאֵינָן מְאַבְּדִין טִיפָּה,

וְכָל דִּבְרֵיהֶם לֵב פְּנִימִי בְּלִי קְלִיפָּה.

They are deep cisterns [of wisdom] that do not lose a drop;

All their words possess an inner heart, without any concealing husk.

RABBI MOSHE BEN NACHMAN (NACHMANIDES, RAMBAN) 1194–1270

Scholar, philosopher, author, and physician. Nachmanides was born in Spain and served as leader of Iberian Jewry. In 1263, he was summoned by King James of Aragon to a public disputation with Pablo Cristiani, a Jewish apostate. Though Nachmanides was the clear victor of the debate, he had to flee Spain because of the resulting persecution. He moved to Israel and helped reestablish communal life in Jerusalem. He authored a classic commentary on the Pentateuch and a commentary on the Talmud.

TEXT 12

Knowing G-d

Sifrei, Ekev 49

רְצוֹנְךָ לְהַכִּיר אֶת מִי שֶׁאָמַר וְהָיָה הָעוֹלָם
לְמוֹד הַגָּדָה שֶׁמִּתּוֹךְ כָּךְ אַתָּה מַכִּיר אֶת מִי
שֶׁאָמַר וְהָיָה הָעוֹלָם וּמִדַּבֵּק בִּדְרָכָיו.

If you wish to recognize the One Who spoke the world into being, study the *agadah*—for through this you will recognize the One Who spoke the world into being, and you will cleave to His ways.

SIFREI

An early rabbinic Midrash on the biblical books of Numbers and Deuteronomy. *Sifrei* focuses mostly on matters of law, as opposed to narratives and moral principles. According to Maimonides, this Halachic Midrash was authored by Rav, a 3rd-century Babylonian Talmudic sage.

TEXT 13

Strange Order

Talmud, Shabbat 77b

רַבִּי זֵירָא אַשְׁכַּח לְרַב יְהוּדָה דַהֲוָה קָאֵי אַפִּיתְחָא
דְבֵי חֲמוּהָ, וְחַזְיֵיהּ דַהֲוָה בְּדִיחָא דַעְתֵּיהּ, וְאִי
בָּעֵי מִינֵיהּ כָּל חֲלָלֵי עָלְמָא הֲוָה אָמַר לֵיהּ.

אֲמַר לֵיהּ: מַאי טַעְמָא עִיזֵּי מַסְגָן בְּרֵישָׁא וַהֲדַר אִימְרֵי.

אֲמַר לֵיהּ: כִּבְרִיָּיתוֹ שֶׁל עוֹלָם, דִבְרֵישָׁא חֲשׁוֹכָא וַהֲדַר נְהוֹרָא.

Rabbi Zeira encountered Rabbi Yehudah, who was standing at the entryway to his father-in-law's house. He observed that Rabbi Yehudah was in an exceptionally positive frame of mind, and realized that he could pose any question at all about the world and would receive an answer.

Rabbi Zeira asked, "Why is it that goats walk ahead and ewes walk behind them?"

Rabbi Yehudah responded, "That corresponds to the pattern of the world's Creation: first darkness, then light."

TEXT 14

Creation Order

Genesis 1:1–3

בְּרֵאשִׁית בָּרָא אֱלֹקִים אֵת הַשָּׁמַיִם וְאֵת הָאָרֶץ. וְהָאָרֶץ
הָיְתָה תֹהוּ וָבֹהוּ וְחֹשֶׁךְ עַל פְּנֵי תְהוֹם וְרוּחַ אֱלֹקִים מְרַחֶפֶת
עַל פְּנֵי הַמָּיִם. וַיֹּאמֶר אֱלֹקִים יְהִי אוֹר וַיְהִי אוֹר.

In the beginning, when G-d created Heaven and earth, the earth was unformed and void, the darkness was over the deep, and the spirit of G-d hovered over the waters. Then G-d said, "Let there be light!" And there was light.

SHEPHERD AND GOATS LANDSCAPE
Nachum Gutman, oil on canvas, Israel, 1935

KEY POINTS

1. During the century and a half following the Mishnah's composition, the sages of the Land of Israel thoroughly examined its teachings. Their own resultant teachings are compiled in the Talmud Yerushalmi (Jerusalem Talmud).

2. The Jewish community in Babylonia became a crucial hub of scholarship, especially during periods of persecution in Israel. The sages of this community produced the Gemara that is most studied today—the Talmud Bavli (Babylonian Talmud).

3. Rav and Shmuel turned the Babylonian Diaspora into the leading center of Torah learning. The debates of Abaye and Rava were a rigorous analysis of Halachic teachings that drew on a comprehensive set of sources.

4. Hundreds of sages participated in Talmudic discussions over the centuries. Rav Ashi and his colleagues organized centuries of teachings into a coherent text that was formalized as the Gemara in its current form.

5. The Gemara's compilers strung together conversations that occurred across centuries. They meticulously tracked names and attributions to ensure the integrity of the teachings.

6 The Gemara's comprehensive approach often leads discussions to meander through various topics. The results are a rich tapestry of Halachic content that travels far beyond the immediate Mishnaic text.

7 *Agadata*, the Talmud's nonlegal content, provides profound insights into the spiritual dimensions of Judaism, offering a deeper understanding of G-d, the soul, and the values underlying Jewish practice.

Continue learning at
myjli.com/talmud

The *Agadot* of the Talmud

The entire corpus of Torah exposition—also known as the "Oral Torah"—is roughly divided into two areas: Halachah and Agadah.

"Halachah" is the field of Torah law, which represents the core function of the Torah—to instruct us on "the path that they should follow and the deeds that they shall do" (Exodus 18:20). *Agadah* is the general name given to the non-Halachic teachings of the Torah. These include moral and ethical aphorisms, philosophical insights, and mystical teachings. The stories, parables, and historic-biographical narratives in the Talmud and Midrash also belong to its *agadic* component.

While the bulk of the Talmud is Halachic in nature, consisting of the expositions, discussions, and disputations in the field of Torah law, a significant part (about one-third) is *agadic*. Presented below are selections from fourteen of the Talmud's sixty-three tractates that showcase this fascinating and illuminating aspect of the Talmud.

Talmud, Berachot 3a

RABBI YOSEI SAID: One time I was traveling on the road, and I entered one of the ruins of Jerusalem to pray. Elijah the Prophet, blessed be his memory, came and watched me at the door until I finished my prayer.

After I had finished, he said to me, "Peace unto you, my teacher!"

I answered, "Shalom, my teacher and master."

"My son," said he, "why did you enter this ruin?"

"To pray," I replied.

"You could have prayed on the road," he said.

"I was afraid lest I be interrupted by travelers."

"You should then have prayed a shortened prayer."

On that occasion, I learned from him three things. I learned that one should not enter a ruin, I learned that one is permitted to pray on the road, and I learned that a person who prays on the road may say a shortened prayer.

He then said to me, "What voice did you hear in this ruin?" I replied, "I heard a Heavenly echo that coos like a dove, saying, 'Woe, that I have destroyed My home, burned My palace, and exiled My children among the nations of the world.'"

He then said to me, "By your life and the life of your head, not only does the voice proclaim this at this time, but each and every day, three times a day does the voice proclaim it. Furthermore, every time the people of Israel enter the synagogues or houses of learning, and they respond, 'Let His great name be praised,' the Holy One, blessed be He, nods His head, and says, 'Happy is the king thus praised in his own house! But what avails a father who has exiled his children? And woe to the children who have been exiled from their father's table!'"

The rabbis taught: There are three reasons why one should not enter a ruin—because it may arouse suspicion, because of the danger of collapse, and because of the demons.

Jerusalem Talmud, Pe'ah 1:1

THEY ASKED REBBI ELIEZER, "How far does honoring one's father and mother go?" He said to them, "You are asking me? Go and ask Dama ben Netinah."

Dama ben Netinah was the head of the city council. Once his mother was slapping him in front of the entire council and a slipper fell from her hand, and he handed it back to her so that she should feel no inconvenience.

Rabbi Chizkiah said: He was a gentile from Ascalon and the head of the city council. He never sat on the stone on which his father used to sit, and when his father died, he worshipped the stone.

Once the jaspis of the tribe Benjamin (one of the twelve precious stones set in the High Priest's breastplate) was lost. They inquired, "Who would have a stone of similar quality?" They were informed that Dama ben Netinah did. They went to him and agreed on a price of one hundred dinars. He went to the upper floor to bring it, and found his father sleeping. Some say that the key to the chest was in his father's fingers; some say his father's foot was resting on the chest.

He came down to them and told them, "I could not bring it to you."

They thought that perhaps he wanted more money, and raised the price to two hundred, then to one thousand. When his father woke up from his sleep, he went up and brought it to them. They wanted to give him according to the amount mentioned last, but he refused. He said: "Do I sell my father's honor for money? I will not have any advantage from honoring my father."

What reward did G-d give him? Rabbi Yosei bar Abun said: "The following night, his cow gave birth to a red heifer, and they gave him its weight in gold for it."

Talmud, Shabbat 12b

[THE RABBIS DECREED:] A person should not read by the light of a lamp on Shabbat, lest they [forget that it is Shabbat] and tilt [the lamp to improve the flow of the oil].

Said Rabbi Yishmael ben Elisha, "I will read, and will not tilt." Yet once he read and wished to tilt. He then exclaimed: "How great are the words of the sages, who said that one must not read by the light of a lamp."

Rabbi Nathan said: He read and did tilt it. He then wrote in his notebook: "I, Yishmael ben Elisha, did read and tilt the lamp on the Sabbath. When the Temple is rebuilt, I will bring a fat sin-offering."

Talmud, Eruvin 53b

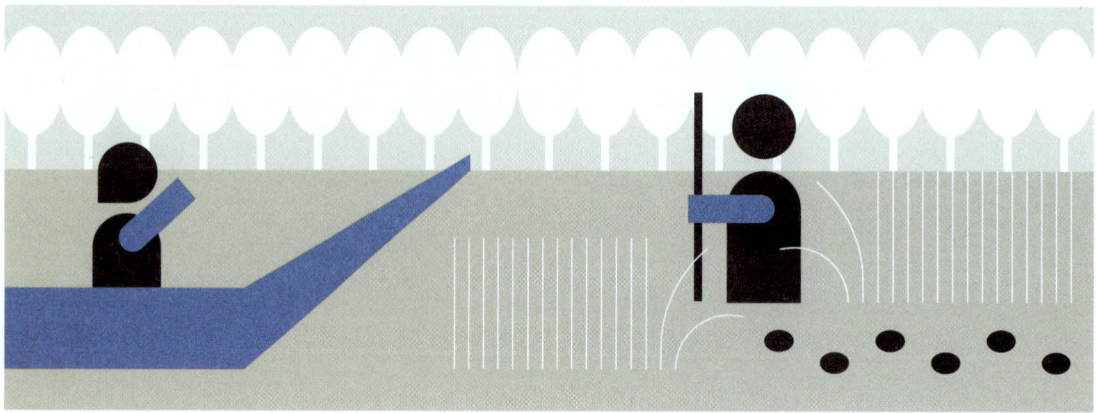

SAID RABBI YEHOSHUA BEN CHANANYAH:

A little girl once got the better of me. I was traveling, and there was a path that cut across a field, and I took that path. This child said to me, "Rabbi, aren't you walking on someone's field? I said to her, "I'm walking on a trodden path." Said she: "Thieves such as yourself have trampled it."

Talmud, Pesachim 119a

JOSEPH GATHERED ALL THE GOLD and silver in the world and brought it to Egypt, as it is written, "And Joseph garnered all the money that was found in the land of Egypt and in the land of Canaan, for the provisions that they were provisioning" (Genesis 47:14). From this verse, I know only regarding the wealth of Egypt and Canaan; from where do I know regarding all other countries? Because it is written, "And the entire world came to Egypt to provision unto Joseph" (Genesis 41:57).

When the Children of Israel went up from Egypt, they brought out this wealth with them, as it is written, "And the Children of Israel did as the word of Moses; and they requested from Egypt vessels of silver and vessels of gold and robes, . . . and they salvaged Egypt" (Exodus 12:35–36). Said Rav Asi: They left Egypt like a trap in which there is no grain. Reish Lakish said: Like a pond without fish.

This treasure remained in Jerusalem until the days of Rehoboam the son of Solomon, when Shishak the king of Egypt came and seized it from Rehoboam (I Kings 14:25–26). Then Zerah the king of Ethiopia came and seized it from Shishak. Then Asa seized it from Zerah king of Ethiopia, and sent it to Hadrimon the son of Tabrimon, the king of Aram. Then the Ammonites came and seized it from Hadrimon the son of Tabrimon. Then Jehoshaphat came and seized it from the Ammonites, and it remained in Jerusalem until the reign of Ahaz, when Sennacherib the king of Assyria came and took it from Ahaz. Then Hezekiah came and took it from Sennacherib, and it remained in Jerusalem until the time of Zedekiah, when the Babylonians came and seized it from Zedekiah. The Persians came and took it from the Babylonians; the Greeks came and took it from the Persians; the Romans came and took it from the Greeks; and it is still there in Rome.

Rabbi Chama ben Rabbi Chanina said: Joseph hid three treasure troves in Egypt. One was discovered by Korah, one by Antoninus the son of Severus, and the third remains hidden away for the righteous in the World to Come.

Talmud, Yoma 69b

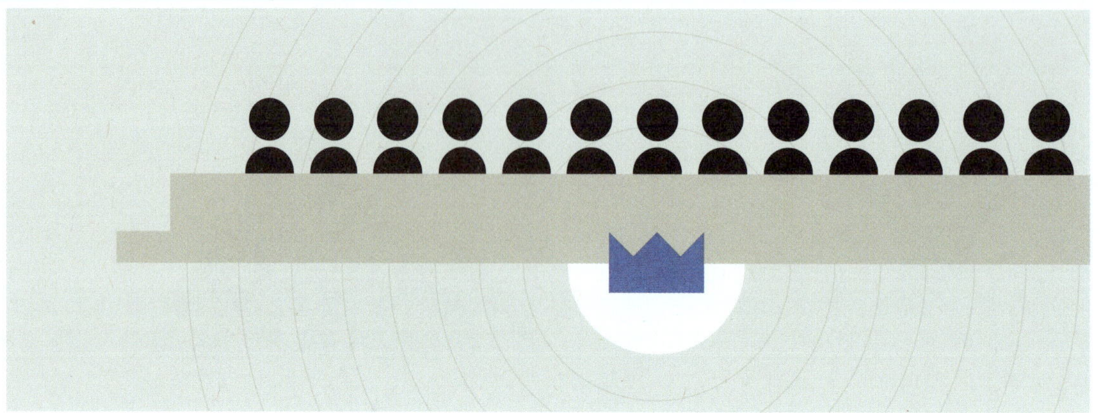

WHY WERE THEY CALLED "the men of the Great Assembly"? Because they restored the crown of the Divine attributes to its ancient completeness.

Moses had come and prayed: "G-d, the great one, the mighty one, and the awesome one" (Deuteronomy 10:17).

Then Jeremiah came and said, "Aliens are prancing about in His Temple. Where is His awesomeness?" So he omitted the attribute "awesome" from his prayer (Jeremiah 32:18).

Daniel came and said, "Aliens are enslaving His children. Where are His mighty deeds?" So he omitted the word "mighty" (Daniel 9:4).

But they (the sages and prophets of the Great Assembly) came and said: "On the contrary! Therein lies His might, in that He suppresses His wrath and extends His tolerance with the wicked. Therein lies His awesomeness. For but for the fear of Him, how could one nation persist among the many nations!"

The rabbis asked, "But how could the earlier ones abolish something established by Moses?" Said Rabbi Elazar, "Because they knew that the Holy One, blessed be He, insists on truth, they would not be false to Him."

Talmud, Sukkah 56b

IT HAPPENED THAT MIRIAM the daughter of (the priestly family) Bilgah apostatized and married an officer of the Greek kings. When the Greeks invaded the Holy Temple, she pounded with her sandal upon the altar, crying out, "Lukos! Lukos! (Wolf! Wolf!) How long will you consume Israel's money? And yet you do not stand by them in the time of oppression!" When the sages heard of the incident, they immobilized Bilgah's bracket and blocked up her alcove.

But it was Miriam the daughter of Bilgah who apostatized; do we then penalize a father on account of his daughter? Yes, replied Abaye, as the proverb goes, "The talk of the child in the marketplace, is either that of their father or of their mother." Do we then penalize the entire clan on account of her father or mother? Said Abaye: "Woe is to the wicked, and woe is to their neighbor; it is good for the righteous and good for their neighbor."

Talmud, Rosh Hashanah 24b–25a

IT ONCE HAPPENED THAT two witnesses came (to testify on the appearance of the new moon) and said, "We saw it in the morning in the east and in the evening in the west." Rabbi Yochanan ben Nuri thereupon said, "They are false witnesses." However, when they came to (the high court in) Yavneh, Rabban Gamliel accepted them.

On another occasion, two witnesses came and said, "We saw it in its season, but on the subsequent night it was not seen," and Rabban Gamliel accepted their testimony. Said Rabbi Dosa ben Harkinas, "They are false witnesses! How could they testify that a woman has given birth to a child when, but on the next day, her belly is still swollen?" Rabbi Yehoshua said to him, "I see your argument." Thereupon Rabban Gamliel sent to Rabbi Yehoshua: "I command you to come to me with your staff and your money on the day on which Yom Kippur falls according to your reckoning."

Rabbi Akiva went to Rabbi Yehoshua and found him in great distress. He said to him, "I can bring proof [from Scripture] that whatever Rabban Gamliel has done is valid. For it is written (Leviticus 23:4), 'These are the appointed times of G-d which you shall proclaim'—whether they are proclaimed at their proper time or not at their proper time, I have no appointed times save these."

Rabbi Yehoshua then went to Rabbi Dosa ben Harkinas, who said to him, "If we are to call into question the decisions of the *beit din* of Rabban Gamliel, we must call into question the decisions of every *beit din* that has existed since the days of Moses up to the present time. For it is written (Exodus 24:9), 'Then went up Moses and Aaron, Nadab and Abihu, and seventy of the elders of Israel.' Why are the names of the elders not mentioned? To tell us that every group of three that has acted as a *beit* din over Israel is on a level with the *beit* din of Moses."

Thereupon Rabbi Yehoshua took his staff and his money and went to Yavneh to Rabban Gamliel on the day on which Yom Kippur fell according to his reckoning. Rabban Gamliel rose and kissed him on his head and said to him: "Come in peace, my teacher and my disciple—my teacher in wisdom and my disciple because you have accepted my decision."

Talmud, Taanit 5b

A MAN WAS TRAVELING through the desert. He was hungry, thirsty, and tired. He came upon a tree that was laden with luscious fruit and gave plentiful shade; under the tree ran a spring of water. He ate of the fruit, drank of the water, and rested in the shade. When he was about to leave, he turned to the tree and said:

"Tree, O tree, with what should I bless you? Should I bless you that your fruit be sweet? Your fruit is already sweet. Should I bless you that your shade be plentiful? Your shade is plentiful. That a spring of water should run beneath you? A spring of water runs beneath you.

"There is one thing with which I can bless you: May the Almighty grant that all the saplings planted from your seeds should be like you."

Talmud, Megilah 15b

WHY DID ESTHER INVITE HAMAN to her wine fest with King Ahasuerus?

Rabbi Elazar said: She set a trap for him, as it is written, "Let their table before them become a snare" (Psalms 69:23).

Rabbi Yehoshua said: She learned to do so from her father's house, as it is written, "If your enemy be hungry give him bread to eat, as you are heaping coals of fire upon his head" (Proverbs 25:21).

Rabbi Me'ir said: So that he should not have a chance to consult and plot a rebellion.

Rabbi Yehudah said: So that they should not discover that she was a Jewess.

Rabbi Nechemiah said: So that Jewish people should not say, "We have a sister in the palace," and thereby neglect to pray to G-d for mercy.

Rabbi Yosei said: So that he should always be close at hand for her.

Rabbi Shimon ben Menasya said: She hoped that this would prompt G-d to perform a miracle.

Rabbi Yehoshua ben Korchah said: She said, "I will encourage him [and make Ahasuerus jealous], so that he may kill us, both Haman and I."

Rabban Gamliel said: She said, "Ahasuerus is always changing his mind." (I.e., if Haman wasn't there when Ahasuerus decided to kill him, he may change his mind again.)

Said Rabban Gamliel: We still require the Modiinite. As it has been taught in the name of Rabbi Eliezer of Modiin: She made the king jealous of him and she made the princes jealous of him.

Rabah said: Because of the verse, "Before destruction comes pride" (Proverbs 16:18).

Abaye and Rava gave the same reason, saying: "With their poison I will prepare their feast" (Jeremiah 51:39).

Rabah ben Avuhah encountered Elijah the Prophet and asked him, "Which of these reasons prompted Esther to act as she did?" He replied, "All the reasons given by all the Mishnaic and Talmudic sages."

Talmud, Gitin 56a-b

VESPASIAN CAME AND BESIEGED Jerusalem for three years. There were three men of great wealth in Jerusalem: Nakdimon ben Gorion, Ben Kalba Shavua, and Ben Tzitzit Hakeset. . . . One of these said to the people of Jerusalem, "I will sustain you with wheat and barley." A second said, "I will supply wine, oil, and salt." The third said, "I will supply firewood." The rabbis considered the offer of firewood the most generous, as Rav Chisda used to entrust all his keys to his servant save that of the firewood, for Rav Chisda used to say, "One storehouse of wheat requires sixty stores of firewood." These men were in a position to keep the city for twenty-one years.

The zealots were then in the city. The rabbis said to them, "Let us go out and make peace with [the Romans]." They would not let them, but on the contrary said, "Let us go out and fight them." The rabbis said, "You will not succeed." The [zealots] then rose up and burned the stores of wheat and barley (in order to force the people to fight), and a famine ensued.

Abba Sikra, the head of the zealots in Jerusalem, was the son of the sister of Rabban Yochanan ben Zakai. [Rabban Yochanan] sent to him, saying, "Come to visit me privately." When he came, he said to him, "How long are you going to carry on in this way, and kill all the people with starvation?" He replied, "What can I do? If I say a word to them, they will kill me." He said, "Devise some plan for me to escape. Perhaps I shall be able to save something." He said to him, "Pretend to be ill, and let everyone come to inquire about you. Bring something evil smelling and put it by you so that they will say you are dead."

When they reached the city gate, some men wanted to put a lance through the bier. [Abba Sikra] said to them, "Shall [the Romans] say, 'They have pierced their master'?" They wanted to give it a push. He said to them,

"Shall they say that they pushed their master?" They opened a gate for them and they got out.

When [Rabban Yochanan] reached [the Roman camp], he said [to Vespasian]: "Peace to you, O king, peace to you, O king." [Vespasian] said, "Your life is forfeit on two counts. First, because I am not a king and you call me king. And again, if I am a king, why did you not come to me before now?"

He replied, "As for your saying that you are not a king, in truth you are a king, since if you were not a king Jerusalem would not be delivered into your hand. As it is written (Isaiah 10:34), 'The Lebanon (a reference to the Holy Temple) shall fall by a mighty one.'"

"As for your question, 'If I am a king, why did you not come to me before now?' the answer is that the zealots among us did not let me."

Said he to him, "If there is a jar of honey around which a serpent is wound, should one not break the jar to get rid of the serpent?" [Rabban Yochanan] was silent.

Rabbi Yosef, or some say Rabbi Akiva, applied to him the verse (Isaiah 44:25), "[G-d] turns wise men backward and makes their knowledge foolish." For he ought to have said to him, "One takes a pair of tongs and removes the snake and kills it, and leaves the jar intact. . . ."

At this point, a messenger came from Rome saying, "Arise, for the emperor is dead, and the notables of Rome have decided to place you at the head." Vespasian had just finished putting on one boot. When he tried to put on the other, he could not. He tried to take off the first, but it would not come off. He said, "What is the meaning of this?" Rabbi Yochanan said to him, "Do not worry. The good news has done it, as it is written (Proverbs 15:30), 'Good tidings fatten the bone.' What is the remedy? Let someone whom you dislike come and pass before you, as it is written (Proverbs 17:22), 'A broken spirit dries up the bones.'" He did so, and the boot went on. He said to him, "Seeing that you are so wise, why did you not come to me until now?" He said, "Have I not told you?" He retorted, "I too have told you."

He then said: "I am going now, and will send someone to take my place. But you make a request of me, and I will grant it."

[Rabban Yochanan] said to him: "Give me Yavneh and its sages, and dynasty of Rabban Gamliel, and physicians to heal Rabbi Tzadok."

Rabbi Yosef, or some say Rabbi Akiva, applied to him the verse, "[G-d] turns wise men backward and makes their knowledge foolish." He ought to have asked him to spare Jerusalem! Rabbi Yochanan, however, thought that so much he would not grant, and then even a little would not be saved.

Talmud, Bava Batra 9

THIS QUESTION WAS PUT BY Turnus Rufus to Rabbi Akiva: "If your G-d loves the poor, why does He not support them?" He replied, "So that through them (i.e., by the merit of giving charity) we may be saved from the punishment of Gehinom." Said he, "On the contrary, it is this that condemns you to Gehinom!

"I will illustrate with a parable. Suppose an earthly king was angry with his servant and put him in prison and ordered that he should be given no food or drink, and a man went and gave him food and drink. If the king heard, would he not be angry with him? And you are called 'servants,' as it is written (Leviticus 25:55), 'For unto Me the Children of Israel are servants.'"

Rabbi Akiva answered him: "I will illustrate with another parable. Suppose an earthly king was angry with his child, and put him in prison and ordered that no food or drink should be given to him, and someone went and gave him food and drink. If the king heard of it, would he not send him a gift? And we are called 'children,' as it is written (Deuteronomy 14:1), 'You are children to the L-rd your G-d.'"

Said he to him: "You are called both children and servants. When you carry out the will of the Omnipresent, you are called 'children,' and when you do not carry out the will of the Omnipresent, you are called 'servants.' At the present time you are not carrying out the will of the Omnipresent."

Rabbi Akiva replied: "The Scripture says, 'Would you not deal your bread to the hungry, and bring the poor that are outcasts into your house?' (Isaiah 58:7). When is the time to 'bring the poor that are outcasts into your house'? It is now. And it says; 'Would you not deal your bread to the hungry?'"

Rabbi Yehudah the son of Rabbi Shalom expounded: In the same way that a person's earnings are determined for them on Rosh Hashanah, so are a person's losses determined for them on Rosh Hashanah. If they merit, this is accomplished through "deal your bread to the hungry." If not, then through "the outcasts into your house" (i.e., the tax collectors).

A case in point is that of the nephews of Rabban Yochanan ben Zakai. He saw in a dream that they were to lose 700 dinars in that year. He accordingly pressured them to give him money for charity until only seventeen dinars were left (of the seven hundred). On the eve of the Day of Atonement, the government sent and arrested them.

Rabban Yochanan ben Zakai said to them, "Do not be afraid. You will not lose more than the seventeen dinars they have taken from you." They said to him, "How did you know that this was going to happen?" He replied, "I saw it in a dream." They asked, "Then why did you not tell us?" He answered, "Because I wanted you to perform the *mitzvah* for its own sake."

Rav Pappa was climbing a ladder when his foot slipped and he narrowly escaped falling. He said, "Had that happened, my enemy would have been punished like Sabbath violators and idolaters!" Chiya bar Rav from Difti said to him, "Perhaps a beggar appealed to you and you did not assist him? For so it has been taught in the name of Rabbi Yehoshua ben Korchah: Whoever turns away his eyes from [one who appeals for] charity is considered as if he were serving idols."

Rabbi Yehudah said: Great is charity, in that it brings the Redemption nearer, as it is written (Isaiah 56:1), "So says G-d: Keep justice and do righteousness (*tzedakah*), for My salvation is near to come and My righteousness to be revealed."

He also used to say: Ten strong things have been created in the world. The rock is hard, but iron cleaves it. Iron is hard, but fire softens it. Fire is hard, but water quenches it. Water is strong, but the clouds bear it. The clouds are strong, but the wind scatters them. The wind is strong, but the body bears it. The body is strong, but fright crushes it. Fright is strong, but wine quashes it. Wine is strong, but sleep sobers it. Death is stronger than all, and charity saves from death, as it is written (Proverbs 10:2), "Charity delivers from death."

Rabbi Dostai son of Rabbi Yanai expounded: Observe that the ways of G-d are not like the ways of flesh and blood. How does flesh and blood act? If a person brings a present to a human king, it may be accepted or it may not be accepted; and even if it is accepted, it is still doubtful whether they will be admitted to the presence of the king or not. Not so G-d. If a person gives a penny to a beggar, they are deemed worthy to receive the Divine Presence, as it is written (Psalms 17:15), "In *tzedek* (righteousness, charity) I shall behold Your face." Rabbi Elazar used to give a coin to a poor person and then pray. He would say: For it is written, "In *tzedek* I shall behold Your face."

Talmud, Nidah 30b

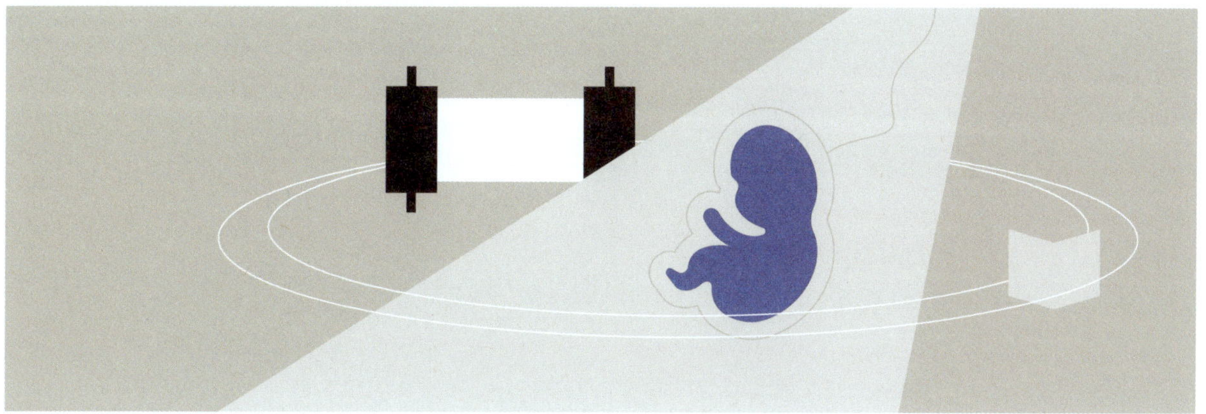

WHAT IS THE FETUS LIKE in its mother's womb? Like a folded writing tablet. Its hands are on its two temples, its two elbows on its two legs, and its two heels against its two buttocks. Its head lies between its knees. Its mouth is closed and its navel is open; and it eats what its mother eats and drinks what its mother drinks, but produces no excrements because otherwise it would kill its mother. As soon as it emerges into the atmosphere of the world, the closed organ opens and the open one closes, for if that does not happen, it could not live even one single hour.

A lamp burns on its head and it looks out and sees from one end of the world to the other, as it is written, "Then His lamp shined above my head, and by His light I walked through darkness" (Job 29:3). Do not be astonished at this, for a person sleeping here might see a dream in Spain.

There is no time in which a person enjoys greater happiness than in those days, as it is written, "O that I were as the months of old, as in the days when G-d watched over me" (Job 29:2). Now, which are the days that make up months and do not make up years? The months of pregnancy.

The child in the womb is also taught the entire Torah, from beginning to end. But as soon as it enters the atmosphere of the world, an angel comes and slaps it on its mouth, and causes it to forget all the Torah completely, as it is written, "Sin crouches at the doorway" (Genesis 4:7).

The child does not emerge from there before it is made to take an oath, as it is written, "As unto Me every knee shall bow, every tongue shall swear" (Isaiah 45:23). "Unto Me every knee shall bow" refers to the day of dying, of which it is written, "All they that go down to the dust shall kneel before Him" (Psalms 22:30); "every tongue shall swear" refers to the day of birth, of which it is written, "The one who has clean hands and a pure heart, who has not taken My name in vain and has not sworn deceitfully" (Psalms 24:4).

What is the nature of the oath that it is made to take? *Be righteous, and do not be wicked. And even if all the world tells you "You are righteous," consider yourself wicked. Always bear in mind that the Holy One, blessed be He, is pure, that His ministers are pure, and that the soul that He gave you is pure. If you preserve it in purity, well and good, but if not, I will take it away from you.*

APPENDIX A

TEXT 15

What's in a Name?

Rabbi Levi Yitzchak Schneerson, *Torat Levi Yitzchak* (*Shas*), p. 60

הַרְבֵּה פְּעָמִים אִיתָא בַּגְמָרָא עַל רַב עַוִּירָא, זִמְנִין אָמַר לָהּ מִשְּׁמֵיהּ דְּרַב אַמִי, וְזִמְנִין אָמַר לָהּ מִשְּׁמֵיהּ דְּרַב אַסִי.

יֵשׁ לוֹמַר עַוִּירָא . . . הוּא גְבוּרָה . . . וְרַב אַמִי וְרַב אַסִי רוֹמְזִים עַל בִּינָה בִּכְלָל . . . מ׳ הוּא תְּבוּנָה, ס׳ הוּא בִּינָה עִלָּאָה.

הִנֵּה רַב עַוִּירָא שֶׁהוּא בְּחִינַת גְבוּרָה עֲנַף הַבִּינָה בִּכְלָל . . . זִמְנִין אָמַר מִשְּׁמֵיהּ דְּרַב אַמִי, תְּבוּנָה, וְזִמְנִין מִשְּׁמֵיהּ דְּרַב אַסִי, בִּינָה עִלָּאָה.

The Gemara includes numerous teachings that were quoted by Rabbi Avira: sometimes, he attributes them to Rabbi Ami, and sometimes to Rabbi Asi.

Rabbi Avira himself . . . corresponds to the Divine *sefirah* (attribute) of *gevurah* (severity) . . . Both Rabbi Ami and Rabbi Asi represent the Divine *sefirah* of *binah* (understanding) . . . but they are not identical: The name Ami is spelled with the letter *mem* that is associated with *tevunah* (discernment) [a lower manifestation of *binah*], whereas the name Asi is spelled with a *samech* that is associated with the higher state of *binah*.

RABBI LEVI YITZCHAK SCHNEERSON 1878–1944

Kabbalist and leader of Jewry in Soviet Russia. Rabbi Levi Yitzchak was a great-grandson of the third Chabad Rebbe, Rabbi Menachem Mendel of Lubavitch. Born in Belarus, he was ordained by Rabbi Chaim Soloveitchik of Brisk and married Chana Yanovski from southern Ukraine. In 1909, Rabbi Levi Yitzchak was appointed chief rabbi of Yekaterinoslav (later called Dnipropetrovsk). He was arrested by the Soviets for the dissemination of Judaism and exiled to Kazakhstan, where he passed away at the age of 66. A fraction of his commentaries written in exile was smuggled to the United States and published by his son, Rabbi Menachem Mendel Schneerson, the seventh Rebbe of Chabad.

APPENDIX B

TEXT 16

Lost and Found

Maimonides, *Mishneh Torah*, Laws Pertaining to Robbery and Returning Lost Property, 14:2–3

זֶה הַכְּלָל בָּאֲבֵידָה:

כָּל דָּבָר שֶׁאֵין בּוֹ סִימָן, כֵּיוָן שֶׁאָבַד וְיָדְעוּ בּוֹ הַבְּעָלִים שֶׁאָבַד, הֲרֵי זֶה בְּחֶזְקַת שֶׁנִּתְיָיאֲשׁוּ מִמֶּנּוּ בְּעָלָיו, כְּגוֹן מַסְמֵר אֶחָד, אוֹ מַחַט אַחַת, אוֹ מַטְבֵּעַ אֶחָד, שֶׁהֲרֵי אֵינָן יְכוֹלִין לִיתֵּן סִימָן לְהַחֲזִירוֹ לָהֶם, וּלְפִיכָךְ הֲרֵי הוּא לְזֶה שֶׁמְּצָאוֹ.

וְכָל דָּבָר שֶׁיֵּשׁ בּוֹ סִימָן, כְּגוֹן שִׂמְלָה וּבְהֵמָה, הֲרֵי זֶה בְּחֶזְקַת שֶׁלֹּא נִתְיָיאֲשׁוּ מִמֶּנּוּ בְּעָלָיו, שֶׁהֲרֵי דַּעְתָּן תְּלוּיָה לִיתֵּן סִימָנִין שֶׁיֵּשׁ בּוֹ וְיַחֲזוֹר לָהֶן. לְפִיכָךְ הַמּוֹצֵא אוֹתָן חַיָּיב לְהַכְרִיז.

The following principle governs the laws of a lost article:

If an article does not have a clear identifying mark, as is the case with a solitary nail, needle, or coin, then as soon as the owners are aware that they have lost such an item, a legal assumption is established: We presume that the owners have despaired of recovering that item, based on the fact they cannot possibly provide an identifying mark by which to prove it is theirs. Based on this presumption, the item belongs to the finder by default.

RABBI MOSHE BEN MAIMON (MAIMONIDES, RAMBAM) 1135–1204

Halachist, philosopher, author, and physician. Maimonides was born in Córdoba, Spain. After the conquest of Córdoba by the Almohads, he fled Spain and eventually settled in Cairo, Egypt. There, he became the leader of the Jewish community and served as court physician to the vizier of Egypt. He is most noted for authoring the *Mishneh Torah*, an encyclopedic arrangement of Jewish law; and for his philosophical work, *Guide for the Perplexed*. His rulings on Jewish law are integral to the formation of Halachic consensus.

By contrast, if an article has an identifying mark, such as an item of clothing or an animal, we presume that the owners will not despair of its recovery. They hope that they will be able to claim its return using its identifying marks or features. Therefore, the finder must publicize their find.

QUESTION

Let's say the finder of a lost object has no way of knowing whether its owner realizes they have lost the object.

Would you suggest the finder can rely on the *yi'ush* principle to keep it? Or do you think the finder must treat the object as still belonging to the owner?

TEXT 17A

Presumption of Awareness

Talmud, Bava Metzi'a 21b

מָעוֹת מְפוּזָרוֹת - הֲרֵי אֵלוּ שֶׁלוֹ.

אַמַאי? הָא לָא יָדַע דְנָפַל מִינֵיהּ!

הָתָם נַמִי כִּדְרַבִּי יִצְחָק דְאָמַר: אָדָם עָשׂוּי לְמַשְׁמֵשׁ בְּכִיסוֹ בְּכָל שָׁעָה וְשָׁעָה.

"Scattered coins belong to their finder."

But why? Perhaps the person has not yet noticed that they dropped?

Here, as well, we can respond using the teaching of Rabbi Yitzchak: "People tend to check their purses (pockets) regularly." [We can safely presume that it would not take long at all before the person noticed their absence.]

TEXT 17B

Conflicting Source

Ibid.

תָּא שְׁמַע:

הַמּוֹצֵא מָעוֹת בְּבָתֵּי כְנֵסִיּוֹת וּבְבָתֵּי מִדְרָשׁוֹת,
וּבְכָל מָקוֹם שֶׁהָרַבִּים מְצוּיִין שָׁם - הֲרֵי אֵלּוּ
שֶׁלוֹ, מִפְּנֵי שֶׁהַבְּעָלִים מִתְיָאֲשִׁין מֵהֶן.

וְהָא לָא יָדַע דְּנָפַל מִינֵּיה?

אָמַר רַבִּי יִצְחָק: אָדָם עָשׂוּי לְמַשְׁמֵשׁ בְּכִיסוֹ בְּכָל שָׁעָה.

Come and hear [the following Baraita]:

If coins are found in an assembly hall, a study hall, or any place where many people gather, they belong to their finder; for their owner abandons hope of recovering them.

But perhaps the owner has not noticed their loss?

Rabbi Yitzchak said: "People tend to check their purses regularly."

TEXT 18

Repeated Questions

Rabbi Meir of Lublin, Bava Metzi'a 21b

הַקּוּשְׁיָא מֵהַבְּרַיְיתָא הִקְשׁוּ מִתְּחִלָּה . . . וְעַלָּהּ אָמַר רַבִּי יִצְחָק לְמִלְתֵּיה. וּמִמֵּילָא הָוֵי מִיתַּרְצָא לְהוּ הַמַּתְנִיתִין, רַק שֶׁהַמַּקְשֶׁה שֶׁהִקְשָׁה כָּאן מִמַּתְנִיתִין לֹא יָדַע מֵהַקּוּשְׁיָא שֶׁל הַבְּרַיְיתָא דְאָמַר עֲלָהּ רַבִּי יִצְחָק לְמִלְתֵּיהּ. וְהֵשִׁיב לוֹ הַתַּרְצָן כִּדְאָמַר רַבִּי יִצְחָק וְכוּ' . . .

וְכֵן דֶּרֶךְ הַגְּמָרָא בְּכַמָּה דוּכְתִּין.

The question on the Baraita had been asked first . . . and the answer had been provided by Rabbi Yitzchak. This answer also resolves the subsequent question on the Mishnah. However, the one who posed the question [on the Mishnah] was unaware of the same question and answer involving the Baraita. [Therefore, he posed his question on the Mishnah] and the responder advised him that Rabbi Yitzchak had already answered that question. . . .

This is the Gemara's style on many occasions.

RABBI MEIR (MAHARAM) OF LUBLIN 1558–1616

Polish rabbi and Talmudist. Rabbi Meir served as rabbi of a number of prestigious Polish communities, most notably the city of Lublin. He is known for his commentary on the Talmud, Halachic responsa, and the famous yeshiva he headed in Lublin.

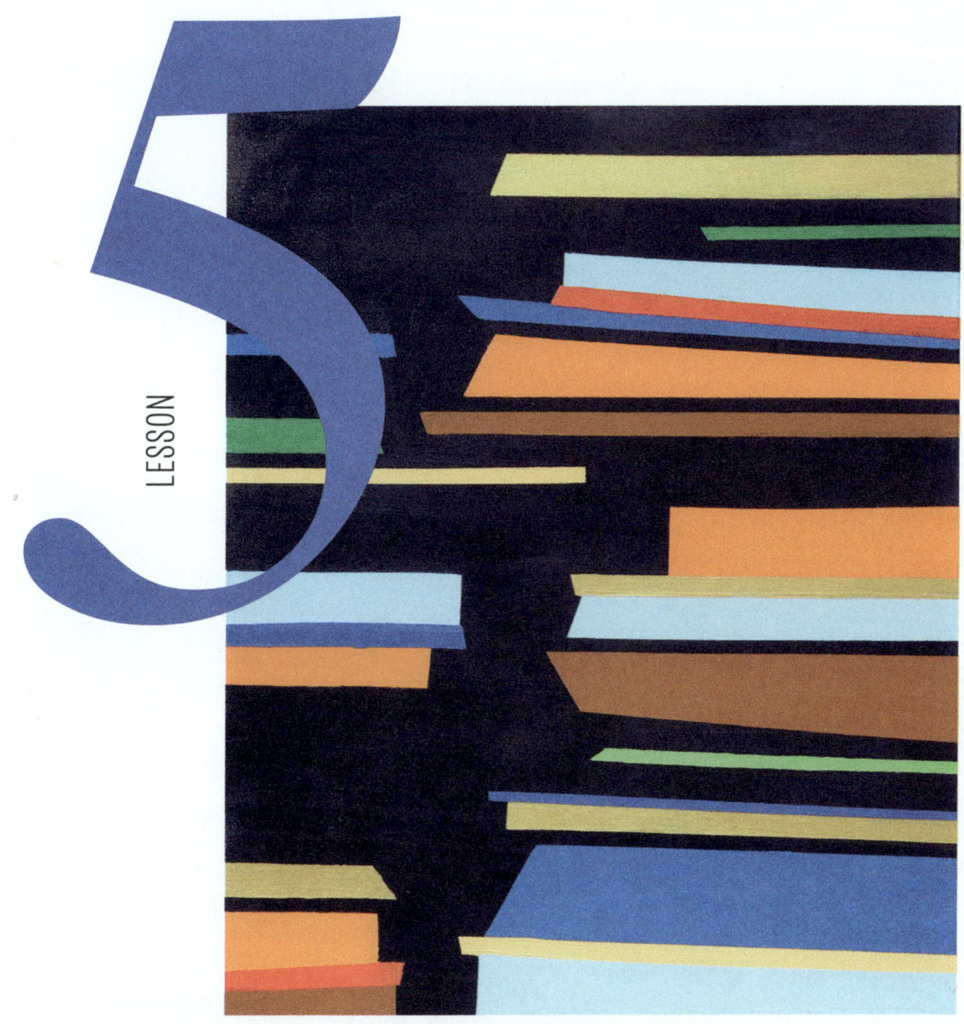

BOOKS III
Alyse Radenovic,
acrylic on canvas, 2024

HOW THE TALMUD THINKS

A unique method of logic—and why it matters

Understand the Babylonian Talmud's rigorous mode of legal reasoning, how it balances dueling principles to arrive at clear legal boundaries, and how its elegant logic fuels deeper learning.

I. TRACKING THE TALMUD'S THINKING

Our present lesson provides an introduction to the unique methods and skills of Talmudic thinking. We begin with the skill referred to popularly in Yiddish as *halten kop* (lit: "hold your head")—the art of following the Talmud's train of thought through a daunting series of logical twists and turns. We review the *sugya* from tractate Pesachim that we explored in the previous two classes, to demonstrate how this skill comes into play in that familiar text.

TORAH STUDIES
Adolf Adi Adler, oil on canvas, c. 1940

TEXT 1

The Key to Success

Talmud, Megilah 6b

אָמַר רַבִּי יִצְחָק, אִם יֹאמַר לְךָ אָדָם: יָגַעְתִּי
וְלֹא מָצָאתִי – אַל תַּאֲמֵן. לֹא יָגַעְתִּי וּמָצָאתִי
– אַל תַּאֲמֵן. יָגַעְתִּי וּמָצָאתִי – תַּאֲמֵן.

Rabbi Yitzchak said: If a person tells you, "I toiled but did not find success," do not believe them. "I did *not* toil but found success," do not believe them. "I toiled and I found success," believe them.

BABYLONIAN TALMUD

A literary work of monumental proportions that draws upon the legal, spiritual, intellectual, ethical, and historical traditions of Judaism. The 37 tractates of the Babylonian Talmud contain the teachings of the Jewish sages from the period after the destruction of the 2nd Temple through the 5th century CE. It has served as the primary vehicle for the transmission of the Oral Law and the education of Jews over the centuries; it is the entry point for all subsequent legal, ethical, and theological Jewish scholarship.

BOOKS
Chana Rivka Schleifer, Jerusalem

TEXT 2

A Closed Book

Rabbi Yosef Chaim of Baghdad, *Ben Yehoyada,* Megilah 6b

ה' יִתְבָּרַךְ נָתַן הַתּוֹרָה סְתוּמָה וַחֲתוּמָה בְּכַמָּה עִזְקִין, שֶׁצָּרִיךְ יְגִיעָה רַבָּה כְּדֵי לִמְצוֹא דְבָרִים הַגְּנוּזִים בָּהּ, כְּדֵי שֶׁלֹּא יִהְיוּ לוֹמְדִים הַתּוֹרָה דֶּרֶךְ טִיּוּל, אֶלָּא לוֹמְדִים מֵרוֹב אַהֲבָתָם אוֹתָהּ, כִּי הַלּוֹמֵד דֶּרֶךְ טִיּוּל אֵינוֹ רוֹצֶה לְיַגֵּעַ וּלְהַטְרִיחַ עַצְמוֹ, אַךְ הַלּוֹמֵד מֵאַהֲבָתוֹ אוֹתָהּ הוּא יָגֵעַ הַרְבֵּה.

G-d gave us the Torah as a closed book, secured with multiple chains, so that it requires much toil to discover the ideas hidden within it. This ensures that we do not study the Torah casually, but rather, out of great love. For one who studies casually does not wish to exert or trouble themselves, whereas one who studies out of love for the material will exert much effort.

RABBI YOSEF CHAIM OF BAGHDAD (*BEN ISH CHAI*) 1834–1909

Sefardic Halachist and kabbalist. Rabbi Yosef Chaim succeeded his father as chief rabbi of Baghdad in 1859, and is best known as author of his Halachic work, *Ben Ish Chai*, by which title he is also known. Also popular is his commentary on the homiletical sections of the Talmud, called *Ben Yehoyada*.

TEXT 3

Mishnah Review

Mishnah, Pesachim 10:1

עַרְבֵי פְסָחִים סָמוּךְ לַמִּנְחָה, לֹא יֹאכַל אָדָם עַד שֶׁתֶּחְשַׁךְ.

One must refrain from eating on the eve of Passover, from close to the time for reciting the Minchah prayers until after darkness has fallen.

**For the full* sugya *discussing this line of the Mishnah, refer back to Lesson Three, Section III.*

MISHNAH

The first authoritative work of Jewish law that was codified in writing. The Mishnah contains the oral traditions that were passed down from teacher to student; it supplements, clarifies, and systematizes the commandments of the Torah. Due to the continual persecution of the Jewish people, it became increasingly difficult to guarantee that these traditions would not be forgotten. Rabbi Yehudah Hanasi therefore redacted the Mishnah at the end of the 2nd century. It serves as the foundation for the Talmud.

FIGURE 5.1

The Two Solutions

SOLUTION AUTHOR	BREAKTHROUGH	REASON THE MISHNAH ONLY MENTIONS "THE EVE OF PESACH"	WHOSE OPINION DOES THE MISHNAH FOLLOW?
RAV HUNA	Although Rabbi Yose rejects such a prohibition for the other festivals, he might agree that it applies to the eve of Passover.	The prohibition is exclusive to Passover.	Rabbi Yose
RAV PAPPA	The prohibition for Shabbat and the other festivals begins 2.5 hours before sundown (3:30 PM), whereas the prohibition for Passover might begin three hours before sundown (3 PM).	It refers to the early-start prohibition (3 PM) that applies exclusively to Passover.	Rabbi Yehudah

FIGURE 5.2

Talmudic Dominoes

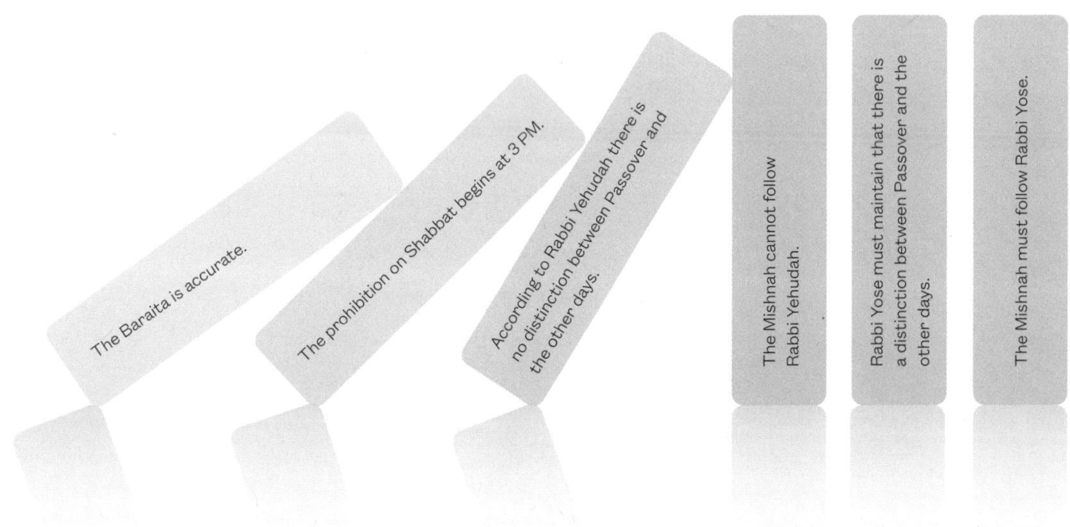

II. THE TALMUDIC BALANCING ACT

We now turn to explore another secret to Talmud study: the idea that every argument that appears in the Talmud has a counterargument. By way of illustration, we cite a law from the regulations of the blessings recited after eating, and we consider arguments that might discredit the law as presented in the Mishnah. This approach trains us to consider arguments in favor of positions with which we disagree, as part of a process of deepening our understanding of the subject matter.

THUMB WAR
Shani Levin, mixed media

TEXT 4

Questioning the Obvious

Talmud, Berachot 47b

וְהַנָּכְרִי אֵין מְזַמְּנִין עָלָיו.

פְּשִׁיטָא!

הָכָא בְּמַאי עָסְקִינַן, בְּגֵר שֶׁמָּל וְלֹא טָבַל.

We do not count a non-Jew toward a *zimun* [for the blessing after a meal].

This is obvious!

What are we dealing with in this case? With a convert who has undergone circumcision but has not yet immersed himself in the *mikveh*.

PARTNERS IN HEAVEN
Tanya Zbili, acrylic on canvas, Toronto, 2024
This painting depicts David Schwartz *z"l* and Yakir Hexter *z"l*, study partners, friends, and fellow IDF soldiers who were killed in battle on the same day.

III. DECEPTIVE EMPLOYEES

We now apply our Talmudic thinking skills to the first *sugya* of the sixth chapter of tractate Bava Metzi'a. The Talmud begins with an assumption regarding the topic of the Mishnah's discussion and proposes four distinct scenarios that may fit the bill. Eventually, the Talmud retreats from its original assumption and adopts an alternative approach to the Mishnah.

OLIVE PICKERS
Yitzchak Devor, oil on canvas, Jerusalem, 2020

FIGURE 5.3

The Super-Tractate Nezikin

BAVA KAMA	Torts and claims of damages
BAVA METZI'A	Loans, bailments, found items, and employment contracts
BAVA BATRA	Property rights, zoning regulations, and real estate transactions

TEXT 5

Laborer Disputes

Talmud, Bava Metzi'a 75b

הַשּׂוֹכֵר אֶת הָאוּמָנִין וְהִטְעוּ זֶה אֶת זֶה - אֵין לָהֶם זֶה עַל זֶה אֶלָּא תַּרְעוֹמֶת. שָׂכַר אֶת הַחַמָּר וְאֶת הַקַּדָּר לְהָבִיא פְּרִייפָרִין וַחֲלִילִים לַכַּלָּה אוֹ לַמֵּת, וּפוֹעֲלִין לְהַעֲלוֹת פִּשְׁתָּנוֹ מִן הַמִּשְׁרָה, וְכָל דָּבָר שֶׁאָבֵד וְחָזְרוּ בָּהֶן, מָקוֹם שֶׁאֵין שָׁם אָדָם - שׂוֹכֵר עֲלֵיהֶן.

If one hired workers but they deceived each other, the parties have no claim of liability against each other; they merely have a right to complain. If one hired a donkey driver or a porter to fetch canopy posts or wedding/funeral flutes, or workers to raise flax from the soaking pit, or any other task involving something that will be lost [if the task is not performed immediately], and they cancel, the individual may hire replacement workers at their expense.

EXERCISE 5.1

Albert owns a field. He asks Barry to hire laborers for specific work in the field, and he stipulates the wages he is prepared to pay. Barry hires Charles and David to do the work, but he informs them that they will get paid at a different rate from the wages Albert had stipulated. Once the work is complete, Charles and David claim the wages they believe they are owed—and the discrepancy is discovered.

What do you believe the law should be in this case?

FIGURE 5.4

Four Solutions

EMPLOYER'S QUOTE	AGENT'S QUOTE	CASE
Three	Four	There is no fixed wage, so the workers have no legal claim. They nevertheless have grounds to complain, because they were led to believe that they would receive four.
Three	Four	The fixed wage is three, but these workers are not laborers. They have grounds to complain because they would not perform manual labor without the incentive of an inflated wage.
Three	Four	The fixed wage is three, but these workers invested extra effort as required for a four-wage, due to the promise of receiving four. However, they have no way to prove their extra effort. They have grounds to complain because the agent's deception caused them to do extra work without extra compensation.
Four	Three	The workers have grounds to complain because the agent caused them to forgo an opportunity to earn higher wages.

EXERCISE 5.2

The Talmudic Balancing Act

Talmud, Bava Metzi'a 76a–b

The Gemara will now present a series of cases. Each case is an attempt by the Gemara to find a case that fits the Mishnah's parameters, where the workers have "the right to complain" but no legal claim.

For each case, draw the ball where you think it belongs, either perfectly balancing on the peak, rolling down into the valley of "legal claim" or into the other valley of "no right to complain".

הֵיכִי דָמֵי? דְאָמַר לֵיהּ בַּעַל הַבַּיִת: זִיל, אוֹגַר
לִי פּוֹעֲלִים, וְאָזַל אִיהוּ וְאַטְעִינְהוּ.

What is the case? The employer directed the agent, "Go ahead and hire workers for me." The agent proceeded to do so, but he deceived them.

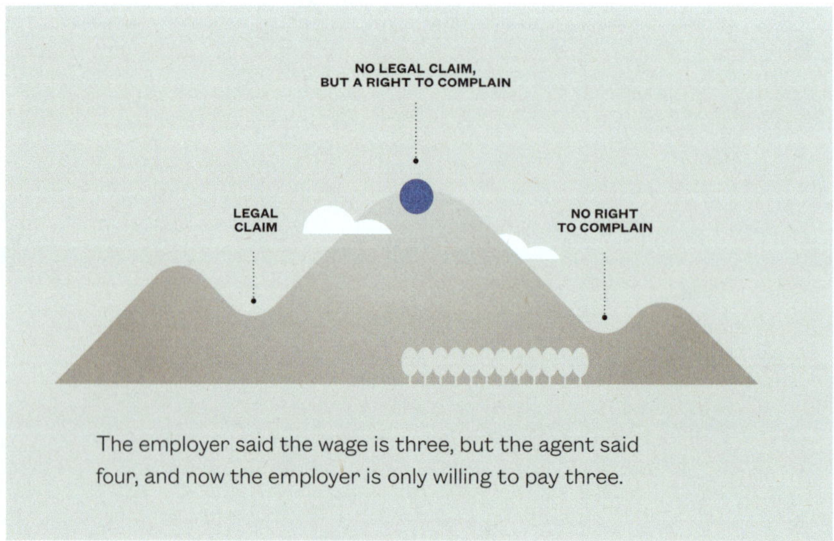

The employer said the wage is three, but the agent said four, and now the employer is only willing to pay three.

CASE 1

הֵיכִי דָמֵי? אִי דְאָמַר לֵיהּ בַּעַל הַבַּיִת בְּאַרְבָּעָה,
וְאָזִיל אִיהוּ אָמַר לְהוּ בִּתְלָתָא,

What is the case? Let's say that the employer told the agent "at four *zuz*," but the agent went and told the workers "at three *zuz*,"

- תַּרְעוֹמֶת מַאי עֲבִידְתֵּיהּ? סָבוּר וְקָבִיל.

What room is there for complaint? They understood and accepted the agent's proposal.

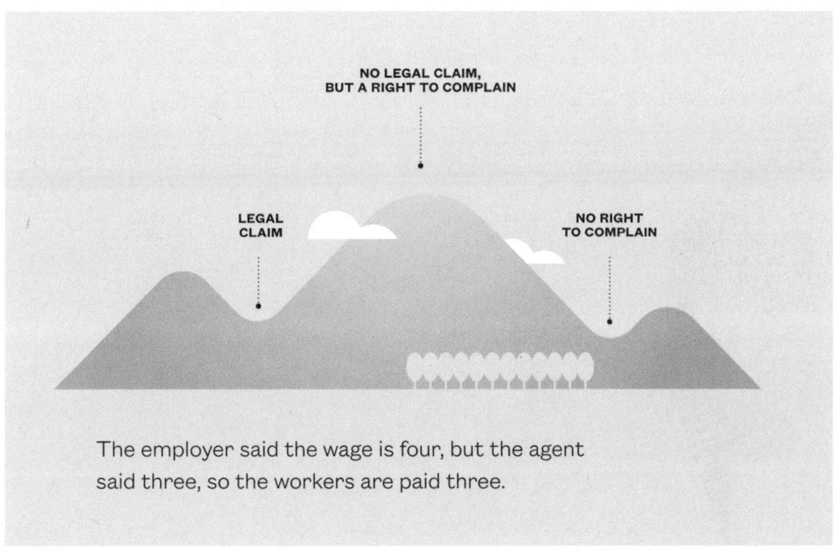

The employer said the wage is four, but the agent said three, so the workers are paid three.

CASE 2

אִי דְאָמַר לֵיהּ בַּעַל הַבַּיִת בִּתְלָתָא, וְאָזֵיל אִיהוּ אָמַר לְהוּ בְּאַרְבָּעָה,

Let's say the employer said "at three," but the agent said "at four,"

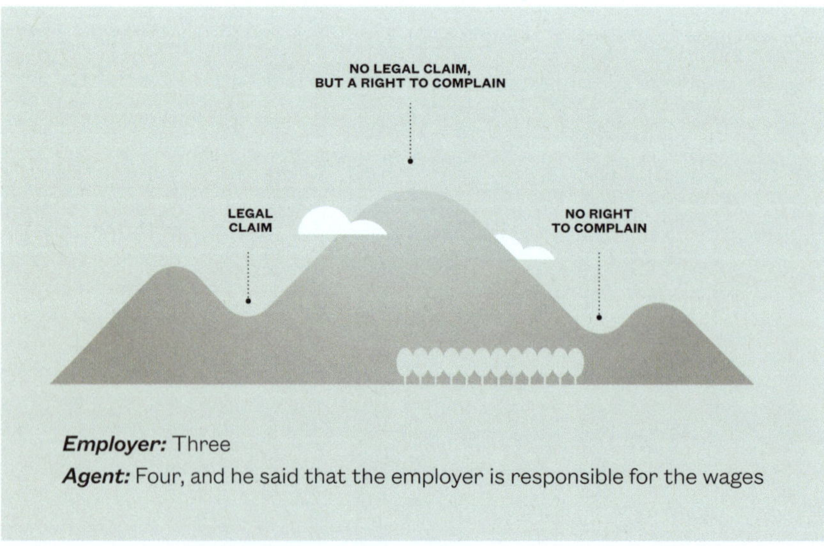

Employer: Three
Agent: Four, and he said that the employer is responsible for the wages

CASE 3

- הֵיכִי דָמֵי? אִי דְאָמַר לְהוּ: "שְׂכַרְכֶם עָלַי" - נֵתֵיב לְהוּ מִדִּידֵיהּ,

What is the precise case? If the agent told them, "Your wages are on me," the agent would have to pay [the addition] from his own resources.

דְתַנְיָא: הַשּׂוֹכֵר אֶת הַפּוֹעֵל לַעֲשׂוֹת בְּשֶׁלּוֹ וְהֶרְאָהוּ בְּשֶׁל חֲבֵירוֹ - נוֹתֵן לוֹ שְׂכָרוֹ מִשָּׁלֵם, וְחוֹזֵר וְנוֹטֵל מִבַּעַל הַבַּיִת מַה שֶּׁהֶהֱנָהוּ.

For we were taught in a Baraita: "If one hires workers to work in his own field, but directs them instead to his fellow's field, he must pay their wages in full, and he can then collect from the owner of the other field according to the amount of benefit he brought to that owner."

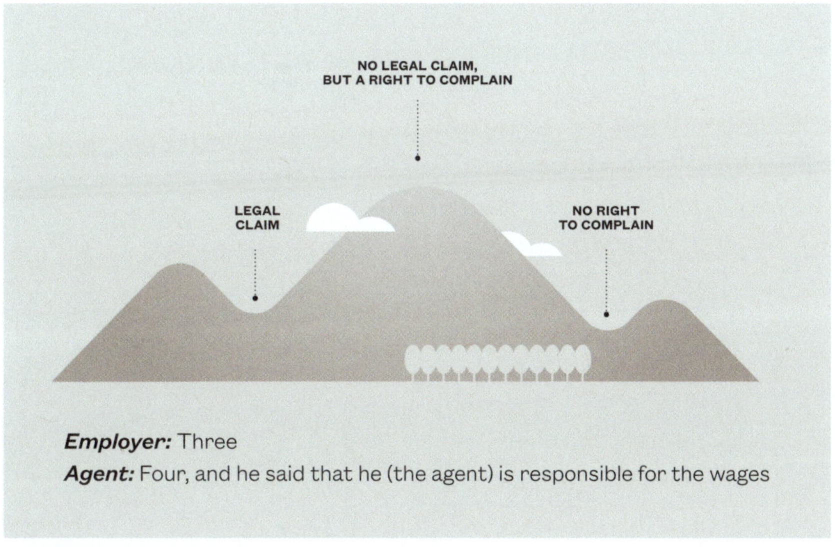

Employer: Three
Agent: Four, and he said that he (the agent) is responsible for the wages

CASE 4

לָא צְרִיכָא, דְאָמַר לְהוּ שְׂכַרְכֶם עַל בַּעַל הַבַּיִת.

Rather, it would work if the agent told them, "Your wages are on the employer."

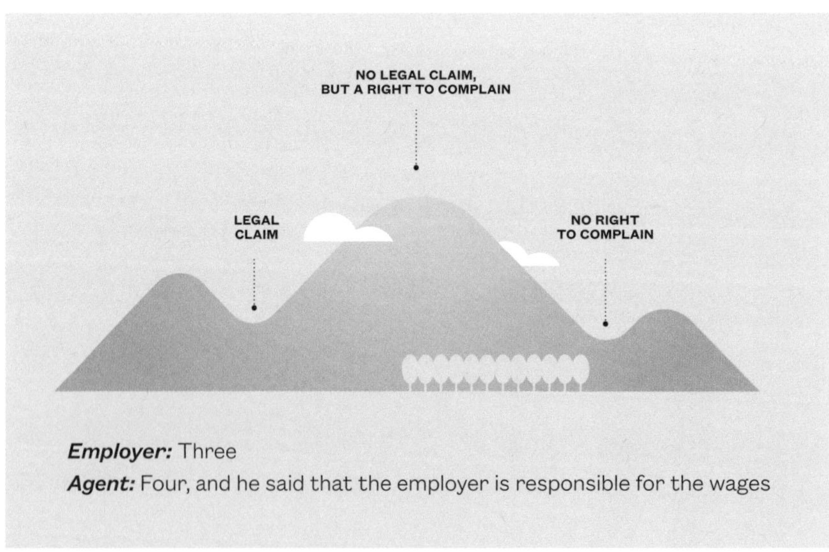

Employer: Three
Agent: Four, and he said that the employer is responsible for the wages

CASE 5 A–B

וְלֶחֱזֵי פּוֹעֲלִים הֵיכִי מִיתַּגְרֵי?

Let's look at the rate at which workers are hired.

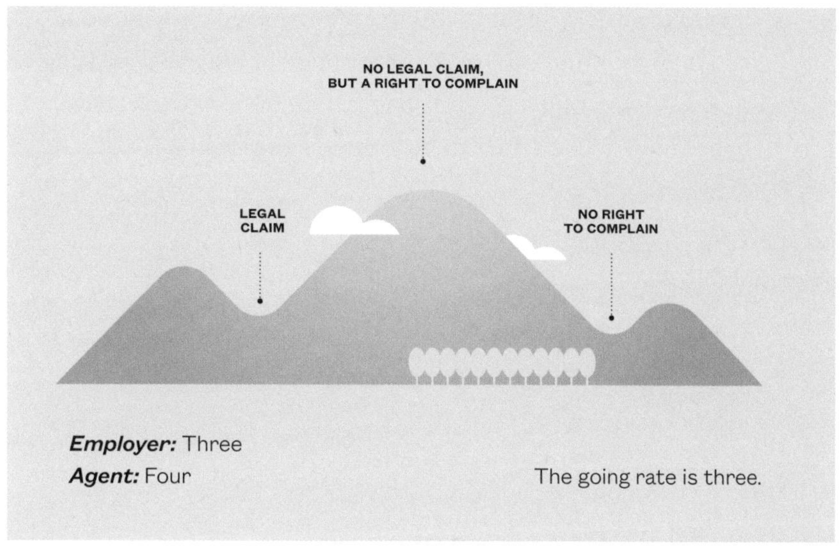

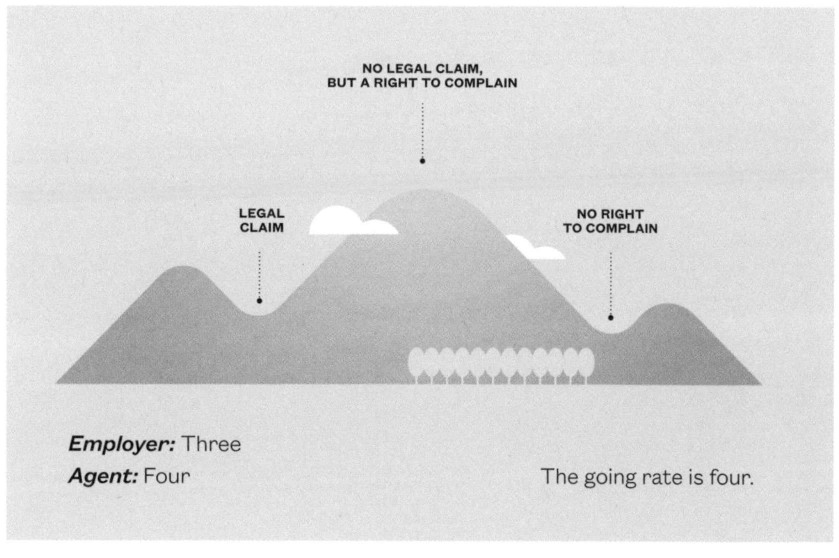

CASE 6

לָא צְרִיכָא, דְאִיכָּא דְמִתְּגַר בְּאַרְבָּעָה וְאִיכָּא
דְמִתְּגַר בִּתְלָתָא, דְאָמְרוּ לֵיהּ: אִי לָאו דַאֲמַרְתְּ לָן
בְּאַרְבָּעָה - טָרְחִינַן וּמִתַּגְרִינַן בְּאַרְבָּעָה.

It would work in a locale where some are typically hired at a rate of four and others at three. They could then tell the agent, "If you had not offered us a rate of four, we would have made more effort to be hired by someone else at a rate of four."

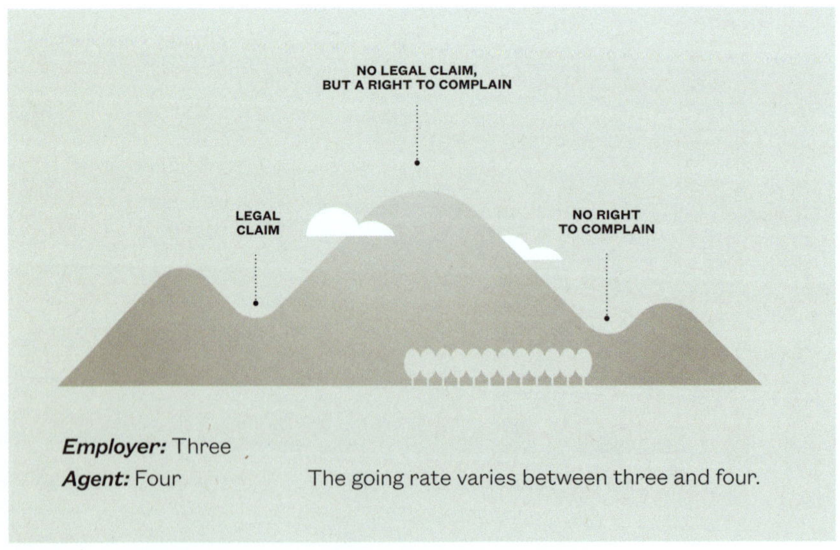

CASE 7

אִיבָּעֵית אֵימָא: הָכָא בְּבַעַל הַבַּיִת עַסְקִינַן, דְּאָמְרוּ לֵיהּ: אִי
לָאו דַּאֲמַרְתְּ לַן בְּאַרְבָּעָה, הֲוָה זִילָא בַּן מִילְּתָא לְאִתְּגוּרֵי.

An alternative suggestion: We are dealing with landowners, who can tell the agent, "If you had not offered us a rate of four, we would have considered it beneath our dignity to be hired."

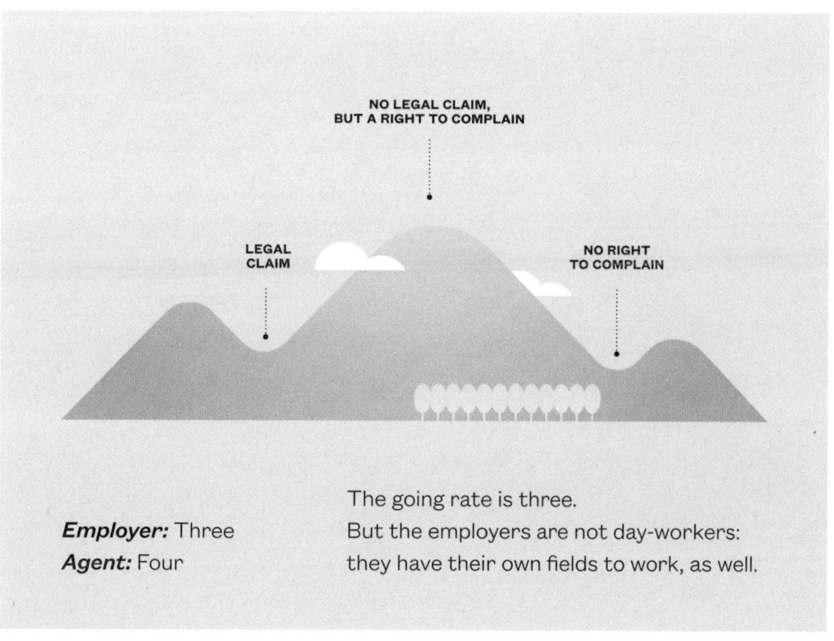

INTRODUCTION TO CASES 8–9

אִיבָּעֵית אֵימָא: לְעוֹלָם בְּפוֹעֲלִים עַסְקִינַן, דְּאָמְרִי לֵיהּ: כֵּיוָן דַּאֲמַרְתְּ לָן בְּאַרְבָּעָה - טָרְחִינַן וְעָבְדִינַן לָךְ עֲבִידְתָּא שַׁפִּירְתָּא.

An alternative suggestion: We are in fact dealing with laborers, but they tell the agent, "Because you offered us a rate of 4, we invested effort and performed exemplary work for you."

CASE 8

וְלֶחֱזֵי עֲבִידְתַּיְיהוּ?

Why don't we just examine their work?

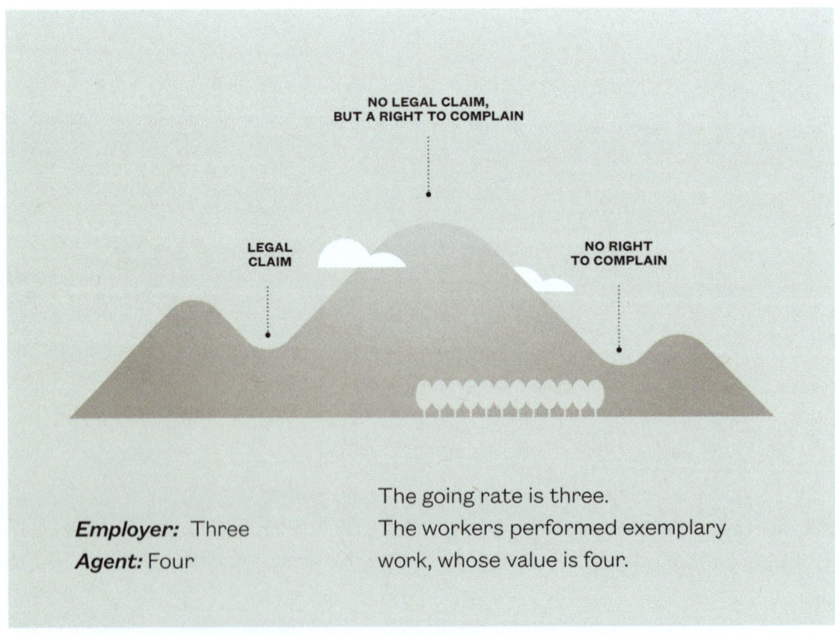

CASE 9

בְּרִיפְקָא.

It was ditch digging.

רִיפְקָא נַמֵּי מֵידַע יְדִיעַ?

Even in ditch digging, one can discern exemplary work!

דְּמָלֵי מַיָּא וְלָא יְדִיעַ.

It has already been filled with water and the quality of work is no longer discernable.

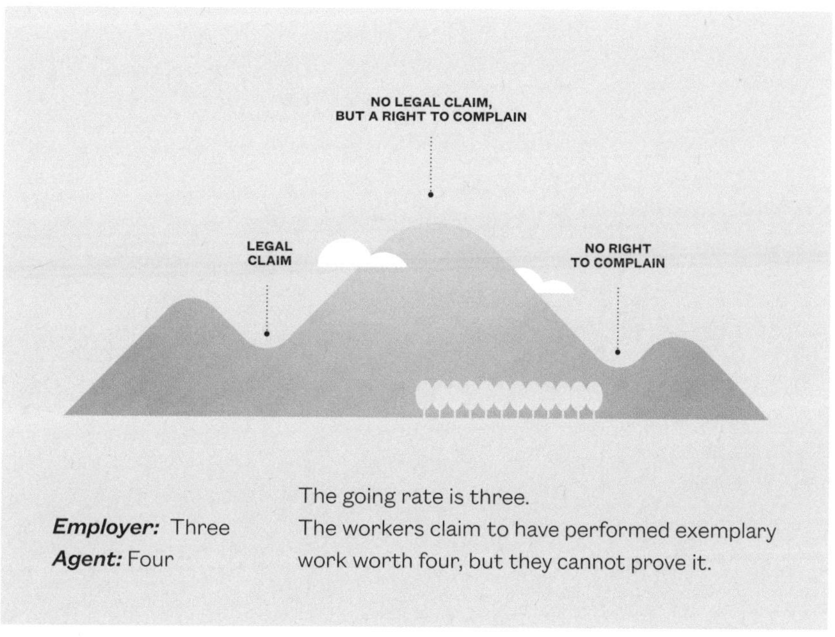

Employer: Three
Agent: Four

The going rate is three.
The workers claim to have performed exemplary work worth four, but they cannot prove it.

CASE 10

אִיבָּעֵית אֵימָא: לְעוֹלָם דְּאָמַר לֵיהּ בַּעַל הַבַּיִת בְּאַרְבָּעָה,
וַאֲזַל אִיהוּ אָמַר לְהוּ בִּתְלָתָא, וּדְקָאָמַרְתְּ סָבוּר וְקָבִיל,
דְּאָמְרִי לֵיהּ, לֵית לָךְ "אַל תִּמְנַע טוֹב מִבְּעָלָיו"?

An alternative suggestion: We are dealing with a case in which the employer stipulated a rate of four but the agent went ahead and offered three. True, we argued earlier that the workers understood and accepted the stipulated wage, but they can now tell the agent, "Do you not subscribe to the principle of 'Do not withhold benefit from its possessor'?"

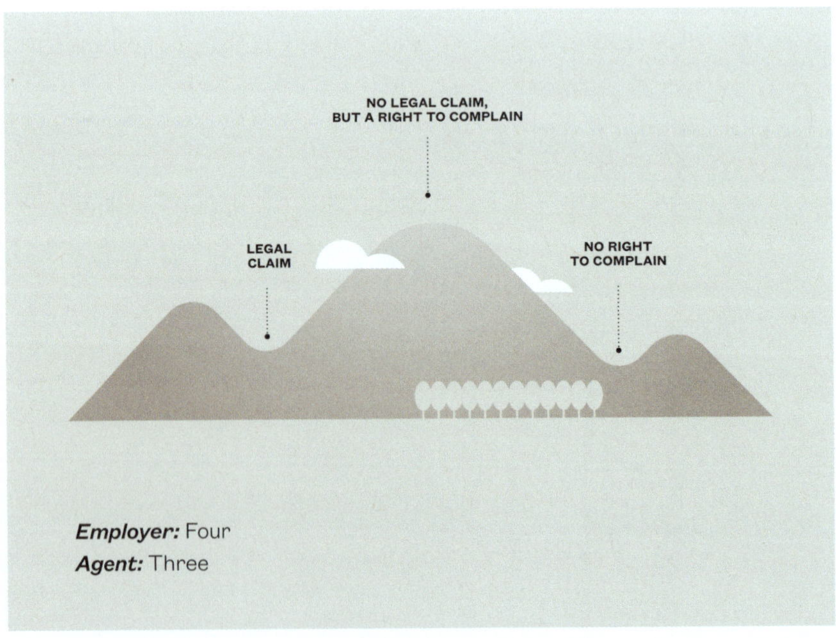

CASE 11

אִיבָּעֵית אֵימָא: הַאי תַּנָּא "חָזְרוּ" נַמֵּי "הִטְעוּ" קָרֵי לֵיהּ.

Alternatively: Our *tanna* uses the term *chazru*, "they canceled," in the sense of *hit'u*, "they deceived."

דְּתַנְיָא: הַשּׂוֹכֵר אֶת הָאוּמָּנִין וְהִטְעוּ אֶת בַּעַל הַבַּיִת, אוֹ בַּעַל הַבַּיִת הִטְעָה אוֹתָן - אֵין לָהֶם זֶה עַל זֶה אֶלָּא תַּרְעוֹמֶת. בַּמֶּה דְּבָרִים אֲמוּרִים? שֶׁלֹּא הָלְכוּ. אֲבָל הָלְכוּ חַמָּרִים וְלֹא מָצְאוּ תְּבוּאָה, פּוֹעֲלִין וּמָצְאוּ שָׂדֶה כְּשֶׁהִיא לַחָה - נוֹתֵן לָהֶן שְׂכָרָן מִשָּׁלֵם.

For we were taught in a Baraita: "If one hires workers and then either they deceive the employer or the employer deceives them, the two parties have nothing more than the right to complain against each other. When is this true? When the workers never turned up. Conversely, if mule drivers showed up but did not find the grain they were meant to transport, or if laborers showed up and found that the field they were hired to irrigate had already been irrigated, the one who hired them must pay their wages in full.

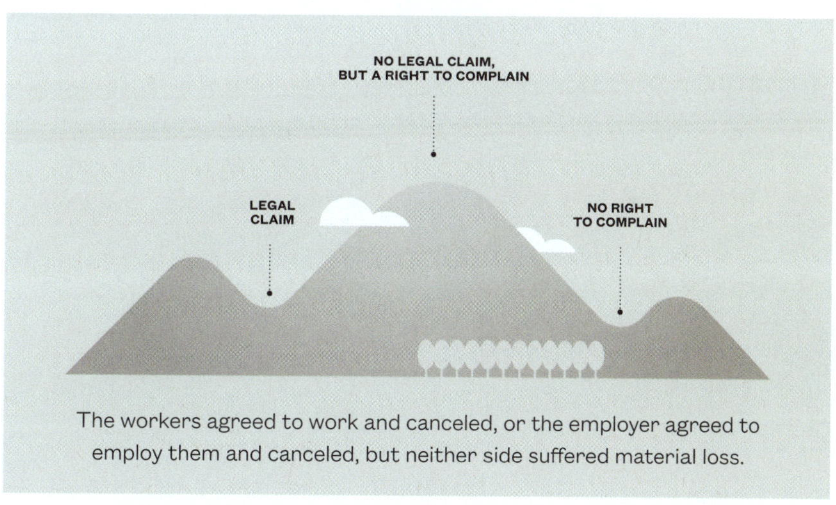

The workers agreed to work and canceled, or the employer agreed to employ them and canceled, but neither side suffered material loss.

IV. QUESTION EVERYTHING

We now turn to contrast our study of the Babylonian Talmud, with the approach of the second, less-studied form of the Talmud, the Jerusalem Talmud. The Jerusalem Talmud handles questions very differently from the Babylonian Talmud; it leaps from a question to the final conclusion, rather than considering many different possibilities that lay in between a problem and its solution.

TALMUDISTS
Ephraim Moses Lilien, engraving, c. 1900

TEXT 6

The Concise Talmud

Jerusalem Talmud, Pesachim 10:1

עֶרֶב פְּסָחִים סָמוּךְ לַמִּנְחָה כו'.

מַתְנִיתָא דְרִבִּי יוּדָה.

On the eve of Passover, from close to the time for reciting the Minchah prayers, etc.

Our Mishnah follows Rabbi Yehudah.

JERUSALEM TALMUD

A commentary to the Mishnah, compiled during the 4th and 5th centuries. The Jerusalem Talmud predates its Babylonian counterpart by 100 years and is written in both Hebrew and Aramaic. While the Babylonian Talmud is the most authoritative source for Jewish law, the Jerusalem Talmud remains an invaluable source for the spiritual, intellectual, ethical, historical, and legal traditions of Judaism.

TEXT 7

The Darkness of Babylonia

Talmud, Sanhedrin 24a

"בְּמַחֲשַׁכִּים הוֹשִׁיבַנִי כְּמֵתֵי עוֹלָם", אָמַר רַב יִרְמְיָה: זֶה תַּלְמוּדָהּ שֶׁל בָּבֶל.

"He set me down in darkness, as those forever dead" (LAMENTATIONS 3:6). Rabbi Yirmiyah said, "This refers to the Babylonian Talmud."

TEXT 8

Darkness Leads to Light

The Rebbe, Rabbi Menachem Mendel Schneerson, *Likutei Sichot*, vol. 5, pp. 61–62

דֶער סֵדֶר הַלִימוּד אִין תַּלְמוּד בַּבְלִי אִיז אוֹיסְגֶעשְׁטֶעלְט אוּן בַּאשְׁטֵייט פוּן קֻשְׁיוֹת אוּן פִּלְפּוּלִים וְכוּ' וָואס זַיְינֶען לִכְאוֹרָה אַ פַּארְשְׁטֶעל אוּן אַ הֶסְתֵּר אוֹיפְן אוֹר הַשֵּׂכֶל פוּן תּוֹרָה (נִיט וִוי תַּלְמוּד יְרוּשַׁלְמִי וָואס אִיז אִין אַן אוֹפֶן פוּן אוֹר יָשָׁר) – אוּן פוּנְדֶעסְטְוֶועגְן אִיז דַוְקָא דוּרְכְן פִּלְפּוּל בְּרִיבּוּי הַקוּשְׁיוֹת וְכוּ' קוּמְט מֶען דֶערְנָאךְ צוּ צוּם עוֹמֶק הַהֲלָכָה, אַ סַך מֶער וִוי דָאס וָואס מְ'קֶען דֶערְגְרֵייכְן דוּרְךְ דֶעם דֶרֶךְ הַלִימוּד פוּן תַּלְמוּד יְרוּשַׁלְמִי.

The Babylonian Talmud is composed of questions and complicated analysis, which seem to conceal and obscure the Torah's intellectual light—unlike the Jerusalem Talmud that uses the "direct light" method. Nevertheless, it is specifically through complex analysis involving a multitude of inquiries that we can reach the depth of the Halachah—far deeper than can be reached through the Jerusalem Talmud's approach.

RABBI MENACHEM MENDEL SCHNEERSON 1902–1994

The towering Jewish leader of the 20th century, known as "the Lubavitcher Rebbe," or simply as "the Rebbe." Born in southern Ukraine, the Rebbe escaped Nazi-occupied Europe, arriving in the U.S. in June 1941. The Rebbe inspired and guided the revival of traditional Judaism after the European devastation, impacting virtually every Jewish community the world over. The Rebbe often emphasized that the performance of just one additional good deed could usher in the era of Mashiach. The Rebbe's scholarly talks and writings have been printed in more than 200 volumes.

TEXT 9

Exile Leads to Redemption

The Rebbe, Rabbi Menachem Mendel Schneerson, ibid.

וָואס דוּרְךְ דֶעם וֶועלְן אִידְן זִיךְ דֶערְהוֹיבְּן צוּ נָאךְ אַ הֶעכֶערֶען עִילוּי וִוי דֶער וָואס אִיז גֶעוֶוען בִּזְמַן הַבַּיִת . . . אִיז דָאךְ פַארְשְׁטַאנְדִיק אַז דִי לֶעצְטֶע יְרִידָה גוּפָא אִיז אַן אָנְהוֹיבּ און אַ חֵלֶק פוּן אָט דֶער קוּמֶענְדִיקֶער עֲלִיָה.

Through the process of Exile, the Jewish people will be elevated to an even greater height than the spiritual height they experienced during the former Temple eras. . . . It is therefore understood that this final descent is the beginning of, and a part of, the imminent ascent.

SIMHA **(JOY) DANCE**
Anna Zarnitsky, oil on canvas,
Jerusalem, Israel, 2019

KEY POINTS

1. The Talmud has its own unique logic system that can only be mastered by experiencing the study of Talmud. This system has shaped Jewish thinking and culture throughout the world.

2. A hallmark of Talmudic thinking is the skill of *halten kop*, keeping track of a line of argument when the Talmud jumps between premises due to unstated logical steps.

3. Talmudic analysis values nuanced arguments that are correct yet not immediately obvious, allowing students to explore deeper layers of Halachic understanding.

4. Talmud study trains students to carefully consider arguments against the views they hold, thereby enhancing the comprehension of the Halachic principles involved.

5. The Jerusalem Talmud offers straightforward answers, contrasting with the Babylonian Talmud's complex, debate-driven approach.

6. The Babylonian Talmud's detailed questioning process is likened to battling through darkness to find light. The experience of studying Talmud teaches us to turn challenges into opportunities for deeper understanding and spiritual growth.

Continue learning at **myjli.com/talmud**

Today, we tackled an original Talmudic text—a selection of Gemara.
Here is how this section we covered appears in a classic printed edition of the Talmud.

מסורת הש"ס　　השוכר את האומנין　פרק ששי　בבא מציעא　　עו.　　עין משפט נר מצוה

אם בעל הבית חוזר בו ידו על התחתונה
כל המשנה ידו על התחתונה וכל החוזר
בו ידו על התחתונה: **גמ'** חזרו זה בזה
לא קתני אלא הטעו זה את זה דאטעו
פועלים אהדדי היכי דמי דאמר ליה בעל
הבית זיל אוגר לי פועלים ואזל איהו
ואטעינהו היכי דמי אי דאמר ליה בעל
הבית בארבעה ואזיל איהו אמר להו בתלתא
תרעומת מאי עבידתיה סבור וקביל אי
דאמר ליה בעל הבית בתלתא ואזיל איהו
אמר להו בארבעה ה"ד אי דאמר להו
שכרכם עלי נתיב להו מדידיה דתניא
השוכר את הפועל לעשות בשלו והראהו
בשל חבירו נותן לו שכרו משלם וחוזר
ונוטל מבעל הבית מה שההנהו לא צריכא
דאמר להו שכרכם על בעל הבית ולחזי
פועלים היכי מיתגרי לא צריכא דאיכא
דמגר בארבעה ואיכא דמתגר בתלתא
דאמרו ליה אי לאו דאמרת לן בארבעה
טרחינן ומתגרינן בארבעה איבעית אימא
הכא בבעל הבית עסקינן דאמרו ליה אי לאו
דאמרת לן בארבעה הוה זילא בן מילתא
לאתגורי איבעית אימא לעולם בפועלים
עסקינן דאמרי ליה כיון דאמרת לן בארבעה
טרחינן ועבדינן לך עבידתא שפירתא
וליחזי עבידתייהו בריפקא ריפקא נמי מידע
ידע דמלי מיא ולא ידיע איבעית אימא
לעולם דאמר ליה בעל הבית בארבעה
ואזל איהו אמר להו בתלתא ודקאמרת
סבור וקביל דאמרי ליה לית לך אל תמנע
טוב מבעליו פשיטא אי אמר ליה בעל
הבית בתלתא ואזל איהו א"ל בארבעה ואמרי
ליה כמו שאמר בעל הבית דעתייהו אעילויא
אלא אי א"ל בעל הבית בארבעה ואזל איהו
אמר להו בתלתא ואמרי כמה שאמר בעל
הבית מאי אדיבורא דידיה קא סמכי דאמרי
ליה מהימנת לן דהכי אמר בעל הבית או
דילמא אדיבורא דבעל הבית קא סמכי
ת"ש הבא לי גיטי ואשתך אמרה התקבל
לי גיטי והוא אומר הילך כמה שאמרה אמר
רב נחמן אמר רבה בר אבוה אמר רב אפי'
הגיע גט לידה אינה מגורשת שמעת
מינה אדיבורא דידיה קא סמיך דאי סלקא
דעתך דאדיבורא דידה קא סמיך מכי מטי
גיטא לידה מיהא תיגרש אמר רב אשי
הכי

Fantastical Cases and Precedents in Talmudic and Halachic Literature

The Talmud and the Midrashim include many case studies which, at first glance, seem highly unlikely to ever occur or to ever have any practical legal relevance. These have generally been viewed either as one-time miraculous occurrences, or as purely theoretical discussions whose purpose is to clarify a legal principle regardless of its practical relevance. But over the centuries, many of these "fantastical" scenarios became quite relevant and applicable, as the following examples illustrate.

CASE STUDY #1

The Flying Tower

אחד עשר סנהדרין

מסורת הש״ס

יודע לדרוש בקל וחומר: במגדל הפורח באויר׳ מתג עליונה שלמעלה מן
הגמ״ד מפני מה כפופ׳ למטה לשון מ״ר מפי השמועה ל״א במגדל הפורח
באויר הנכנס לארץ העמים בשיד׳ תיבה ומגדל אם הוא טמא אם לאו

TEXT SHOWN:

Rabbi Shlomo Yitzchaki (Rashi) on Talmud, Sanhedrin 108b

SECOND CENTURY CE AND ELEVENTH CENTURY CE

In Talmudic and Halachic Literature

The Talmud, its commentaries, and the early Halachists discuss the case of a person who traverses a space in a "tower flying through the air." At issue is the laws of ritual purity and impurity. Entering or passing over certain spaces (e.g., stepping over or leaning over a grave) renders a person ritually impure. Subsequently, a ritually impure person may not enter the Holy Temple in Jerusalem until they undergo a purification process. But what is the law in the case that a person enters an impure space, or an impure person enters a sacred space, in "a tower flying through the air"—i.e., an enclosed structure that enters the space without being in contact with the ground? (Mishnah, Ohalot 4:1; Talmud, Gittin 8b; Rashi on Talmud, Sanhedrin 108b; Maimonides, *Mishneh Torah*, Laws of Entering the Sanctuary, 3:19)

Modern-Day Applications

Today, with the absence of a Holy Temple and Temple service, the extensive body of law governing ritual purity is mostly inapplicable in practice. However, the law remains that a *Kohen* is forbidden to become ritually impure through contact with a corpse. This raises the question of whether a *Kohen* is permitted to travel in an airplane that flies over a cemetery. The Talmudic precedent of the "tower flying through the air" is cited and analyzed by modern-day *poskim* (halachic authorities) who tackle this question.

CASE STUDY #2

A Virgin Giving Birth?

וכ׳ יש נהסתפק אשה שנתעברה
באמבטי אם קיים האב פ״ו ואם מקרי
בנו לכל דבר. ובלקוטי מהרי״ל נמלא
שבן סירא היה בנו של ירמיה שרחץ

TEXT SHOWN:

Rabbi Moshe ben Yitzchak Yehudah Lima, *Chelkat Mechokek* on Shulchan Aruch, *Even Ha'ezer* 1:8

THIRD CENTURY CE AND SEVENTEENTH CENTURY CE

In Talmudic and Halachic Literature

The Talmud (Chagigah 14b–15a) raises the question: Is it possible for a woman to become pregnant without coitus? The legal question at hand is if such a woman may marry a *Kohen Gadol* (High Priest), whom the Torah instructs to only marry a virgin (Leviticus 21:13). The scenario proposed for this possibility is if a man has a seminal emission while bathing in a bathtub, and a woman subsequently bathes in the same bathwater. Later Halachic authorities further probe this discussion, asking if a person who fathers a child in such a manner has fulfilled their obligation "to be fruitful and multiply" (e.g., *Chelkat Mechokek* on Shulchan Aruch, *Even Ha'ezer* 1:8).

Modern-Day Applications

This seemingly theoretical discussion has become highly relevant in recent decades, as medical advances in infertility treatments have given rise to numerous legal and moral dilemmas: Is it permissible for a married woman to be impregnated by the sperm of a man who is not her husband? Do we need to be concerned with the possibility that a child born from the sperm of an anonymous donor may end up marrying their biological sibling?

CASE STUDY #3

The Transported Fetus

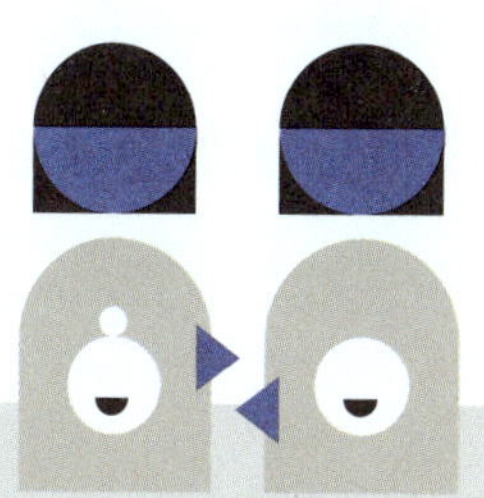

בזריעת נקבה תחלה והרא"ש ז] כתב בזה בדחוקים עיין שם ואין להאריך ודו"ק: **ואת דינה**
בתו תלה הזכרים בנקבות ונקבות בזכרים כו'. יש להקשות דהא דינה זכר היה
ונהפכה לנקבה כדאיתא פרק הרואה י] וא"כ עיקר יצירתה זכר היה ולאה הזריעה תחלה
ונהפכה לנקבה ע"י תפלת האמהות והרא"ש תירצו בדחוקים וגם ספר פענ"ח רז"י שמעתי
לתרץ הא דנהפכה דינה לבת היינו שהזכר שבבטן לאה ניתן בבטן רחל והנקבה שבבטן רחל ניתן
בבטן לאה דהשתא אתי שפיר עיקר יצירתה של דינה נקבה עכ"ד וכן מוכיחין דברי הפייטן
ביולד של ר"ה עובר להמיר בבטן אחות כו' סלוף דינה ביוסף כו' ותו לא מידי ח]: **מרבים**

TEXT SHOWN:

Rabbi Shmuel Eidels (Maharsha) on Talmud, Nidah 31a

SEVENTH AND SIXTEENTH CENTURIES

In Talmudic and Halachic Literature

As related in the thirtieth chapter of the Book of Genesis, Leah, the wife of Jacob, gave birth to six sons, after which she gave birth to a daughter, Dinah. A talmudic analysis of the text deduces that Leah's seventh pregnancy was actually with a male fetus. But Leah knew that Yaakov would have a total of twelve sons who would generate the twelve tribes of Israel. At the time, Yaakov had already fathered ten sons while Rachel was still childless, and Leah did not want to deprive her sister Rachel of giving birth to at least two tribes. So Leah prayed that she should give birth to a female. Indeed, shortly after Dinah's birth Rachel gave birth to a son, Joseph (Talmud, Berachot 60a; Rashi on Genesis 30:21).

While this is commonly understood to mean that the fetus in Leah's womb was changed from male to female, an alternative interpretation, implied by other Talmudic statements about Dinah's conception, is that Leah was carrying a male fetus in her womb and Rachel was carrying a female, and the two fetuses miraculously switched places (*Targum Yonatan ben Uzi'el* on Genesis 30:21; Maharsha on Talmud, Nidah 31a).

Some sources seem to indicate that, based on this tradition, Dinah's true mother was Rachel, not Leah, even though Leah carried her to term and gave birth to her.

Modern-Day Applications

With the advent of reproductive surrogacy, contemporary *poskim* grapple with a host of Halachic questions, including: Who is the Halachic mother of the child—the woman who provided the ovum, the woman in whose womb the fetus was implanted and carried to term, or perhaps both? Thus, an esoteric discussion concerning a one-time miraculous event becomes relevant to a contemporary phenomenon.

CASE STUDY #4

Temporary Death

ימים בא הכתוב ולמד על המת שמטמא טומאת שבעה. [יא]הנוגע
במת, נוגע במת טמא ואין מת עצמו טמא. נוגע במת טמא ואין
בנה של שונמית טמא. אמרו בנה של שונמית כשמת כל שהיה
עמו בבית טמא טומאת שבעה, וכשחיה היה טהור לקדש חזרו
ונגעו בו וטמאוהו הם. הרי זה אומר מטמאיך לא טמאוני ואתה
טומאתני. השורף פרה ופרים הנשרפים ושעירים הנשרפים מטמאין

TEXT SHOWN:

Midrash, *Yalkut Shimoni*, Numbers 19:11

FOURTH AND THIRTEENTH CENTURIES

In Talmudic and Halachic Literature

The "son of the Shunamite woman" was a child who died and was miraculously brought back to life by the prophet Elisha, as related in the fourth chapter of the biblical book of II Kings. The Halachic Midrashim speculate on the legal ramifications of this event as it would pertain to the laws of ritual purity. For example: The basic premise is that while the child was dead, anyone touching his corpse would become ritually impure, and having attained this status, would remain so even after the child was revived. But what about the boy himself? Should he be considered ritually impure, after having been in contact with his own dead body? (*Sifrei Zuta* on Numbers 19:11, cited in *Yalkut Shimoni*, ad loc.)

Modern-Day Applications

Advances in the medical sciences have made the miraculous "resurrection of the dead" an almost everyday occurrence. During open heart surgery, for example, a cardiopulmonary bypass machine takes over the function of the heart and lungs, meaning that the person is technically, and perhaps also Halachically, dead for many hours. This led one prominent *posek*, who underwent such a procedure himself, to raise a fascinating Halachic question. According to Torah law, the death of a husband or wife effectively ends the marriage, allowing the other spouse to marry someone else (Mishnah, Kidushin 1:1). So, is a person who underwent such a procedure now required to remarry their spouse?

APPENDIX

TEXT 10

Mice Problems

Talmud, Pesachim 9b–10b

תֵּשַׁע צִיבּוּרִין שֶׁל מַצָּה וְאֶחָד שֶׁל חָמֵץ, וַאֲתָא עַכְבָּר
וּשְׁקַל. וְלָא יָדְעִינַן אִי מַצָּה שְׁקַל אִי חָמֵץ שְׁקַל . . .

שְׁנֵי צִיבּוּרִין, אֶחָד שֶׁל מַצָּה וְאֶחָד שֶׁל חָמֵץ, וְלִפְנֵיהֶם
שְׁנֵי בָתִּים, אֶחָד בָּדוּק וְאֶחָד שֶׁאֵינוֹ בָּדוּק. וַאֲתוֹ
שְׁנֵי עַכְבָּרִים, אֶחָד שְׁקַל מַצָּה, וְאֶחָד שְׁקַל חָמֵץ.
וְלָא יָדְעִינַן הֵי לְהַאי עָיֵיל וְהֵי לְהַאי עָיֵיל . . .

צִבּוּר אֶחָד שֶׁל חָמֵץ וּלְפָנָיו שְׁנֵי בָתִּים בְּדוּקִין, וַאֲתָא
עַכְבָּר וּשְׁקַל, וְלָא יָדְעִינַן אִי לְהַאי עָל אִי לְהַאי עָל . . .

סָפֵק עָל, סָפֵק לָא עָל . . .

עַכְבָּר נִכְנָס וְכִכָּר בְּפִיו, וְעַכְבָּר יוֹצֵא וְכִכָּר בְּפִיו . . .

עַכְבָּר לָבָן נִכְנָס וְכִכָּר בְּפִיו, וְעַכְבָּר שָׁחוֹר יוֹצֵא וְכִכָּר בְּפִיו . . .

עַכְבָּר נִכְנָס וְכִכָּר בְּפִיו, וְחוּלְדָּה יוֹצְאָה וְכִכָּר בְּפִיהָ . . .

עַכְבָּר נִכְנָס וְכִכָּר בְּפִיו, וְחוּלְדָּה יוֹצְאָה
וְכִכָּר וְעַכְבָּר בְּפִי חוּלְדָּה.

There were nine bundles of matzah and one of *chametz*. A mouse appeared and took one [and carried it into the house], and we do not know whether the mouse took matzah or *chametz*. . . .

There were two bundles, one of matzah and one of *chametz*, in front of two houses—one home had already been searched and the other had not been searched. Two mice arrived: one took the bundle of matzah and the other took the bundle of *chametz*. We do not know which mouse entered this house and which entered the other house. . . .

There was one bundle of *chametz* in front of two homes. A mouse appeared and carried the bundle into a home, but we do not know if it was this home or the other. . . .

We are uncertain whether the mouse entered a house altogether. . . .

A mouse entered a house with a loaf in its mouth, and a mouse subsequently exited the same house with a loaf in its mouth. . . .

A white mouse entered a home with a loaf in its mouth, and a black mouse subsequently exited the same home with a loaf in its mouth. . . .

A mouse entered a home with a loaf in its mouth, and a weasel subsequently exited the same house with a loaf in its mouth. . . .

A mouse entered a home with a loaf in its mouth, and a weasel subsequently exited the same house with a mouse and a loaf in its mouth.

TEXT 11

Theoretical Value

Hershey Friedman, "Talmudic Humor and the Establishment of Legal Principles," *Thalia, Studies in Literary Humor,* vol. 21, 2004, pp. 14–28

Purely theoretical cases are discussed because the sages felt that principles derived from these discussions would clarify the law and thus provide a more thorough understanding of it.

HERSHEY FRIEDMAN

Business professor. Hershey Friedman is a professor of business at Brooklyn College. He has written extensively about business ethics and leadership, and his academic work often incorporates wisdom and lessons from the Bible and Talmud.

TEXT 12

Expressing G-d's Mind

Rabbi Shneur Zalman of Liadi, *Tanya*, *Kuntres Acharon* 5

גַם הַפְּרָטִים שֶׁיוּכַל לִהְיוֹת שֶׁלֹּא הָיוּ וְלֹא יִהְיוּ לְעוֹלָם בִּמְצִיאוּת . . . מִכָּל מָקוֹם, עַל כָּל פָּנִים יֶשְׁנוֹ בִּמְצִיאוּת, לְהַבְדִּיל, בְּחָכְמָה עִילָּאָה, שֶׁנִּתְפַּשְּׁטָה בִּפְרָט זֶה לְמֹשֶׁה רַבֵּינוּ עָלָיו הַשָּׁלוֹם בְּסִינַי.

Even those details that may never have occurred and might never occur . . . at the very least, they do exist in G-d's Supernal Wisdom, which extended and expressed itself in these particular details, as taught by G-d to Moses at Mount Sinai.

RABBI SHNEUR ZALMAN OF LIADI (ALTER REBBE) 1745–1812

Chasidic rebbe, Halachic authority, and founder of the Chabad movement. The Alter Rebbe was born in Liozna, Belarus, and was among the principal students of the Magid of Mezeritch. His numerous works include the *Tanya*, an early classic containing the fundamentals of Chabad Chasidism; and *Shulchan Aruch HaRav*, an expanded and reworked code of Jewish law.

THE TALMUD UNTIL TODAY

Talmudic literature and fifteen centuries of constant study

See how and why the Talmud became the core of Jewish law, and discover the vast literature of responsa, legal codes, and commentaries that continue the conversation until today.

UNTITLED
Robert Kremnitzer, oil on canvas, Israel, 2020

I. THE AUTHORITY OF THE TALMUD

Our previous lessons traced the Talmud's origins and explored its unique structure and logic. In this section, we focus on the Talmud's practical gifts—the ways in which the Talmud's rulings have guided Jewish life from the era of its completion until modern times. We learn that in normative Halachic practice, all post-Talmudic rulings must align with the Talmud's teachings, making the Talmud a universal and unifying guide across all Jewish communities.

Illustrated title page from a Talmud printed in Frankfurt, Germany in 1699, featuring drawings of Moses, Aaron, King David, and King Solomon

FIGURE 6.1

Development of Talmudic Scholarship

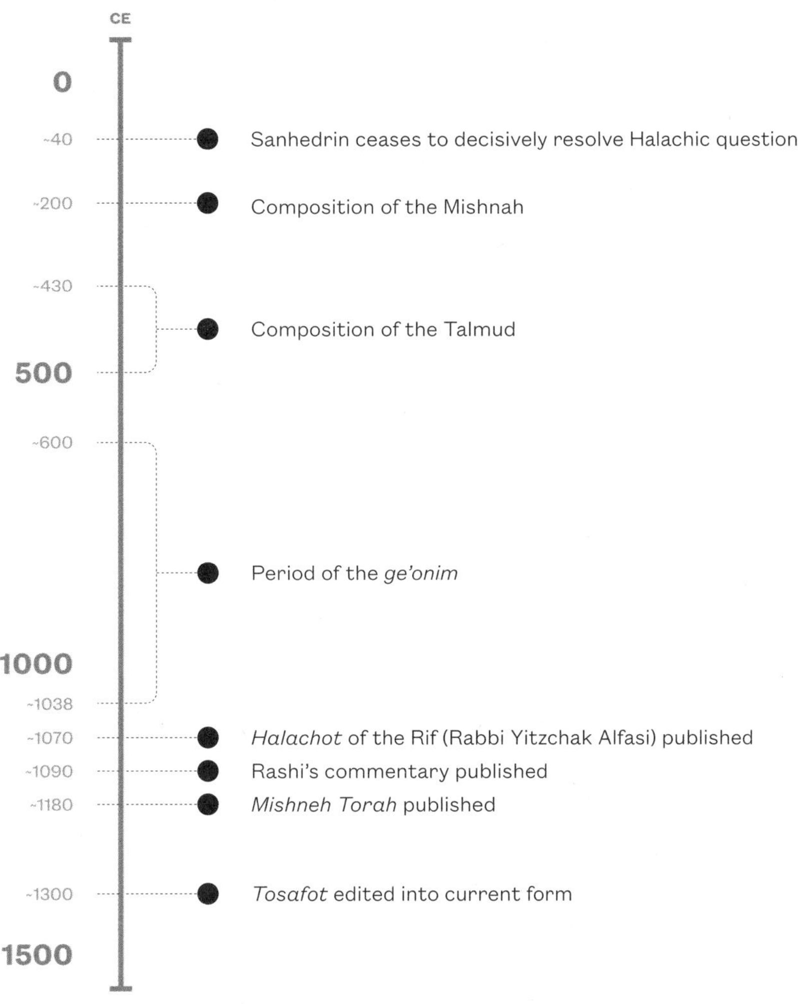

TEXT 1

Universal Acceptance

Maimonides, *Mishneh Torah*, introduction

רָבִינָא וְרַב אַשִׁי וַחֲבֵרֵיהֶם, סוֹף גְדוֹלֵי חַכְמֵי יִשְׂרָאֵל הַמַעְתִּיקִים תּוֹרָה שֶׁבְּעַל פֶּה, וְשֶׁגָּזְרוּ גְזֵרוֹת וְהִתְקִינוּ תַּקָנוֹת וְהִנְהִיגוּ מִנְהָגוֹת וּפָשְׁטוּ גְזֵרוֹתָם וְתַקָנוֹתָם וּמִנְהֲגוֹתָם בְּכָל יִשְׂרָאֵל . . .

וְכָל בֵּית דִין שֶׁעָמַד אַחַר הַתַּלְמוּד בְּכָל מְדִינָה וּמְדִינָה וְגָזַר אוֹ הִתְקִין אוֹ הִנְהִיג לִבְנֵי מְדִינָתוֹ, אוֹ לִבְנֵי מְדִינוֹת - לֹא פָּשְׁטוּ מַעֲשָׂיו בְּכָל יִשְׂרָאֵל . . .

לְפִיכָךְ . . . אִם לִמֵד אֶחָד מִן הַגְאוֹנִים שֶׁדֶרֶךְ הַמִשְׁפָּט כָּךְ הוּא, וְנִתְבָּאֵר לְבֵית דִין אַחֵר שֶׁעָמַד אַחֲרָיו שְׁאֵין זֶה דֶרֶךְ הַמִשְׁפָּט הַכָּתוּב בַּתַּלְמוּד - אֵין שׁוֹמְעִין לָרִאשׁוֹן, אֶלָא לְמִי שֶׁהַדַעַת נוֹטָה לִדְבָרָיו, בֵּין רִאשׁוֹן, בֵּין אַחֲרוֹן . . .

אֲבָל כָּל הַדְבָרִים שֶׁבַּתַּלְמוּד הַבַּבְלִי, חַיָבִין כָּל בֵּית יִשְׂרָאֵל לָלֶכֶת בָּהֶם.

Ravina and Rav Ashi and their colleagues constituted the end of the era of the sages who authoritatively transmitted the Oral Torah, and who set in place ordinances, decrees, and customs that became accepted as normative practice by all the Jewish people. . . .

By contrast, any ordinance, decree, or custom instituted by any court that arose after the Talmud, in any land, whether it was instituted

RABBI MOSHE BEN MAIMON (MAIMONIDES, RAMBAM) 1135–1204

Halachist, philosopher, author, and physician. Maimonides was born in Córdoba, Spain. After the conquest of Córdoba by the Almohads, he fled Spain and eventually settled in Cairo, Egypt. There, he became the leader of the Jewish community and served as court physician to the vizier of Egypt. He is most noted for authoring the *Mishneh Torah*, an encyclopedic arrangement of Jewish law; and for his philosophical work, *Guide for the Perplexed*. His rulings on Jewish law are integral to the formation of Halachic consensus.

for the inhabitants of that land or for an entire region, did not become accepted as normative by the entire Jewish people. . . .

Therefore . . . if one of the post-Talmudic scholars taught that, in a specific case, the judgment ought to be a certain way, and then a later court subsequently determined that the earlier ruling was an inaccurate interpretation of the Talmud, we need not follow the earlier conclusion; we follow whichever ruling is more logically correct and in greater accordance with the Talmud, whether its author lived in an earlier or a later generation. . . .

All decisions recorded in the Babylonian Talmud, however, are obligatory upon the entire Jewish people.

MOSES WOULD SPEAK AND G-D WOULD RESPOND TO HIM WITH A VOICE (EXODUS 19:19)
Yossi Rosenstein, Israel, 1997

KEY TERM 6.1

HEBREW TERM	פּוֹסֵק/פּוֹסְקִים
TRANSLITERATION	***posek/poskim***
PRONUNCIATION	POH-sek/POHS-keem
LITERAL MEANING	**decisor/s**
MEANING	a rabbi with the authority to render a verdict on a question of Halachah

TEXT 2

Post-Talmudic Dispersion

Maimonides, *Mishneh Torah*, introduction

וְאַחַר בֵּית דִּינוֹ שֶׁל רַב אַשִׁי . . . נִתְפַּזְּרוּ יִשְׂרָאֵל בְּכָל הָאֲרָצוֹת פִּזּוּר יָתֵר, וְהִגִּיעוּ לַקְּצָוֹות וְלָאִיִּים הָרְחוֹקִים; וְרָבְתָה קְטָטָה בָּעוֹלָם, וְנִשְׁתַּבְּשׁוּ הַדְּרָכִים בְּגְיָסוֹת. וְנִתְמַעֵט תַּלְמוּד תּוֹרָה, וְלֹא נִתְכַּנְסוּ יִשְׂרָאֵל לִלְמֹד בִּישִׁיבוֹתֵיהֶם אֲלָפִים וּרְבָבוֹת כְּמוֹ שֶׁהָיוּ מִקֹּדֶם.

After the era of Rav Ashi . . . the people of Israel grew increasingly dispersed throughout the world, reaching the furthest geographic extremes and the most remote islands. War became more prevalent and travel was impeded by armed forces. The study of Torah dwindled and students no longer attended *yeshivot* in their thousands and myriads, as before.

II. DERIVING HALACHAH FROM THE TALMUD

With the Talmud's authority in Jewish law established, we now move from theory to practice. Answering a Halachic question begins with consulting the Talmud—a complex endeavor. This section explores how scholars simplified this process by creating digests and codes that made Talmudic Halachah more accessible.

***BEIT MIDRASH* (STUDY HALL)**
Nechama Shaish, oil on canvas, Israel, 2007

FIGURE 6.2

The Flow of the *Sugya*, Pesachim 99b–100a

STEP		
STEP 1	THE PROBLEM	The Mishnah draws a distinction between Passover and the other festivals (including Shabbat). This seems to contradict the view of Rabbi Yose, who apparently denies the legitimacy of the restriction under discussion altogether, and it also contradicts the view of Rabbi Yehudah, who apparently sees no distinction between Passover and other festivals.
STEP 2	RAV HUNA'S SOLUTION	Rabbi Yose draws a distinction between Passover and the other festivals. He concedes that this restriction is legitimate in the case of Passover. The Mishnah accords with Rabbi Yose's view.
STEP 3	RAV PAPPA'S SOLUTION	Rabbi Yehudah draws a time distinction between the restriction in the case of Passover and the restriction on other festivals. It begins earlier for Passover. The Mishnah accords with Rabbi Yehudah's view.
STEP 4	THE SECOND BARAITA	A Baraita proves that Rabbi Yehudah believes that the restriction timing is uniform for all occasions. This undermines the solution suggested by Rav Pappa. We therefore assume that Rav Huna's solution is correct.
STEP 5	MAR ZUTRA'S SUGGESTION	The text of the second Baraita might be inaccurate, in which case, it would not undermine Rav Pappa's solution.
STEP 6	MAREIMAR'S TESTIMONY	The second Baraita was taught at Rav Pinchas's public lecture, proving its authenticity. It certainly undermines Rav Pappa's solution. We therefore reaffirm our conclusion that Rav Huna's solution is accurate.

EXERCISE 6.1

Using the above information, try to determine whether one may eat a meal on Friday afternoon before sunset.

TEXT 3

The Challenge of Talmud Study

Maimonides, *Mishneh Torah*, introduction

שֶׁדֶּרֶךְ עֲמוּקָה דַּרְכּוֹ עַד לִמְאוֹד. וְעוֹד שֶׁהוּא בְּלָשׁוֹן
אֲרַמִּי מְעֹרָב עִם לְשׁוֹנוֹת אֲחֵרוֹת, לְפִי שֶׁאוֹתָהּ הַלָּשׁוֹן
הָיְתָה בְּרוּרָה לַכֹּל בְּשִׁנְעָר בְּעֵת שֶׁחֻבַּר הַתַּלְמוּד;
אֲבָל בִּשְׁאָר הַמְּקוֹמוֹת וְכֵן בְּשִׁנְעָר בִּימֵי הַגְּאוֹנִים,
אֵין אָדָם מַכִּיר אוֹתָהּ לָשׁוֹן עַד שֶׁמְּלַמְּדִים אוֹתוֹ.

The Talmud's manner of expression is extremely profound. Furthermore, it is composed in Aramaic with some other languages thrown in as well. That vernacular was well understood by all the Jews of Babylonia during the era in which the Talmud was composed. In other locations, however, and even within Babylonia during the subsequent era of the *ge'onim*, no one could understand this language without being taught.

KEY TERM 6.2

HEBREW TERM	גָּאוֹן/גְאוֹנִים
TRANSLITERATION	***Ga'on/Ge'onim***
PRONUNCIATION	Gah-ON/Geh-oh-NIM
LITERAL MEANING	**splendor or pride**
MEANING	a leader/s of one of the great Talmudic academies of Babylonia during the seventh to the eleventh centuries

JEWISH TIMELINE: EARLY MIDDLE AGES—MUSLIM CONQUESTS AND THEIR INFLUENCE ON JEWISH LIFE
Elena Kalman, mixed media and acrylic on paper, 2022

FIGURE 6.3

Ge'onic Responsa Samples

QUESTIONER	RESPONDER	QUESTION	ANSWER	SOURCE
UNKNOWN	Rabbi Natronai Ga'on (d. 858)	Is the custom of reciting Kol Nidrei on Yom Kippur appropriate?	We have heard that this prayer is recited in other lands; however, it is not our custom in Babylonia.	*Otzar Hage'onim*, Nedarim 63
RABBI YAAKOV BEN NISSIM OF KAIROUAN, TUNISIA (D. 1006)	Rabbi Sherira Ga'on (906–1006)	How and when was the Mishnah compiled? What are *Baraitot*, and why are they not part of the Mishnah?	[Quotes from Rabbi Sherira's lengthy responsive exposition are presented throughout this course, especially in Lessons Two and Three.]	*Igeret DeRabbi Sherira Ga'on*
UNKNOWN	Rabbi Sherira Ga'on (906–1006)	Is astrology authentic?	Even if astrology is authentic, it can only determine a particular inclination. However, individuals always maintain the free choice to commit or to refrain from a specific action.	*Teshuvot Upirushei Rav Sherira Ga'on*, vol. 2, p. 524
RABBI BAHALUL OF KAIROUAN, TUNISIA	Rabbi Hai Ga'on (939–1038)	The Talmud explains that there were three distinct customs regarding the shofar sounds on Rosh Hashanah until Rabbi Avahu instituted that all three should be sounded. How did such varied practices originally emerge concerning a *mitzvah* that is performed every year?	All three customs were valid, and each community followed its preferred practice. Rabbi Avahu standardized the practice for everyone to avoid confusion.	*Otzar Hage'onim*, Rosh Hashanah 117

EXERCISE 6.2

Rabbi Yitzchak Alfasi ("Rif") composed a digest of the *sugya* in Pesachim that we have studied.

Read through Rif's digest (Text 4a). Note that for the sake of clarity, we emphasized the material that Rif added on to the base of the Talmud's text. For a fuller picture of what Rif's digest did to the original *sugya*, visually review Text 4b, which indicates all of the changes Rif made to the *sugya*.

TEXT 4A

Halachic Digest

Rabbi Yitzchak Alfasi (Rif), Pesachim 19a

עֶרֶב פְּסָחִין סָמוּךְ לַמִּנְחָה לֹא יֹאכַל אָדָם עַד שֶׁתֶּחְשַׁךְ . . .

גְּמָרָא: תַּנְיָא לֹא יֹאכַל אָדָם בְּעַרְבֵי שַׁבָּתוֹת וּבְעַרְבֵי יָמִים טוֹבִים מִן הַמִּנְחָה וּלְמַעְלָה כְּדֵי שֶׁיִּכָּנֵס לַשַּׁבָּת כְּשֶׁהוּא מִתְאַוֶּה, דִּבְרֵי רַבִּי יְהוּדָה. רַבִּי יוֹסֵי אוֹמֵר אוֹכֵל וְהוֹלֵךְ עַד שֶׁתֶּחְשַׁךְ, **וְהִילְכְתָא כְּרַבִּי יוֹסֵי דְקַיְמָא לָן הִילְכְתָא כְּרַבִּי יוֹסֵי מֵחֲבֵירוֹ, וּמַתְנִיתִין דְעֶרֶב פְּסָחִין דִּבְרֵי הַכֹּל הִיא,** דְּמוֹדֶה רַבִּי יוֹסֵי **בְּעֶרֶב פְּסָחִין** מִשּׁוּם חִיּוּבָא דְמַצָּה.

Mishnah: One must refrain from eating on the eve of Passover, from close to the time for reciting the Minchah prayers until after darkness has fallen. . . .

Gemara: We learned in a Baraita:

"One should not eat on the eves of Shabbat or festivals from the time of Minchah and onward so

RABBI YITZCHAK ALFASI (RIF) 1013–1103

Halachist. A native of the North African Maghreb, Rabbi Yitzchak Alfasi (Rif) studied with Rabbi Chananel of Kairouan, Tunisia. He lived and taught in the Maghreb for most of his life and lived his final years in Spain. Rabbi Alfasi authored a digest of the Talmud, known as Rif, containing only the practical conclusions of the Talmud, excluding the lengthy debates and nonlegal material. As the first comprehensive work of practical Jewish law, Rif had a decisive influence in shaping the consensus of Jewish law.

that one enters Shabbat [or the festivals] with an appetite. This is the opinion of Rabbi Yehudah. [Conversely,] Rabbi Yose says that one may continue eating until it grows dark."

The law follows the view of Rabbi Yose, because there is a rule that "the law favors Rabbi Yose over his colleagues." And our Mishnah regarding Passover eve concurs with all views, because Rabbi Yose will concede [that eating is prohibited] **on the eve of Passover** due to the obligation to eat matzah.

A SYNAGOGUE IN SAFED, 1950
Nachum Gutman, gouache, Safed, Israel, 1950

TEXT 4B

Talmud Cuts

Rif's Edits to Pesachim 99b–100a

Mishnah: One must refrain from eating on the eve of Passover, from close to the time for reciting the Minchah prayers until after darkness has fallen.

Why does it specify "the eve of Passover"? Even the eve of Shabbat and [other] festivals also [trigger this prohibition]! For we learned in a Baraita: "One should not eat on the eves of Shabbat or festivals from the time of Minchah and onward so that one enters Shabbat [or the festivals] with an appetite. This is the opinion of Rabbi Yehudah. [Conversely,] Rabbi Yose says that one may continue eating until it grows dark." **The law follows Rabbi Yose, because there is a rule that "the law favors Rabbi Yose over his colleagues." And our Mishnah regarding Passover eve concurs with all views,** Rav Huna said: This [distinction between Passover and Shabbat or the other festivals] is necessary for Rabbi Yose, who said, "One may continue eating until it grows dark." That will apply to the eve of Shabbat and other festivals, but on the eve of Passover, he will concede [that it is prohibited] **because** Rabbi Yose will concede [that eating is prohibited] **on the eve of Passover** due to the obligation to eat matzah. Rav Pappa said: We can explain the Mishnah in a way that conforms with Rabbi Yehudah's view: [The distinction between

Passover and other occasions is that] there, in the case of the eve of Shabbat and other festivals, the prohibition is in force from the time of Minchah and onward. However, in proximity to the time of Minchah [eating is still] permitted. Conversely, on the eve of Passover, the prohibition comes into force even during the time that is proximate to Minchah [shortly prior to Minchah]. But is it the case that on the eve of Shabbat, [eating] is permitted in proximity to the time for Minchah? Surely we learned [the contrary] in a Baraita: "One may not eat on the eve of Shabbat or festivals, from the ninth hour and onward so that they enter Shabbat with an appetite. That is the opinion of Rabbi Yehudah. [However,] Rabbi Yose maintains that one may continue eating until it grows dark." Mar Zutra said: Who can tell us whether [this Baraita] is accurate? Perhaps it is erroneous? Mareimar (some claim that it was Rav Yeimar) responded, "I visited the public lecture of Rav Pinchas, son of Rav Ami; there, a Reciter arose and recited [this same Baraita] in the presence of [Rav Pinchas]—and he accepted it!" If so, we indeed have a difficulty [with Rav Pappa's suggestion]. Rav Huna's answer is therefore more plausible.

EXERCISE 6.3

Using the Rif's text, answer the following two questions:

1. **Is a meal permitted on the eve of Passover?**
2. **Is a meal permitted on the eve of Shabbat/other festivals?**

TEXT 5

The Creation of a Code

Maimonides, *Mishneh Torah*, introduction

וּמִפְּנֵי זֶה נָעַרְתִּי חָצְנִי, אֲנִי מֹשֶׁה בְּרַבִּי מַיְמוֹן הַסְּפָרַדִּי, וְנִשְׁעַנְתִּי עַל הַצּוּר בָּרוּךְ הוּא, וּבִינוֹתִי בְּכָל אֵלּוּ הַסְּפָרִים, וְרָאִיתִי לְחַבֵּר דְּבָרִים הַמִּתְבָּרְרִים מִכָּל אֵלּוּ הַחִבּוּרִים בְּעִנְיַן הָאָסוּר וְהַמֻּתָּר וְהַטָּמֵא וְהַטָּהוֹר עִם שְׁאָר דִּינֵי תוֹרָה כֻּלָּם בְּלָשׁוֹן בְּרוּרָה וְדֶרֶךְ קְצָרָה, עַד שֶׁתְּהֵא תוֹרָה שֶׁבְּעַל פֶּה כֻּלָּהּ סְדוּרָה בְּפִי הַכֹּל בְּלֹא קֻשְׁיָא וְלֹא פֵּרוּק.

Therefore, I, Moses the son of Maimon of Spain, girded my loins. I relied upon the Rock, blessed be He. I examined all these texts and set out to compile the conclusions that can be extracted from all these texts as to what is forbidden and what is permitted, what is ritually impure and what is ritually pure, and the rest of the Torah's laws. I will present all the conclusions in clear language and a concise format, so that the entire Oral Law will be easily accessible to everyone, without questions or objections.

TEXT 6

Codifying Pesachim

Maimonides, *Mishneh Torah*, Laws of *Chametz* and Matzah 6:12

אָסוּר לֶאֱכוֹל עֶרֶב הַפֶּסַח מִקּוֹדֶם הַמִּנְחָה כִּמְעַט כְּדֵי שֶׁיִּכָּנֵס לַאֲכִילַת מַצָּה בְּתַאֲוָה. אֲבָל אוֹכֵל הוּא מְעַט פֵּירוֹת אוֹ יְרָקוֹת וְלֹא יְמַלֵּא כְּרֵיסוֹ מֵהֶן . . . אֲבָל בִּשְׁאַר עַרְבֵי שַׁבָּתוֹת אוֹ עַרְבֵי יָמִים טוֹבִים אוֹכֵל וְהוֹלֵךְ עַד שֶׁתֶּחְשַׁךְ.

It is forbidden to eat on the eve of Passover, from a little before the time for Minchah, so that we arrive at the eating of matzah with an appetite. However, we may eat a small quantity of fruit or vegetables, as long as we do not eat enough to feel full. . . . By contrast, on the eves of Shabbat or the other festivals, we may continue eating until dark.

***LA TABLE DU SEDER* (THE *SEDER* TABLE): *ACHILAT MATZAH* (EATING MATZAH)**
Engraving (artist unknown), from a French and Hebrew Passover *Haggadah*, published in Vienna, 1930. (National Archives, Washington, D.C.)

FIGURE 6.4

Stages of Halachic Derivation

HALACHIC WORK	TYPE	DESCRIPTION	AUTHOR(S)	TIME	LOCATION
TESHUVOT HAGE'ONIM	Responses to questions posed	Complied in various collections, including a series titled *Teshuvot Hage'onim*	Various *Ge'onim*	7th–11th centuries	Babylonia
HILCHOT HARIF	Halachic Digest	A Halachic digest of the Babylonian Talmud, covering all Halachah relevant to Jews living in the post-Temple era	Rabbi Yitzchak Alfasi	11th century	North Africa
MISHNEH TORAH	Halachic Code	Covering every Halachic subject, including laws relevant only in the Temple era. Variant opinions are rarely cited. Mostly limited to Halachic questions addressed in the Talmud.	Maimonides	12th century	Egypt
SHULCHAN ARUCH	Halachic Code	Covering only Halachah relevant to Jews in the post Temple era. Includes variant opinions. Includes Halachic questions not addressed in the Talmud. The main text reflects the consensus of Sefardic *poskim*; the glosses reflect the Ashkenazi consensus. Numerous commentaries round out the Halachic spectrum. Shulchan Aruch and its related commentaries represent a consensus of Halachah, similar to the Talmud.	Rabbi Yosef Karo, with glosses by Rabbi Moshe Issereles	16th century	Land of Israel, Poland

III. EXPLAINING THE TALMUD

To help students navigate the Talmud's complexity, scholars such as Rashi and the authors of the *Tosafot* crafted foundational commentaries. Rashi's clear explanations guide readers through each passage, whereas the *Tosafot* selectively add innovative insights, challenging and expanding upon particular points of the text. This legacy continues today, with every committed student encouraged to uncover new layers of meaning, adding their personal contributions to the collective study of the Torah.

SCHOLAR IN RESIDENCE
Brocha Teichman, oil on canvas, New York, 2011

FIGURE 6.5

Talmud Page Layout

השוכר את האומנין פרק ששי בבא מציעא עו.

מסורת הש"ס

עין משפט נר מצוה

תורה אור השלם

הגהות הב"ח

מוסף רש"י

אם בעל הבית חוזר בו ידו על התחתונה (א)אכל המשנה ידו על התחתונה בוכל החוזר בו ידו על התחתונה: **גמ'** חזרו זה בזה לא קתני אלא הטעו זה את זה דאטעו פועלים אהדדי גהיכי דמי דאמר ליה בעל הבית זיל אוגר לי פועלים ואזל איהו ואטעינהו היכי דמי אי דאמר ליה בעל הבית בארבעה ואזיל איהו אמר להו בתלתא תרעומת מאי עבידתיה סבור וקביל אי דאמר ליה בעל הבית בתלתא ואזיל איהו אמר להו בארבעה ה"ד אי דאמר להו שכרכם עלי גנתיב להו מדידיה דתניא ג)דהשוכר את הפועל לעשות בשלו והראהו בשל חבירו נותן לו שכרו משלם וחוזר ונוטל מבעל הבית מה שההנהו לא צריכא הדאמר להו שכרכם על בעל הבית ולחזי פועלים היכי מיתגרי לא צריכא ודאיכא (א) דמגר בארבעה ואיכא דמתגר בתלתא דאמרו ליה אי לאו דאמרת לן בארבעה טרחינן ומתגרינן בארבעה איבעית אימא הכא בבעל הבית עסקינן דאמרו ליה אי לאו דאמרת לן בארבעה הוה זילא בן מילתא לאתגורי איבעית אימא לעולם בפועלים עסקינן ידאמרי ליה כיון דאמרת לן בארבעה טרחינן ועבדינן לך עבידתא שפירתא וליחזי עבידתייהו בריפקא ריפקא נמי מידע ידע דמלי מיא חולא ידיע איבעית אימא טלעולם דאמר ליה בעל הבית בארבעה ואזל איהו אמר להו בתלתא ודקאמרת סבור וקביל דאמרי ליה לית לך יאל תמנע טוב מבעליו יפשיטא אי אמר ליה בעל הבית בתלתא ואזל איהו א"ל בארבעה ואמרי ליה כמו שאמר בעל הבית דעתייהו אעילויא כאלא אי א"ל בעל הבית בארבעה ואזל איהו אמר להו בתלתא ואמרי כמה שאמר בעל הבית מאי אדיבורא דידיה קא סמכי דאמרי ליה מהימנת לן דהכי אמר בעל הבית או דילמא אדיבורא דבעל הבית קא סמכי ת"ש ד)להבא לי גיטי ואשתך אמרה התקבל לי גיטי והוא אומר הילך כמה שאמרה אמר רב נחמן אמר רבה בר אבוה אמר רב מאפי' הגיע גט לידה אינה מגורשת שמעת מינה אדיבורא דידיה קא סמיך דאי סלקא דעתך דאדיבורא דידה קא סמיך מכי מטי גיטא לידה מיהא תיגרש אמר רב אשי הכי

FIGURE 6.6

Talmud, Bava Metzi'a 76a, as It Appears in the Munich Manuscript of the Talmud

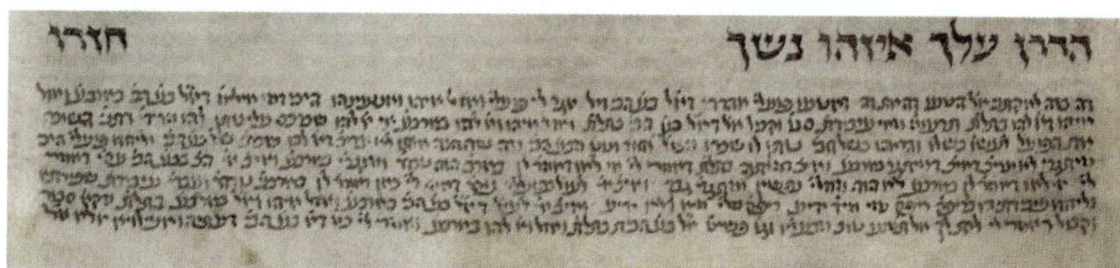
הדרן עלך איזהו נשך
חזרו

TEXT 7

The Raw Talmud

Talmud, Bava Metzi'a 76a

What is the case if that the employer said to them at four and he went and said to them at three what is the function of complaint he knew and accepted if the employer said to him at three and he went and said to them at four what is the case if he told them your wages are on me he gives them from his own.

EXERCISE 6.4

1. **Read the direct, literal translation of the Talmud's text presented above.**

2. **Review Lesson 5, Section 3, where the *sugya* is explained at length.**

3. **Make the text more accessible by filling in punctuation (question marks, exclamation points, commas, periods, etc.) to indicate the Gemara's series of questions and answers.**

BABYLONIAN TALMUD

A literary work of monumental proportions that draws upon the legal, spiritual, intellectual, ethical, and historical traditions of Judaism. The 37 tractates of the Babylonian Talmud contain the teachings of the Jewish sages from the period after the destruction of the 2nd Temple through the 5th century CE. It has served as the primary vehicle for the transmission of the Oral Law and the education of Jews over the centuries; it is the entry point for all subsequent legal, ethical, and theological Jewish scholarship.

TEXT 8

Sample Rashi

Rashi, Bava Metzi'a 76a

הֵיכִי דָמֵי - דְתַרְעוֹמֶת יִהְיֶה לָהֶן וְלֹא יוֹתֵר.

"What is the case": that gives them a right to complain but nothing more?

RABBI SHLOMO YITZCHAKI (RASHI) 1040–1105

Most noted biblical and Talmudic commentator. Born in Troyes, France, Rashi studied in the famed *yeshivot* of Mainz and Worms. His commentaries on the Pentateuch and the Talmud, which focus on the straightforward meaning of the text, appear in virtually every edition of the Talmud and Bible.

TEXT 9

Rounding Out the Talmud

Rabbi Shlomo Luria, *Yam Shel Shlomo*, Bava Kama, introduction

הֵם עָשׂוּ אֶת הַתַּלְמוּד כְּכַדוּר, וַהֲפָכוּהוּ וְגִלְגְלוּהוּ מִמָּקוֹם לְמָקוֹם, וְנִמְצָא מְיוּשָׁר הַתַּלְמוּד וּמְקוּשָׁר.

They made the Talmud like a ball, spinning it and rolling it from place to place, until it was all smooth and interconnected.

RABBI SHLOMO LURIA (MAHARSHAL, RASHAL) 1510–1574

Talmudist and Halachist. Maharshal was born in Posen to a prestigious rabbinic family. He authored *Yam Shel Shlomo*, a Talmudic commentary, and *Chochmat Shlomo*, a work mostly dedicated to establishing the proper text of the Talmud and its primary commentaries. Rabbi Luria succeeded Rabbi Shalom Shachna as head of the famed Yeshivah of Lublin, Poland.

TEXT 10

It's All in the Talmud

Mishnah, Avot 5:22

בֶּן בַּג בַּג אוֹמֵר, הֲפֹךְ בָּהּ וַהֲפֹךְ בָּהּ, דְכוּלָּהּ בָּהּ.

וּבָהּ תֶּחֱזֵי, וְסִיב וּבְלֵה בָּהּ, וּמִינָהּ לֹא תָזוּעַ,
שֶׁאֵין לְךָ מִדָּה טוֹבָה הֵימֶנָּה.

Ben Bag Bag said: Turn it over, and turn it over again, for it contains everything.

Look into it; grow gray and old over it, and do not budge from it, for you have no better portion than it.

AVOT
(ETHICS OF THE FATHERS; PIRKEI AVOT)

A 6-chapter work on Jewish ethics that is studied widely by Jewish communities, especially during the summer. The first 5 chapters are from the Mishnah, tractate Avot. Avot differs from the rest of the Mishnah in that it does not focus on legal subjects; it is a collection of the sages' wisdom on topics related to character development, ethics, healthy living, piety, and the study of Torah.

TEXT 11

Insights from Sinai

Midrash, *Vayikra Rabah* 22

מַה שֶׁתַּלְמִיד וָתִיק עָתִיד לוֹמַר לִפְנֵי
רַבּוֹ, כֻּלָּן נֶאֶמְרוּ לְמֹשֶׁה בְּסִינַי.

The insights that a veteran student will, in the future, say in front of his teacher were all given to Moses at Mount Sinai.

VAYIKRA RABAH

An early rabbinic commentary on the Book of Leviticus. This Midrash, written in Aramaic and Hebrew, provides textual exegeses and anecdotes, expounds upon the biblical narrative, and develops and illustrates moral principles. It was first printed in Constantinople in 1512 together with 4 other Midrashic works on the other 4 books of the Pentateuch.

TEXT 12A

Old and New

The Rebbe, Rabbi Menachem Mendel Schneerson, *Likutei Sichot*, vol. 19, p. 253

וִויבַּאלְד אָבֶּער אַז אַלֶע חִידוּשִׁים אִין תּוֹרָה מוּזְן זַיין גֶעבּוֹיט אוֹיף דִי כְּלָלִים וָואס מֹשֶׁה הָאט מְקַבֵּל גֶעוֶוען בְּסִינַי, קוּמְט אוֹיס אַז "הַכֹּל נִיתַּן לְמֹשֶׁה בְּסִינַי" . . .

וּבְכָל זֹאת, דָאס וָואס דֶער תַּלְמִיד וָתִיק הָארֶעוֶועט אוֹיס מִיט זַיין שֵׂכֶל צוּ מְגַלֶה זַיין אַן עִנְיָן פְּרָטִי פוּן תּוֹרָה שֶׁבְּעַל פֶּה (לוֹיט דִי כְּלָלֵי הַתּוֹרָה), טוּט עֶר דֶערְמִיט אוֹיף אַ חִידוּשׁ אִין תּוֹרָה.

Seeing that all the innovations in Torah must be built on the principles that Moses received from Mount Sinai, it emerges that "all [was] given to Moses at Sinai." . . .

Nonetheless, when a veteran student toils with their mind to reveal a specific idea within the Oral Torah—an idea that accords with thc Torah's principles—they create something truly original in Torah.

RABBI MENACHEM MENDEL SCHNEERSON 1902–1994

The towering Jewish leader of the 20th century, known as "the Lubavitcher Rebbe," or simply as "the Rebbe." Born in southern Ukraine, the Rebbe escaped Nazi-occupied Europe, arriving in the U.S. in June 1941. The Rebbe inspired and guided the revival of traditional Judaism after the European devastation, impacting virtually every Jewish community the world over. The Rebbe often emphasized that the performance of just one additional good deed could usher in the era of Mashiach. The Rebbe's scholarly talks and writings have been printed in more than 200 volumes.

TEXT 12B

The Obligation to Innovate

The Rebbe, ibid.

עֶס אִיז אַ חִיוּב אוֹיף "כָּל אִישׁ יִשְׂרָאֵל" נִיט נָאר צוּ לֶערְנֶען דָאס וָואס שְׁטֵייט שׁוֹין אִין סְפָרִים וְכוּ', נָאר אוֹיךְ לְחַדֵּשׁ.

Every Jew has the obligation not only to study that which is already published in sacred books, but also to innovate.

FLOATING LETTERS
Art by Abish, digital painting, New York, 2023

IV. STUDYING THE TALMUD

In this section, we reflect on the Talmud's development into the central treasure of Jewish religion and culture. We examine the diverse ways in which Jews study the Talmud today, from rapid daily regimens to in-depth explorations. We subsequently discover that each of us, regardless of background, can engage in this timeless tradition of study and growth.

A WISE WOMAN
Yaron Goldfarb, paper cutting, Israel, 2008

FIGURE 6.7

Reasons for Studying Talmud

LESSON 1	Source of Halachah	The Talmud is the repository of Halachah—the instructions through which we can live up to the covenant we made with G-d at Mount Sinai.
LESSON 1	Communing with G-d	The struggle to clarify the Divine Will and Wisdom (as expressed in Halachah) is itself an experience of bonding with G-d. In the study of Talmud, our minds are immersed in the Divine.
LESSON 2	The Oral Torah	The written Torah is G-d's message to us. The Oral Torah, which is intended to be engraved in our memories, allows us to assume an active role in our relationship with G-d.
LESSON 3	Valuing Diversity	The Talmud teaches us to find value even in views that are not accepted as the final Halachah.
LESSON 4	Deeper Meanings	All of the Talmud's teachings (and especially its *agadeta* sections) contain deeper spiritual, philosophical, and ethical messages.
LESSON 5	Thinking like a Talmudist	The Talmudic approach trains us in critical thinking—to question every premise and reach the core of every issue.

EXERCISE 6.5

Take a minute to reflect on the primary ideas that we encountered over the course of our lessons. Which of these ideas resonates most with you?

TEXT 13

Shared Credit

Rabbi Chaim Chizkiyahu Medini, *Sedei Chemed*, *maarechet mem*, *klal* 198

וּמִצְוָוה שֶׁעוֹשִׂין אוֹתָהּ הַרְבֵּה בְּנֵי אָדָם בְּשׁוּתָּפוּת, כָּל אֶחָד נוֹטֵל שָׂכָר כְּאִילוּ עֲשָׂאָהּ כּוּלָּהּ לְבַדָּהּ, וּמִטַּעַם זֶה נוֹהֲגִים כָּל בְּנֵי יִשְׂרָאֵל לַעֲשׂוֹת חֶבְרַת שַׁ"ס וּמְחַלְּקִים אֶת הַשַּׁ"ס בֵּין כַּמָּה בְּנֵי אָדָם.

If a *mitzvah* is performed by several people jointly, each participant is rewarded as if they had performed the entire *mitzvah* alone. For this reason, the entire Jewish people have embraced the practice of forming *chevrot Shas* (Talmud study clubs) for the sake of dividing the study of the entire Talmud between many individuals.

RABBI CHAIM CHIZKIYAHU MEDINI
1833–1905

Scholar and prolific author. A Jerusalem native, Rabbi Medini was born into a distinguished Sephardic family. He served as the rabbi of Constantinople and later in the Crimea, during which time he authored many volumes of Torah scholarship. His most famous work is the 18-volume *Sedei Chemed*, a comprehensive encyclopedia of the Talmud. He eventually returned to Israel where he passed away in 1905.

KEY TERM 6.3

HEBREW TERM	דַף
TRANSLITERATION	*daf*
PRONUNCIATION	dahf
LITERAL MEANING	**folio**
MEANING	a two-sided page of Talmud or another Hebrew text

FIGURE 6.8

Talmud Study Programs

TALMUD STUDY PROGRAM	SUBJECT MATTER	SCHEDULE
***IYUN*: IN-DEPTH STUDY**	A selected section of the Talmud, studied carefully with several commentaries	Classes or study groups might cover as few as a handful of pages in a year.
CHALUKAS HASHAS	One tractate of the Talmud per person, with the entire Talmud covered by the group	Each person completes their tractate in a year, and the entire Talmud is completed by the group each year.
EIN YAAKOV	The *agadeta* sections of the Talmud	Typically studied in a daily class presented in a synagogue. A few paragraphs of *agadeta* are covered each day.
DAF YOMI	The entire Talmud	Each participant studies one *daf* each day, completing the Talmud in 7.5 years.
RAMBAM (MAIMONIDES)	The Halachic rulings that emerge from the Talmud, as recorded in Maimonides's *Mishneh Torah*	Each participant studies three (or 1) chapter(s) each day, completing the entire text each year (or in three years).

TEXT 14

Late Bloomer

Avot DeRabbi Natan 6:2

מָה הָיָה תְּחִלָּתוֹ שֶׁל רַבִּי עֲקִיבָא? אָמְרוּ, בֶּן אַרְבָּעִים שָׁנָה הָיָה וְלֹא שָׁנָה כְּלוּם. פַּעַם אַחַת הָיָה עוֹמֵד עַל פִּי הַבְּאֵר, אָמַר: מִי חָקַק אֶבֶן זוֹ? אָמְרוּ, לֹא הַמַּיִם שֶׁתָּדִיר [נוֹפְלִים] עָלֶיהָ בְּכָל יוֹם? . . .

רַבִּי עֲקִיבָא דָן קַל וָחוֹמֶר בְּעַצְמוֹ, מָה רַךְ פָּסַל אֶת הַקָּשֶׁה, דִּבְרֵי תּוֹרָה שֶׁקָּשֶׁה כַּבַּרְזֶל עַל אַחַת כַּמָּה וְכַמָּה שֶׁיְּחַקְקוּ אֶת לִבִּי שֶׁהוּא בָּשָׂר וָדָם. מִיָּד חָזַר לִלְמוֹד תּוֹרָה. הָלַךְ הוּא וּבְנוֹ וְיָשְׁבוּ אֵצֶל מְלַמְּדֵי תִּינוֹקוֹת, אָמַר לֵיהּ, רַבִּי לַמְּדֵנִי תּוֹרָה. אָחַז רַבִּי עֲקִיבָא בְּרֹאשׁ הַלּוּחַ וּבְנוֹ בְּרֹאשׁ הַלּוּחַ, כָּתַב לוֹ אָלֶף בֵּית וְלָמְדָהּ . . . הָיָה לוֹמֵד וְהוֹלֵךְ עַד שֶׁלָּמַד כָּל הַתּוֹרָה כּוּלָּהּ.

How did Rabbi Akiva begin his journey to scholarship? It is told that he was forty years old and had never studied in his life, but he was once standing at the mouth of a well and asked, "Who carved a hole in this stone over here?" The people there told him, "It was formed by the water that constantly drips onto it, striking the same spot day after day." . . .

Rabbi Akiva told himself, "If a substance so soft can carve its way through material so hard, then surely the words of Torah that are like iron can

AVOT DERABBI NATAN

A commentary on, and an elaboration of, the Mishnaic tractate Avot, bearing the name of Rabbi Natan, one of the sages of the Mishnah. The work exists in two very different versions, one of which appears in many editions of the Talmud.

engrave themselves within my heart, which is mere flesh and blood! He immediately set out to start studying Torah. He went with his young son and they sat down before the teachers of young children. He said to one, "Rabbi, teach me Torah!" He then took hold of one end of the tablet, and his son took hold of the other end. The teacher wrote down *aleph* and *bet* for him, and he studied those two letters. . . . He continued studying until he had mastered the entire Torah.

RABBI AKIVA
Ahuva Manes, oil on board, Jerusalem, Israel, 2019

KEY POINTS

1. The Talmud's rulings became binding for the entire Jewish nation because they are the consensus of the sages and were accepted by the Jewish people worldwide. After its completion, Jewish communities were dispersed in exile; new Halachic decisions by local rabbis were binding within their own communities, not universally.

2. Deriving Halachah from the Talmud has always been challenging, and expert scholars were consulted for guidance through responsa. Halachic digests like the Halachot of the Rif simplified the Talmud's discussions, making practical rulings more accessible by omitting lengthy debates.

3. Rambam's *Mishneh Torah* organized Jewish law systematically, offering clear presentations of Halachic rulings derived from the Talmud. The Shulchan Aruch, by Rabbi Yosef Karo with Rabbi Moshe Isserlis's glosses, became the most accepted code, incorporating numerous Halachic opinions and addressing new questions and customs.

4. Rashi's explanatory commentaries help students understand the Talmud's complex, unpunctuated text. The *Tosafot*, created by Rashi's students, uncover new depths of Talmudic insight by resolving questions and contradictions in the Talmud's text.

5 All true Torah innovations were already given to Moses at Mount Sinai. Every generation of scholars builds on previous works, uncovering new insights and layers of meaning. Every Jew has the potential to contribute novel insights to the Talmud.

6 Today there are various methods for studying Talmud, making the study of Talmud accessible to everyone. These approaches allow for both in-depth study and faster-paced learning, accommodating learners at all levels.

7 Rabbi Akiva's story inspires all Jews to pursue Talmud study, regardless of prior knowledge. Each of us is able to begin the journey to scholarship.

Continue learning at
myjli.com/talmud

Major Milestones in the Publication of the Talmud

200 CE

Compilation of the Mishnah

First officially written record of the Oral Law, compiled by Rabbi Yehudah Hanasi in Sepphoris, Israel

350 CE

Redaction of the Jerusalem Talmud

Compiled primarily by Rabbi Yochanan and his disciples in Tiberias, Israel

THE MESOPOTAMIAN BASIN

5th century CE

Babylonian Talmud redacted

Rav Ashi, Ravina, and their disciples edit 300 years of Talmudic discourse to form the Babylonian Talmud

6th century CE

Mosaic of Mishnaic text

From the Rehov synagogue in northern Israel

750 CE

Oldest extant Talmudic manuscript

Fragment of the Babylonian Talmud discovered in the Cairo Genizah

10th or 11th century

Vowelized manuscript of the Mishnah

Dating from the 10th or 11th century

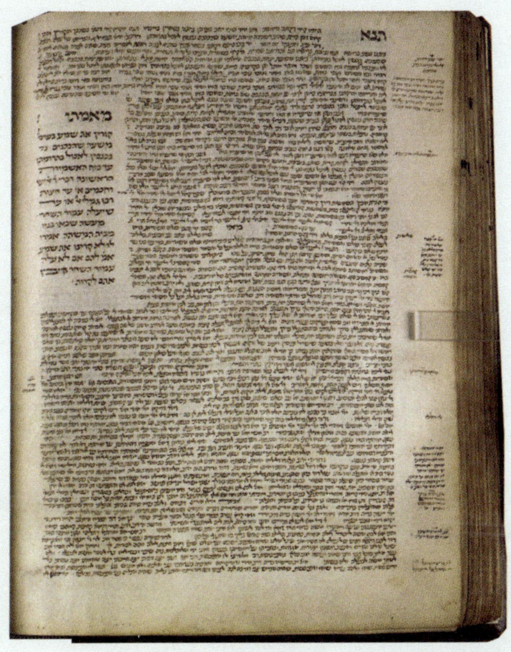

1342

The Munich Manuscript

Oldest surviving copy of the entire Babylonian Talmud

1470

Printing the Talmud

The first printed editions of the Talmud were published in the Iberian Peninsula in the 1480s, just 30 years after the invention of the printing press by Johannes Gutenberg. Pictured here is the edition published by Rabbi Shlomo Alkabetz in Guadalajara, Spain. Rashi's commentary appears alongside the Talmudic text.

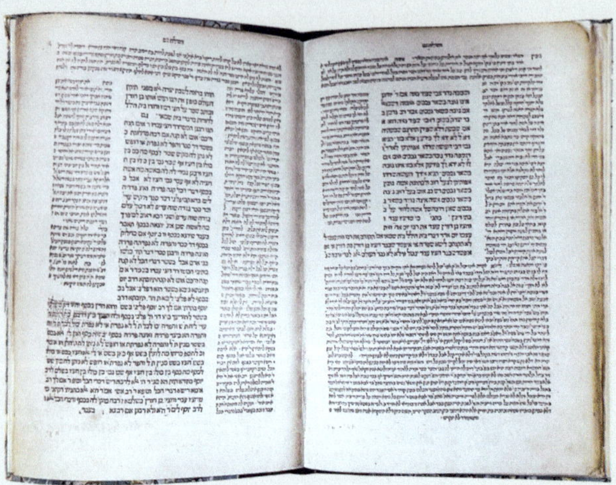

1520–1523

The Bomberg Talmud

Daniel Bomberg, a Christian printer of Hebrew books in Venice, Italy, was the first to produce a complete set of the entire Babylonian Talmud. His edition of the Talmud was prized for the high quality of its letterforms and physical production. The layout of his folio pages (i.e., the first and last words of each page) became the standard for all subsequent publications of the Talmud.

1484

Creation of the *daf* format

The Soncino family pioneered Hebrew printing in Italy and later in Turkey, Greece, and Egypt. They created the first known *daf* format (*tzurat hadaf*), which places the text of the Talmud in the center of the page, Rashi's commentary on its inner margin, and the Tosafot commentaries on the outer margin—a format followed by almost all subsequent printings of the Talmud.

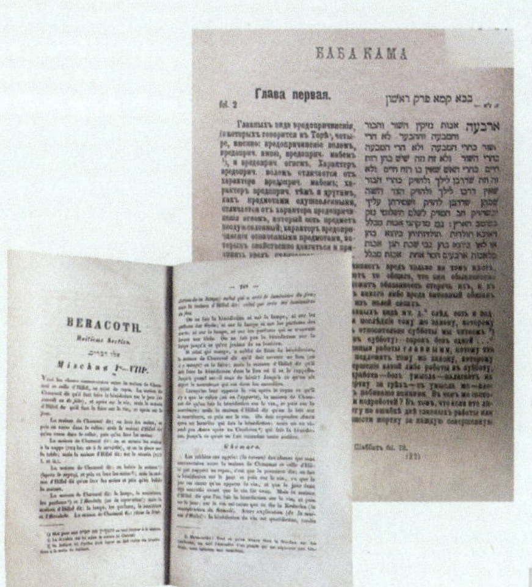
БАБА КАМА

Глава первая.

בבא קמא פרק ראשון

BERACOTH

I. N. D. N. J. C.

מסכת עבודה זרה
מתלמוד בבלי
פרק ראשון

TRACTATUS TALMUDICI DE IDOLOLATRIA.

CAPUT I.

MISCHNA I. Triduo ante festa idololatrarum prohibitum est negociari cum illis, commodare illis, aut commodato ab illis accipere, mutuum dare illis, aut mutuum ab illis accipere (1), solvere debitum illis, aut solutionem debiti ab illis accipere, (*idque ideo, quia idola sua propterea in festo celebrant.*) R. Juda dicit, solutionem licite ab illis accipi, quia Judæus hoc ipso affligit ethnicum. Alii vero ipsi regesserunt, quod licet gentilis se propterea angat in præsens, lætetur tamen deinceps (*in festo, se ab ære alieno esse liberatum; atque hinc rectius statuerunt, nec debiti solutionem esse ab illo admittendam*).

GEMARA. Raf & Samuel (2) circa lectionem vocis אידיהן dissentiunt. Alter docet, legendum esse אידיהן per Aleph, alter vero statuit, legendum esse עידיהן per Ain. Qui dicit, legendum esse אידיהן, non errat, itemque qui legendum esse statuit עידיהן, non errat.

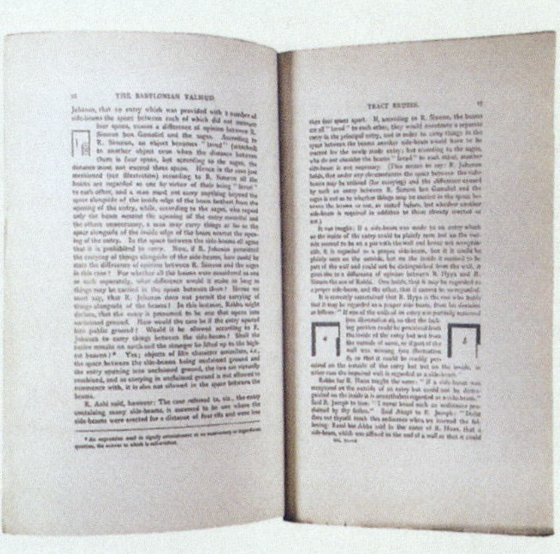
THE BABYLONIAN TALMUD.

מאימתי

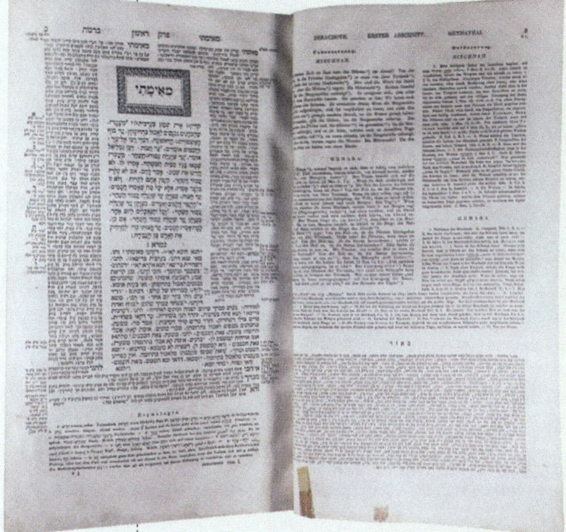
מאימתי

Talmud Babli

Babylonischer Talmud.

Tractat

Berachoth

Segensprüche.

deutscher Uebersetzung

Dr. E. M. PINNER,

BERLIN 1842.

1523–1524

First printing of the Jerusalem Talmud

Bomberg was also the first to print the Jerusalem Talmud. This first edition was printed without any commentaries.

16th–19th centuries

Translating the Talmud

Latin translations of portions of the Talmud were produced as early as 1519. Pictured here is a translation of the tractate Avodah Zarah, produced by George Eliezer Edzard and published in Hamburg in 1705. Also shown are translations into French (1831), German (1842), Russian (1892), and English (1897).

1820

The Slavita Shas

In the ensuing centuries, multiple editions of the Talmud were produced, with printers adding additional commentaries and glosses both in the margins of the folio page itself as well as to the back pages of each Talmudic volume. A particularly sought-after edition is the "Slavita *Shas*," produced by the saintly Shapiro brothers in the early 19th century in Slavuta in the Russian Empire.

1880

Vilna *Shas*

Rivaling the Slavuta edition was the famed "Vilna *Shas*," published in Vilnius, Lithuania beginning in 1880, which became a household name in the Jewish world.

1941–1946

Amidst the ashes

Jews persisted in publishing the Talmud wherever they lived and in virtually whatever circumstances they found themselves. The Talmud was published a number of times in Hungary in the years 1941 and 1942, even as the mass slaughter of Jews was already underway in neighboring Poland and Ukraine. The Talmud was also printed in 1943 in Japanese-occupied Shanghai, China, where many Jews, including the students of several *yeshivot*, had taken refuge. Another landmark edition of the Talmud is the one published in Munich, Germany, for use of the Holocaust survivors still in the Displaced Persons' camps.

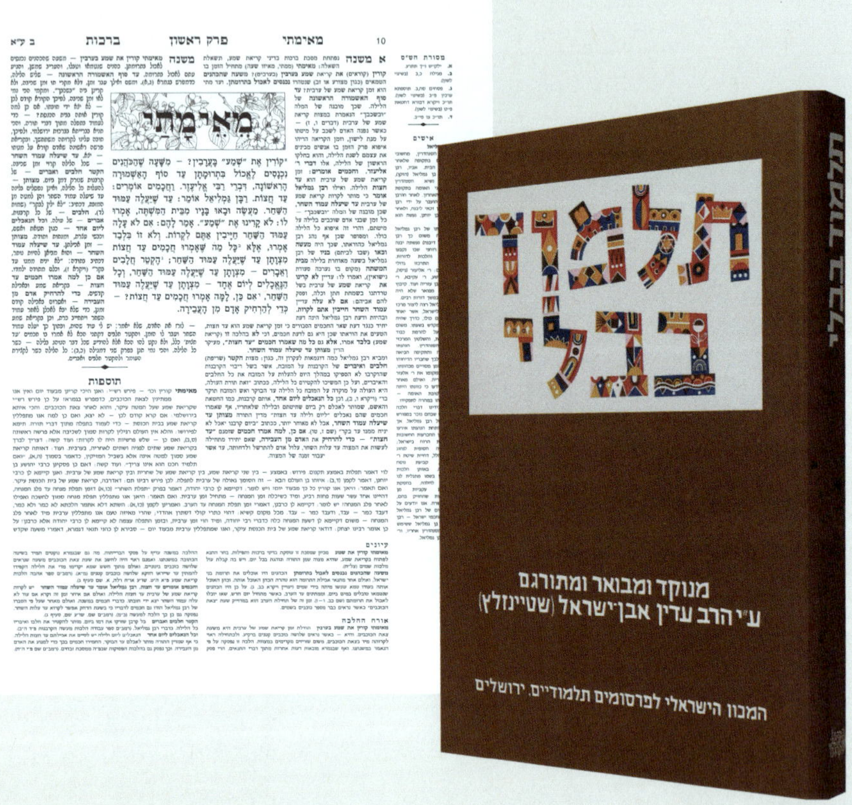

1965

The Steinsaltz Talmud

Compiled by Rabbi Adin Even-Israel (Steinsaltz), this edition of the Talmud revolutionized Talmud study, making it accessible to many for whom the Talmud was a closed book, by adding *nekudot* (vowel points), punctuation, illustrations, and a running commentary in contemporary Hebrew to the Aramaic text. An English edition of some volumes was published by Random House beginning in 1989, and the work has been translated into a number of other languages as well.

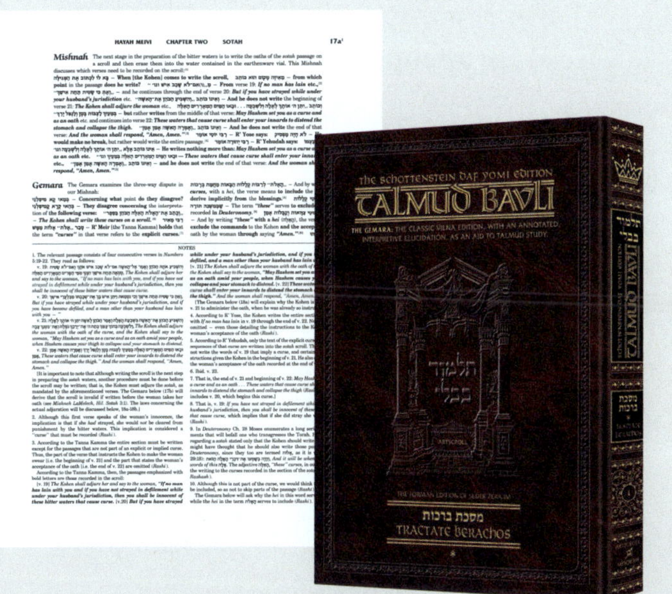

1990 | 2012

The Talmud in English

Over the last few decades English editions of the Talmud have appeared, providing translation and elucidation that have made Talmudic learning broadly accessible to English-speaking students of all levels. Artscroll's *Schottenstein Edition of the Babylonian Talmud* was published between 1990–2005 and spans 73 volumes. The *Koren Talmud Bavli*, based on Rabbi Adin Even-Israel's Hebrew Talmud commentary, was published by Koren Publishers between 2012–2019, spanning 42 volumes.

APPENDIX

TEXT 15

Defining the Restriction

Tosafot, Pesachim 99b

וְאִם תֹּאמַר, וּמָה לֹא יֹאכַל?

אִי מַצָּה אֲפִילוּ קוֹדֶם נַמִי אָסוּר כִּדְאַמְרִינָן בִּירוּשַׁלְמִי . . . וְאִי בְּמִינֵי תַּרְגִימָא הָא אָמַר בַּגְּמָרָא (קז, ב) אֲבָל מְטַבֵּל הוּא בְּמִינֵי תַּרְגִימָא.

וְיֵשׁ לוֹמַר דְאַיירִי בְּמַצָּה עֲשִׁירָה דְלָא אָסַר בִּירוּשַׁלְמִי אֶלָא בְּמַצָּה הָרְאוּיָה לָצֵאת בָּהּ חוֹבָתוֹ וְאוֹכְלָהּ קוֹדֶם זְמַנָּהּ אֲבָל מַצָּה עֲשִׁירָה שַׁרְיָא וְכֵן הָיָה נוֹהֵג רַבֵּינוּ תָּם.

If you will ask: What exactly are we supposed to refrain from eating at close to Minchah time?

Matzah? Why, that is forbidden even *earlier* than the late afternoon, as stated explicitly in the Jerusalem Talmud! . . . Small snacks? Those are *permitted*, as the Talmud informs us later (PESACHIM 107B)—"However, we may snack on small snacks."

We can answer that the prohibition relates to *matzah ashirah* (enriched matzah), because the Jerusalem Talmud only prohibits the consumption of matzah that is fit to be used for fulfilling

TOSAFOT

A collection of French and German Talmudic commentaries written during the 12th and 13th centuries. Among the most famous authors of *Tosafot* are Rabbi Yaakov Tam, Rabbi Shimshon ben Avraham of Sens, and Rabbi Yitzchak ("the Ri"). Printed in almost all editions of the Talmud, these commentaries are fundamental to basic Talmudic study.

that night's obligation of eating matzah on the eve of Passover. Conversely, *matzah ashirah* is permitted earlier in the day. In fact, that was the custom as practiced by Rabbeinu Tam.

Acknowledgments

We are grateful to the following individuals for their contributions to this course:

Flagship Director
RABBI SHMULY KARP

Curriculum Coordinator
RIVKI MOCKIN

Flagship Administrator
NAOMI HEBER

Author
RABBI YOCHANAN RIVKIN

Curriculum Development Team
RABBI MORDECHAI DINERMAN
RABBI SHMUEL SUPER
RABBI YANKI TAUBER

Instructors Advisory Board
RABBI MICHOEL GOLDMAN
RABBI YOSSI MENDELSON
RABBI SHOLOM NOTIK
RABBI AVROHOM STERNBERG
RABBI JOSH ZEBBERMAN

Research
RABBI YAKOV GERSHON

Copywriters
RABBI YONI BROWN
RABBI YAAKOV PALEY
RABBI SCHNEUR PRUSS

Proofreading
LEIBA ESTRIN
RACHEL MUSICANTE
YA'AKOVAH WEBER

Hebrew Punctuation
RABBI MOSHE WOLFF

Permissions
SHULAMIS NADLER

Instructor Support
RABBI TZALY DUBOV
RABBI LEVI GOLDSHMID
RABBI AVREMI RAPOPORT

Design and Layout Administrator
SARA OSDOBA

Textbook and Marketing Design
LEAH FAINZILBER
CHAYA MUSHKA KANNER
CHAYA KATZ
ESTIE KLEIN
RABBI LEVI WEINGARTEN

Textbook Layout
RABBI MOTTI KLEIN

Imagery
CHAYA BARNETT
SARA ROSENBLUM

Publication and Distribution
RABBI MOSHE RAICHIK
RABBI MENDEL SIROTA

PowerPoint Presentations
CHAYA BARNETT
SARA ROSENBLUM

Course Videos
GETZY RASKIN
MOSHE RASKIN

Key Points Videos
RABBI AVREMI RAPOPORT

Artists
YARON GOLDFARB ARTOMANUT.COM
TANYA ZBILI KATZ TANYAZBILIART.COM
YOSSI ROSENSTEIN YOSSIROSENSTEIN.COM
CHAVA ROTH JUDAICAFINEART.COM
RHONDA ROTH RHONDAROTHART.COM

Rabbi Moshe Kotlarsky, *z"l*, our beloved mentor, friend, and JLI chairman saw the potential of JLI from its very inception, supporting and shepherding its growth and expansion wholeheartedly, along with the countless other Chabad programs and services he directed across the globe. May the merit of the Torah study by JLI students worldwide serve to honor Rabbi Kotlarsky's legacy, continuing to be a source of *nachas* to him on high, as it always was during his lifetime.

It is thanks to Rabbi Kotlarksy, that we are fortunate to have the unwavering support of JLI's principal benefactor, **Mr. George Rohr**, who is fully invested in our work, continues to be instrumental in JLI's monumental growth, and is largely responsible for the Jewish renaissance that is being spearheaded by JLI and its affiliates worldwide.

The commitment and sage direction of JLI's dedicated executive board—**Rabbis Chaim Block**, **Hesh Epstein**, **Ronnie Fine**, **Yosef Gansburg**, **Shmuel Kaplan**, **Yisrael Rice**, and **Avrohom Sternberg**—and the countless hours they devote to the development of JLI are what drive the vision, growth, and tremendous success of the organization.

Finally, JLI represents an incredible partnership of more than 1,600 *shluchim* and *shluchot* in more than 1,000 locations across the globe who contribute their time and talent to furthering Jewish adult education. We thank them for generously sharing feedback and making suggestions that steer JLI's development and growth. They are our most valuable critics and our most cherished contributors.

Inspired by the call of the **Lubavitcher Rebbe**, of righteous memory, it is the mandate of the Rohr JLI to provide a community of learning for all Jews throughout the world where they can participate in their precious heritage of Torah learning and experience its rewards. May this course succeed in fulfilling this sacred charge!

On behalf of the Rohr Jewish Learning Institute,

RABBI EFRAIM MINTZ
Executive Director

RABBI YISRAEL RICE
Chairman, Editorial Board

Rosh Chodesh Kislev, 5785

The Rohr Jewish Learning Institute

AN AFFILIATE OF MERKOS L'INYONEI CHINUCH,
THE EDUCATION ARM OF THE CHABAD-LUBAVITCH MOVEMENT
832 EASTERN PARKWAY, BROOKLYN, NY 11213

CURRICULUM DEVELOPMENT

Rabbi Mordechai Dinerman
Rabbi Naftali Silberberg
EDITORS IN CHIEF

Rabbi Shmuel Klatzkin, PhD
ACADEMIC CONSULTANT

Rabbi Yanki Tauber
SENIOR EDITOR

Rabbi Eli Block
Rabbi Yoni Brown
Rabbi Mendy Goldberg
Rabbi Eliezer Gurkow
Rabbi Meir Kerzner
Rabbi Berel Polityko
Rabbi Schneur Pruss
Rabbi Yochanan Rivkin
Rabbi Levi Shmotkin
Rabbi Shmuel Super
CURRICULUM AUTHORS

Rabbi Ahrele Loschak
EDITOR, TORAH STUDIES

Rabbi Yaakov Paley
WRITER

Rabbi Moshe Wolff
EDITORIAL SUPPORT

Rabbi Yakov Gershon
RESEARCH

Rabbi Michoel Lipskier
EXPERIENTIAL LEARNING

Mrs. Rivki Mockin
CONTENT COORDINATOR

MARKETING AND BRANDING

Mr. David Kaplan
CHIEF MARKETING OFFICER

Ms. Miriam Posner
MARKETING ADMINISTRATOR

Yonatan Azrielant
Rabbi Mendel Backman
Sholom Baitelman
Risa Bursk
Lazer Cohen
Yosef Feigelstock
Rochel Horowitz
Avremi Rapoport
Chana Wrubel
MARKETING AND SOCIAL MEDIA

Ms. Sara Osdoba
DESIGN ADMINISTRATOR

Ms. Leah Fainzilber
Mrs. Chaya Mushka Kanner
Mrs. Chaya Katz
Mrs. Estie Klein
Rabbi Levi Weingarten
GRAPHIC DESIGN

Rabbi Sholom Gurary
Rabbi Motti Klein
Rabbi Zalman Korf
Rabbi Moshe Wolff
PUBLICATION DESIGN

Rabbi Yaakov Paley
COPYWRITER

Rabbi Yossi Grossbaum
Rabbi Mendel Lifshitz
Rabbi Shraga Sherman
Rabbi Ari Sollish
Rabbi Mendel Teldon
MARKETING COMMITTEE

MARKETING CONSULTANTS

Alan Rosenspan
ALAN ROSENSPAN & ASSOCIATES
Sharon, MA

Gary Wexler
PASSION MARKETING
Los Angeles, CA

JLI CENTRAL

Mrs. Mimi Brawer
Ms. Chanie Chesney
Rabbi Tzali Dubov
Rabbi Levi Goldshmid
Ms. Mushka Majeski
Rabbi Avremi Rapoport
Ms. Mimi Schapiro
Mrs. Aliza Scheinfeld
Ms. Mushka Silberstein
Rabbi Yosef Vogel
ADMINISTRATION

Ms. Liba Leah Gutnick
Rabbi Motti Klein
Mrs. Chana Marasow
Mrs. Rochel Perlstein
Rabbi Shlomie Tenenbaum
PROJECT MANAGERS

Mrs. Mindy Wallach
AFFILIATE ORIENTATION

Ms. Chaya Barnett
Ms. Tova Farro
Rabbi Motti Klein
Getzy Raskin
Moshe Raskin
Mrs. Sara Rosenblum
Mrs. Chana Zajac
MULTIMEDIA DEVELOPMENT

Rabbi Mendel Ashkenazi
Yoni Ben-Oni
Rabbi Mendy Elishevitz
Rabbi Yirmi Emmer
Mendel Grossbaum
Rabbi Aron Liberow
Mrs. Chana Weinbaum
ONLINE DIVISION

Mrs. Ya'akovah Weber
SENIOR PROOFREADER
& COPY EDITING

Mrs. Rachel Musicante
Ms. Chaya Barnett
Mrs. Leiba Estrin
PROOFREADERS

Rabbi Moshe Raichik
Rabbi Mendel Sirota
PRINTING AND DISTRIBUTION

Mrs. Shaina B. Mintz
Mrs. Shulamis Nadler
Ms. Chinkah Zirkind
ACCOUNTING

Ms. Tova Farro
Mrs. Chaya Katz
Mrs. Shulamis Nadler
Mrs. Mindy Wallach
CONTINUING EDUCATION

JLI FLAGSHIP

Rabbi Yisrael Rice
CHAIRMAN

Rabbi Shmuly Karp
DIRECTOR

Mrs. Naomi Heber
ADMINISTRATOR

PAST FLAGSHIP AUTHORS

Rabbi Yitzchak M. Kagan
of blessed memory

Rabbi Zalman Abraham
Brooklyn, NY

E. David Klonsky, PhD
Lisa Miller, PhD
Laura H. Mufson, PhD
Tayyab Rashid, PhD
Sylvia J. Sandler, LMFT
Bella Schanzer, M.D.
Andrew Shatté, PhD
Arielle H. Sheftall, PhD
Jonathan Singer, PhD, LCSW
Casey Skvorc, PhD, JD
Darcy Wallen, LCSW, PC

JLI INTERNATIONAL

Rabbi Avrohom Sternberg
CHAIRMAN

Rabbi Dubi Rabinowitz
DIRECTOR

Rabbi Eli Wolf
ADMINISTRATOR, JLI IN THE CIS

In Partnership with the Federation of Jewish Communities of the CIS

Flor Setton
COORDINATOR,
CHABAD OF ARGENTINA

Rabbi Nochum Schapiro
REGIONAL REPRESENTATIVE, AUSTRALIA

Rabbi Avrohom Steinmetz
REGIONAL REPRESENTATIVE, BRAZIL

Rabbi Shevach Zlatopolsky
EDITOR, JLI IN THE CIS

Rabbi Shlomo Cohen
FRENCH COORDINATOR,
REGIONAL REPRESENTATIVE

Rabbi Avraham Golovacheov
REGIONAL REPRESENTATIVE, GERMANY

Rabbi Shlomo Koves
REGIONAL REPRESENTATIVE, HUNGARY

Rabbi Shmuel Katzman
REGIONAL REPRESENTATIVE,
NETHERLANDS

Rabbi Bentzi Sudak
REGIONAL REPRESENTATIVE,
UNITED KINGDOM

NATIONAL JEWISH RETREAT

Rabbi Hesh Epstein
CHAIRMAN

Mrs. Shaina B. Mintz
DIRECTOR

Bruce Backman
HOTEL LIAISON

Rabbi Shabsy Katz
PROGRAM COORDINATOR

Rabbi Isaac Mintz
SHLUCHIM LIAISON

Rabbi Mendel Rosenfeld
LOGISTICS COORDINATOR

Mrs. Aliza Scheinfeld
Ms. Mushka Silberstein
SERVICE AND SUPPORT

THE LAND & THE SPIRIT
Israel Experience

Rabbi Isaac Mintz
DIRECTOR

Mrs. Shaina B. Mintz
ADMINISTRATOR

Rabbi Levi Moscowitz
PROJECT MANAGER

Ms. Esty Donin
PARTICIPANT LIAISON

Rabbi Yechiel Baitelman
Rabbi Dovid Flinkenstein
Rabbi Chanoch Kaplan
Rabbi Levi Klein
Rabbi Mendy Mangel
Rabbi Sholom Raichik
STEERING COMMITTEE

SHABBAT IN THE HEIGHTS

Rabbi Isaac Mintz
DIRECTOR

Rabbi Avremi Rapoport
SHLUCHIM LIAISON

Mrs. Shulamis Nadler
SERVICE AND SUPPORT

Rabbi Chaim Hanoka
CHAIRMAN

Rabbi Mordechai Dinerman
Rabbi Zalman Marcus
STEERING COMMITTEE

MYSHIUR
Advanced Learning Initiative

Rabbi Shmuel Kaplan
CHAIRMAN

Rabbi Shlomie Tenenbaum
ADMINISTRATOR

TORAHCAFE.COM
Online Learning

Rabbi Mendy Elishevitz
WEBSITE DEVELOPMENT

Moshe Levin
CONTENT MANAGER

Mendel Laine
FILMING

OMEK

Ms. Sara Weiss
COORDINATOR

Mrs. Chana Marasow
ADMINISTRATOR

Rabbi Dr. Seth Grauer
Rabbi Zalman Leib Markowitz
ADVISORY BOARD

MACHON SHMUEL
The Sami Rohr Research Institute

Rabbi Zalman Korf
ADMINISTRATOR

Rabbi Moshe Miller, OBM
Rabbi Gedalya Oberlander
Rabbi Chaim Rapoport
Rabbi Levi Yitzchak Raskin
Rabbi Chaim Schapiro
RABBINIC ADVISORY BOARD

Rabbi Yakov Gershon
RESEARCH FELLOW

FOUNDING DEPARTMENT HEADS

Rabbi Mendel Bell
Rabbi Zalman Charytan
Rabbi Mendel Druk
Rabbi Menachem Gansburg
Rabbi Meir Hecht
Rabbi Levi Kaplan
Rabbi Yoni Katz
Rabbi Chaim Zalman Levy
Rabbi Benny Rapoport
Dr. Chana Silberstein
Rabbi Elchonon Tenenbaum
Rabbi Mendy Weg

JLI Chapter Directory

ALABAMA

BIRMINGHAM

Rabbi Yossi Friedman 205.970.0100

MOBILE

Rabbi Yosef Goldwasser 251.265.1213

ALASKA

ANCHORAGE

Rabbi Yosef Greenberg
Rabbi Mendy Greenberg 907.357.8770

ARIZONA

CHANDLER

Rabbi Mendy Deitsch 480.855.4333

FLAGSTAFF

Rabbi Dovie Shapiro 928.255.5756

FOUNTAIN HILLS

Rabbi Mendy Lipskier 480.776.4763

GLENDALE

Rabbi Sholom Lew 623.252.1759

LAKE HAVASU CITY

Rabbi Mendel Super 928.706.6602

ORO VALLEY

Rabbi Ephraim Zimmerman 520.477.8672

PARADISE VALLEY

Rabbi Shlomo Levertov 480.788.9310

PHOENIX

Rabbi Dovber Dechter 347.410.0785
Rabbi Mendy Levertov 602.861.1600
Rabbi Yossi Friedman 602.944.2753

PRESCOTT

Rabbi Elie Filler 928.362.8924

SCOTTSDALE

Rabbi Yossi Levertov 480.998.1410
Rabbi Mendel Vaisfiche 929.309.7811

SEDONA

Rabbi Mendel Kessler 928.985.0667

TUCSON

Rabbi Yehuda Ceitlin 520.881.7956

VAIL

Rabbi Yisroel Shemtov 347.372.3092

ARKANSAS

LITTLE ROCK

Rabbi Pinchus Ciment 501.217.0053

CALIFORNIA

AGOURA HILLS

Rabbi Moshe Bryski 818.516.0444

ALAMEDA

Rabbi Meir Shmotkin 510.640.2590

ARCADIA

Rabbi Sholom Stiefel 626.539.4578

BAKERSFIELD

Rabbi Shmuli Schlanger 661.834.1512

BEL AIR

Rabbi Chaim Mentz 310.475.5311

BEL AIR WEST

Rabbi Mendy Mentz 310.666.2302

BEVERLY HILLS

Rabbi Dovid Begun 310.242.7750

BEVERLYWOOD

Rabbi Menachem Mendel Piekarski 310.597.0967

BURBANK

Rabbi Shmuly Kornfeld 818.954.0070

CARLSBAD

Rabbi Yeruchem Eilfort
Mrs. Nechama Eilfort 760.943.8891

CERRITOS

Rabbi Mendel Lehrer 917.717.8704

CHATSWORTH

Rabbi Yossi Spritzer 818.307.9907

CHULA VISTA

Rabbi Mendy Begun 347.587.0979

CONCORD

Rabbi Berel Kesselman 925.326.1613

CONTRA COSTA

Rabbi Dovber Berkowitz 925.937.4101

CORONADO

Rabbi Eli Fradkin 619.365.4728

DANA POINT

Rabbi Eli Goorevitch 949.290.0628

DANVILLE

Rabbi Shmuli Raitman 213.447.6694

EMERYVILLE

Rabbi Menachem Blank 510.859.8808

ENCINO

Rabbi Aryeh Herzog 818.784.9986
Chapter founded by Rabbi Joshua Gordon, OBM

FOLSOM

Rabbi Yossi Grossbaum 916.608.9811

FREMONT

Rabbi Eli Landes 510.300.4090

GLENDALE

Rabbi Simcha Backman 818.240.2750

HIGHLAND PARK

Rabbi Mendel Korf 323.872.4876

HOLLYWOOD

Rabbi Zalman Partouche 818.964.9428

HUNTINGTON BEACH

Rabbi Aron David Berkowitz 714.846.2285

IRVINE

Rabbi Elly Andrusier 949.786.5000

LAGUNA NIGUEL

Rabbi Mendy Paltiel 949.831.7701

LA JOLLA

Rabbi Baruch Shalom Ezagui 858.455.5433

LAKE BALBOA

Rabbi Eli Gurary 347.403.6734

LOMITA

Rabbi Sholom Pinson 310.326.8234

LONG BEACH

Rabbi Abba Perelmuter 562.773.1350

LOS ANGELES

Rabbi Yigal Begun 347.933.8174
Rabbi Yossi Elifort 310.515.5310
Rabbi Leibel Korf 323.660.5177
Rabbi Zalmy Labkowsky 213.618.9486
Rabbi Mendel Zajac 310.770.9051

MALIBU

Rabbi Levi Cunin 310.456.6588

MAR VISTA

Rabbi Shimon Simpson 646.401.2354

MARINA DEL REY

Rabbi Danny Yiftach-Hashem
Rabbi Dovid Yiftach 310.859.0770

MILL VALLEY

Rabbi Hillel Scop 415.336.3055

MISSION VIEJO

Rabbi Zalman Marcus 949.689.5159

NEWHALL

Rabbi Choni Marosov 661.254.3434

NEWPORT BEACH

Rabbi Reuven Mintz 949.375.3707

NORTHRIDGE

Rabbi Eli Rivkin 818.368.3937

OJAI

Rabbi Mordechai Nemtzov 805.613.7181

OXNARD

Rabbi Dov Muchnik 805.844.9989

PACIFIC PALISADES

Rabbi Avi Cunin 310.454.7783

PALO ALTO

Rabbi Yosef Levin
Rabbi Ber Rosenblatt 650.424.9800

PASADENA

Rabbi Zushe Rivkin 626.788.3343

PLEASANTON

Rabbi Josh Zebberman 925.846.0700

PORTOLA VALLEY

Rabbi Mayer Brook 650.304.2098

POWAY

Rabbi Mendel Goldstein 858.208.6613

RANCHO CUCAMONGA

Rabbi Sholom Ber Harlig 909.949.4553

RANCHO MIRAGE

Rabbi Shimon H. Posner 760.770.7785

RANCHO PALOS VERDES

Rabbi Yitzchok Magalnic 310.544.5544

RANCHO S. FE

Rabbi Levi Raskin 858.756.7571

REDONDO BEACH

Rabbi Yossi Mintz
Rabbi Zalman Gordon 310.214.4999

RESEDA

Rabbi Hershy Spritzer 818.881.1033

RIVERSIDE

Rabbi Shmuel Fuss 951.329.2747

S. ANSELMO

Rabbi Moshe Berkowitz 415.910.8186

S. CLEMENTE

Rabbi Menachem M. Slavin 949.489.0723

S. CRUZ

Rabbi Yochanan Friedman 831.454.0101

S. DIEGO

Rabbi Rafi Andrusier 619.387.8770
Rabbi Yechiel Cagen 832.216.1534
Rabbi Motte Fradkin 858.547.0076

S. FRANCISCO

Rabbi Yakov Barber 424.499.9868
Rebbetzin Mattie Pil 415.933.4310
Rabbi Gedalia Potash 415.648.8000
Rabbi Shlomo Zarchi 415.752.2866

S. LUIS OBISPO

Rabbi Meir Gordon 347.675.3383

S. MATEO

Rabbi Yossi Marcus 650.341.4510

S. RAFAEL

Rabbi Yisrael Rice 415.492.1666

SHERMAN OAKS

Rabbi Nachman Abend 818.989.9539

SONOMA

Rabbi Mendel Wolvovsky 707.292.6221

SOUTH LAKE TAHOE

Rabbi Mordechai Richler 530.539.4363

SOUTH PASADENA

Rabbi Dovid Harlig 626.921.6256

STOCKHOLM

Rabbi Avremel Brod 209.952.2081

SUNNYVALE

Rabbi Yisroel Hecht 408.720.0553

TEMECULA

Rabbi Yonason Abrams 951.234.4196

TIBURON

Rabbi Levi Mintz 415.378.9364

TOPANGA

Rabbi Menachem Piekarski 858.335.7197

TUSTIN

Rabbi Yehoshua Eliezrie 714.508.2150

VACAVILLE

Rabbi Chaim Zaklos 707.592.5300

WEST HILLS

Rabbi Avi Rabin 818.337.4544

WEST HOLLYWOOD

Rabbi Mordechai Kirschenbaum 310.691.9988

WEST LOS ANGELES

Rabbi Mordechai Zaetz 424.652.8742

WOODLAND HILLS

Rabbi Menachem Mendel Gordon 818.917.8456

YORBA LINDA

Rabbi Dovid Eliezrie 714.693.0770

COLORADO

ASPEN

Rabbi Mendel Mintz 970.544.3770

BROOMFIELD

Rabbi Yossi Rapoport 720.968.0086

DENVER

Rabbi Mendel Popack 720.515.4337
Rabbi Yossi Serebryanski 303.744.9699
Rabbi Mendy Sirota 720.940.3716

FORT COLLINS

Rabbi Yerachmiel Gorelik 970.407.1613

HIGHLANDS RANCH

Rabbi Avraham Mintz 303.694.9119

LONGMONT

Rabbi Yakov Borenstein 303.678.7595

VAIL

Rabbi Dovid Mintz 970.476.7887

WESTMINSTER

Rabbi Benjy Brackman 303.429.5177

CONNECTICUT

FAIRFIELD

Rabbi Shlame Landa 203.373.7551

GLASTONBURY

Rabbi Yosef Wolvovsky 860.659.2422

GREENWICH

Rabbi Yossi Deren
Rabbi Menachem Feldman 203.629.9059

GUILFORD

Rabbi Yossi Yaffe 203.645.4635

HAMDEN

Rabbi Moshe Hecht 203.635.7268

LITCHFIELD

Rabbi Joseph Eisenbach 860.567.3377

MILFORD

Rabbi Schneur Wilhelm 203.887.7603

NEW HAVEN

Rabbi Mendy Hecht 203.589.5375
Rabbi Chanoch Wineberg 203.479.0313

NEW LONDON

Rabbi Avrohom Sternberg 860.437.8000

ORANGE

Rabbi Hershy Hecht 203.464.7809

OXFORD

Rabbi Shmaya Hecht 203.514.0622

SHELTON

Rabbi Schneur Brook 203.364.4149

STAMFORD

Rabbi Yisrael Deren
Rabbi Levi Mendelow 203.3.CHABAD

WEST HARTFORD

Rabbi Shaya Gopin 860.232.1116

WESTPORT

Rabbi Yehuda Kantor 561.460.3758

DELAWARE

WILMINGTON

Rabbi Chuni Vogel 302.529.9900

DISTRICT OF COLUMBIA

Rabbi Levi Shemtov
Rabbi Yitzy Ceitlin 202.332.5600

FLORIDA

ALTAMONTE SPRINGS

Rabbi Mendy Bronstein 407.280.0535

AVENTURA

Rabbi Yossi Itkin 347.300.0439
Rabbi Mendel Rosenblum 412.807.0584

BOCA RATON

Rabbi Zalman Bukiet 561.487.2934
Rabbi Moishe Denburg 561.526.5760
Rabbi Arele Gopin 561.994.6257
Rabbi Ruvi New 561.394.9770

BONITA SPRINGS

Rabbi Mendy Greenberg 239.949.6900

BOYNTON BEACH

Rabbi Sholom Ciment 561.732.4633
Rabbi Yosef Yitzchok Raichik 561.740.8738

BRADENTON

Rabbi Menachem Bukiet 941.388.9656

CAPE CORAL

Rabbi Yossi Labkowski 239.963.4770

CLERMONT

Rabbi Moshe Dubinsky 862.812.2174

CORAL GABLES

Rabbi Avraham Stolik 305.490.7572

CORAL SPRINGS

Rabbi Hershy Bronstein 954.798.6023
Rabbi Yankie Denburg 954.471.8646

CUTLER BAY

Rabbi Yossi Wolff 305.975.6680

DAVIE

Rabbi Aryeh Schwartz 954.376.9973

DELRAY BEACH

Rabbi Yaakov Perman 561.666.2770

FISHER ISLAND

Rabbi Efraim Brody 347.325.1913

FLEMING ISLAND

Rabbi Shmuly Feldman 904.290.1017

FORT LAUDERDALE

Rabbi Schneur Kaplan 954.667.8000
Rabbi Yitzchok Naparstek 954.568.1190

FORT MYERS

Rabbi Yitzchok Minkowicz 239.433.7708

HALLANDALE BEACH

Rabbi Mordy Feiner 954.458.1877

HOLLYWOOD

Rabbi Leizer Barash 954.549.5012
Rabbi Leibel Kudan 954.801.3367

JUPITER

Rabbi Berel Barash 561.317.0968

KENDALL

Rabbi Yossi Harlig 305.234.5654

KEY BISCAYNE

Rabbi Avremel Caroline 305.365.6744

LAKE WORTH

Rabbi Zalmen Itkin 917.445.1973

LAUDERHILL

Rabbi Shmuel Heidingsfeld 323.877.7703

LONGWOOD

Rabbi Yanky Majesky 407.636.5994

MAITLAND

Rabbi Sholom Dubov
Rabbi Levik Dubov 470.644.2500
Rabbi Tzviki Dubov 407.529.8256

MARION COUNTY

Rabbi Yossi Hecht 352.330.4466

MIAMI

Rabbi Mendy Cheruty 305.219.3353
Rabbi Yakov Fellig 305.445.5444
Rabbi Shmuel Gopin 305.573.9995
Rabbi Chaim Lipskar 305.373.8303

MIAMI BEACH

Rabbi Yisroel Frankforter 305.534.3895
Rabbi Sholom Korf 786.423.6483
Rabbi Shmuel Mann 305.674.8400

NAPLES

Rabbi Fishel Zaklos 239.404.6993

N. MIAMI BEACH

Rabbi Leib Ezagui 561.596.0530
Rabbi Yehoshua Karp 862.226.2869
Rabbi Eli Laufer 305.770.4412

ORLANDO

Rabbi Yosef Konikov 407.354.3660

ORMOND BEACH

Rabbi Asher Farkash 386.672.9300

OVEIDO

Rabbi Tzviky Dubov 407.529.8256

PALM BEACH

Rabbi Zalman Levitin 561.659.3884

PALM BEACH GARDENS

Rabbi Dovid Vigler 561.624.2223

PALM CITY

Rabbi Shlomo Uminer 772.485.5501

PALM HARBOR

Rabbi Pinchas Adler 727.789.0408

PARKLAND

Rabbi Mendy Gutnick 954.600.6991

PEMBROKE PINES

Rabbi Mordechai Andrusier 954.874.2280

PENSACOLA

Rabbi Mendel Danow 850.291.9600

PLANTATION

Rabbi Pinchas Taylor 954.644.9177

PONTE VEDRA BEACH

Rabbi Nochum Kurinsky 904.543.9301

PORT ORANGE

Rabbi Mendel Niasoff 386.679.5756

ROYAL PALM BEACH

Rabbi Nachmen Zeev Schtroks 561.714.1692

S. AUGUSTINE

Rabbi Levi Vogel 904.521.8664

S. JOHNS

Rabbi Mendel Sharfstein 347.461.3765

S. PETERSBURG

Rabbi Alter Korf 727.344.4900

SARASOTA

Rabbi Chaim Shaul Steinmetz 941.925.0770
Rabbi Levi Steinmetz 941.928.9267

SATELLITE BEACH

Rabbi Zvi Konikov 321.777.2770

SINGER ISLAND

Rabbi Berel Namdar 347.276.6985

SOUTH PALM BEACH

Rabbi Leibel Stolik 561.889.3499

SOUTH TAMPA

Rabbi Mendy Dubrowski 813.922.1723

SOUTHWEST BROWARD COUNTY

Rabbi Aryeh Schwartz 954.252.1770

SUNNY ISLES BEACH

Rabbi Alexander Kaller 305.803.5315

SURFSIDE

Rabbi Dov Schochet 305.790.8294

TAMARAC

Rabbi Kopel Silberberg 954.882.7434

TAMPA

Rabbi Chaim Lipszyc 954.882.7434

VENICE

Rabbi Sholom Ber Schmerling 845.238.0770

VERO BEACH

Rabbi Motty Rosenfeld 772.245.6712

WATERWAYS

Rabbi Yisroel Brusowankin 786.663.8731

WESLEY CHAPEL

Rabbi Mendy Yarmush
Rabbi Mendel Friedman 813.731.2977

WEST DELRAY BEACH

Rabbi Yossi Schapiro 561.221.1618

WEST PALM BEACH

Rabbi Yoel Gancz 561.659.7770

WESTON

Rabbi Yisroel Spalter 954.349.6565

GEORGIA

ALPHARETTA

Rabbi Hirshy Minkowicz 770.410.9000

ATLANTA

Rabbi Yossi New
Rabbi Isser New 404.843.2464
Rabbi Alexander Piekarski 678.267.6418
Rabbi Ari Sollish 404.898.0434

ATLANTA: INTOWN

Rabbi Eliyahu Schusterman
Rabbi Chanan Rose 415.370.1333

AUGUSTA

Rabbi Zalman Fischer 706.836.1576

CUMMING

Rabbi Levi Mentz 310.666.2218

DUNWOODY

Rabbi Mendy Wineberg 347.770.2414

GAINESVILLE

Rabbi Nechemia Gurevitz 770.906.4970

GWINNETT

Rabbi Yossi Lerman 678.595.0196

MARIETTA

Rabbi Ephraim Silverman 770.565.4412

ROSWELL

Rabbi Chaim Schwartz 770.363.4644

HAWAII

KAILUA-KONA

Rabbi Levi Gerlitzky 917.853.2787

KAPA'A

Rabbi Michoel Goldman 808.647.4293

IDAHO

BOISE

Rabbi Mendel Lifshitz 208.853.9200

ILLINOIS

ARLINGTON HEIGHTS

Rabbi Yaakov Kotlarsky 224.357.7002

CHAMPAIGN

Rabbi Dovid Tiechtel 217.355.8672

CHICAGO

Rabbi Mendy Benhiyoun 312.498.7704
Rabbi Mordechai Gershon 773.412.5189
Rabbi Dovid Kotlarsky 773.495.7127
Rabbi Yosef Moscowitz 773.772.3770
Rabbi Levi Notik 773.274.5123

ELGIN

Rabbi Mendel Shemtov 847.440.4486

GLENVIEW

Rabbi Yishaya Benjaminson 847.910.1738

GURNEE

Rabbi Sholom Tenenbaum 847.782.1800

HIGHLAND PARK

Mrs. Michla Schanowitz 847.266.0770

NAPERVILLE

Rabbi Mendy Goldstein 630.957.8122

NORTHBROOK

Rabbi Meir Moscowitz 847.564.8770

NORWOOD PARK

Rabbi Mendel Perlstein 312.752.8894

OAK PARK

Rabbi Yitzchok Bergstein 708.524.1530

PARK RIDGE

Rabbi Lazer Hershkovich 224.392.4442

PEORIA

Rabbi Eli Langsam 309.370.7701

RIVERWOODS

Rabbi Sholom Notik 847.208.8794

SKOKIE

Rabbi Yochanan Posner 847.677.1770

VERNON HILLS

Rabbi Shimmy Susskind 718.755.5356

WILMETTE

Rabbi Dovid Flinkenstein 847.251.7707

INDIANA

INDIANAPOLIS

Rabbi Avraham Grossbaum
Rabbi Dr. Shmuel Klatzkin 317.251.5573

IOWA

BETTENDORF

Rabbi Shneur Cadaner 563.355.1065

KANSAS

OVERLAND PARK

Rabbi Mendy Wineberg 913.649.4852

KENTUCKY

LOUISVILLE

Rabbi Avrohom Litvin 502.459.1770

LOUISIANA

BATON ROUGE

Rabbi Peretz Kazen 225.267.7047

METAIRIE

Rabbi Yossie Nemes
Rabbi Mendel Ceitlin 504.454.2910

NEW ORLEANS

Rabbi Mendel Rivkin 504.302.1830

MAINE

BANGOR

Rabbi Chaim Wilansky 207.650.7223

PORTLAND

Rabbi Levi Wilansky 207.650.1783

MARYLAND

BALTIMORE

Rabbi Velvel Belinsky 410.764.5000
Classes in Russian

Rabbi Dovid Reyder 781.796.4204

BEL AIR

Rabbi Kushi Schusterman 443.353.9718

BETHESDA

Rabbi Sender Geisinsky 301.913.9777

CHEVY CHASE

Rabbi Zalman Minkowitz 301.260.5000

COLUMBIA

Rabbi Hillel Baron
Rabbi Yosef Chaim Sufrin 410.740.2424

FREDERICK

Rabbi Boruch Labkowski 301.996.3659

GAITHERSBURG

Rabbi Sholom Raichik 301.926.3632

OLNEY

Rabbi Bentzy Stolik 301.660.6770

OWINGS MILLS

Rabbi Nochum Katsenelenbogen 410.356.5156

POTOMAC

Rabbi Mendel Bluming 301.983.4200
Rabbi Mendel Kaplan 301.983.1485

ROCKVILLE

Rabbi Shlomo Beitsh 646.773.2675
Rabbi Moishe Kavka 301.836.1242

MASSACHUSETTS

ANDOVER

Rabbi Asher Bronstein 978.470.2288

ARLINGTON

Rabbi Avi Bukiet 617.909.8653

BOSTON

Rabbi Yosef Zaklos 617.297.7282

BRIGHTON

Rabbi Dan Rodkin 617.787.2200

CAPE COD

Rabbi Yekusiel Alperowitz 508.775.2324

CHESTNUT HILL

Rabbi Mendy Uminer 617.738.9770

LEXINGTON

Rabbi Yisroel New 646.248.9053

LONGMEADOW

Rabbi Yakov Wolff 413.567.8665

NEWTON

Rabbi Shalom Ber Prus 617.244.1200

PEABODY

Rabbi Nechemia Schusterman 978.977.9111

SHARON

Rabbi Naftoli Minkowitz 781.363.7066

SOUTH SHORE

Rabbi Levi Lezell 617.862.2770

SUDBURY

Rabbi Yisroel Freeman 978.443.0110

SWAMPSCOTT

Rabbi Yossi Lipsker 781.581.3833

VINEYARD HAVEN

Rabbi Tzvi Alperowitz 508.560.8650

MICHIGAN

ANN ARBOR

Rabbi Aharon Goldstein 734.995.3276

BLOOMFIELD HILLS

Rabbi Levi Dubov 248.949.6210

GRAND RAPIDS

Rabbi Mordechai Haller 616.957.0770

TROY

Rabbi Menachem Caytak 248.873.5851

WEST BLOOMFIELD

Rabbi Zelig Shemtov 248.788.4000
Rabbi Elimelech Silberberg 248.855.6170
Rabbi Schneur Silberberg 248.207.5513

MINNESOTA

MINNETONKA

Rabbi Mordechai Grossbaum
Rabbi Shmuel Silberstein 952.929.9922

PLYMOUTH

Rabbi Nissan Naparstek 310.430.0960

S. PAUL

Rabbi Shneur Zalman Bendet 651.998.9298

MISSOURI

CHESTERFIELD

Rabbi Avi Rubenfeld 314.258.3401

S. LOUIS

Rabbi Yosef Abenson 314.448.0927
Rabbi Yosef Landa 314.725.0400

MONTANA

BOZEMAN

Rabbi Chaim Shaul Bruk 406.600.4934

KALISPELL

Rabbi Shneur Wolf 406.885.2541

NEVADA

LAS VEGAS

Rabbi Yosef Rivkin 702.217.2170

RENO

Rabbi Levi Sputz 347.262.4531

SUMMERLIN

Rabbi Yisroel Schanowitz
Rabbi Tzvi Bronchtain 702.855.0770

NEW JERSEY

BASKING RIDGE

Rabbi Mendy Herson
Rabbi Mendel Shemtov 908.604.8844

CHERRY HILL

Rabbi Mendel Mangel 856.874.1500

CLINTON

Rabbi Eli Kornfeld 908.623.7000

ENGLEWOOD

Rabbi Shmuel Konikov 201.519.7343

FAIR LAWN

Rabbi Avrohom Bergstein 201.794.3770

FANWOOD

Rabbi Avrohom Blesofsky 908.790.0008

FLANDERS

Rabbi Yaacov Shusterman 973.723.6868

FORT LEE

Rabbi Meir Konikov 201.886.1238

GREATER MERCER COUNTY

Rabbi Dovid Dubov
Rabbi Yaakov Chaiton 609.213.4136

HASKELL

Rabbi Mendy Gurkov 201.696.7609

HOLMDEL

Rabbi Shmaya Galperin 732.772.1998

JACKSON

Rabbi Shmuel Naparstek 732.668.7702

JERICHO

Rabbi Mendy Brownstein 516.850.4486

MADISON

Rabbi Shalom Lubin 973.377.0707

MANALAPAN

Rabbi Boruch Chazanow
Rabbi Levi Wolosow 732.972.3687

MEDFORD

Rabbi Yitzchok Kahan 609.451.3522

MENDHAM

Rabbi Ari Herson 732.619.8829

MONTCLAIR

Rabbi Yaacov Leaf 862.252.5666

MORRISTOWN

Rabbi Moishe Gurevitz 973.216.8077

MOUNTAIN LAKES

Rabbi Levi Dubinsky 973.551.1898

MULLICA HILL

Rabbi Avrohom Richler 856.733.0770

OLD TAPPAN

Rabbi Mendy Lewis 201.767.4008

RANDOLPH

Rabbi Avraham Bekhor 973.723.0933

RED BANK

Rabbi Dovid Harrison 973.895.3070

ROCKAWAY

Rabbi Asher Herson
Rabbi Mordechai Baumgarten 973.625.1525

RUTHERFORD

Rabbi Yitzchok Lerman 347.834.7500

SCOTCH PLAINS

Rabbi Avrohom Blesofsky 908.790.0008

SHORT HILLS

Rabbi Mendel Solomon
Rabbi Avrohom Levin 973.725.7008

SOUTH BRUNSWICK

Rabbi Levi Azimov 732.398.9492

TENAFLY

Rabbi Mordechai Shain 201.871.1152

TOMS RIVER

Rabbi Moshe Gourarie 732.349.4199

VENTNOR

Rabbi Avrohom Rapoport 609.822.8500

WEST ORANGE

Rabbi Mendy Kasowitz 973.325.6311

WOODCLIFF LAKE

Rabbi Dov Drizin 201.476.0157

NEW MEXICO

LAS CRUCES

Rabbi Bery Schmukler 575.524.1330

S. FE

Rabbi Berel Levertov 505.920.4324

NEW YORK

ALBANY

Rabbi Mordechai Rubin 518.368.7886

BEDFORD

Rabbi Arik Wolf 914.666.6065

BENSONHURST

Rabbi Avrohom Hertz 718.753.7768

BINGHAMTON

Mrs. Rivkah Slonim 607.797.0015

BRIGHTON BEACH

Rabbi Dovid Okonov 718.368.4490

BRONXVILLE

Rabbi Sruli Deitsch 917.755.0078

BROOKVILLE

Rabbi Mendy Heber 516.626.0600

CEDARHURST

Rabbi Zalman Wolowik 516.295.2478

CLIFTON PARK

Rabbi Yossi Rubin 518.495.0772

COMMACK

Rabbi Mendel Teldon 631.543.3343

DELMAR

Rabbi Zalman Simon 518.866.7658

DOBBS FERRY

Rabbi Benjy Silverman 914.693.6100

EAST HAMPTON

Rabbi Leibel Baumgarten
Rabbi Mendy Goldberg 631.329.5800

ELLENVILLE

Rabbi Shlomie Deren 845.647.4450

FOREST HILLS

Rabbi Yossi Mendelson 917.861.9726

GLEN OAKS

Rabbi Shmuel Nadler 347.388.7064

GREAT NECK

Rabbi Yoseph Geisinsky 516.487.4554

HOWARD BEACH

Rabbi Avrohom Richler 917.541.7374

ISLIP

Rabbi Shimon Stillerman 631.913.8770

KINGSTON

Rabbi Yitzchok Hecht 845.334.9044

LARCHMONT

Rabbi Mendel Silberstein 914.834.4321

LITTLE NECK

Rabbi Eli Shifrin 718.423.1235

LONG BEACH

Rabbi Eli Goodman 516.574.3905

LONG ISLAND CITY

Rabbi Zev Wineberg 347.218.2927

MANHASSET

Rabbi Mendel Paltiel 516.984.0701

MELVILLE

Rabbi Yosef Raskin 631.276.4453

MINEOLA

Rabbi Anchelle Perl 516.739.3636

NEW HARTFORD

Rabbi Levi Charitonow 716.322.8692

NEW YORK

Rabbi Yakov Bankhalter 917.613.1678
Rabbi Nissi Eber 347.677.2276
Rabbi Berel Gurevitch 212.518.3122
Rabbi Daniel Kraus 917.294.5567
Rabbi Shmuel Metzger 212.758.3770

NYC TRIBECA

Rabbi Zalman Paris 212.566.6764

NYC UPPER EAST SIDE

Rabbi Uriel Vigler 212.369.7310

NYC WEST SIDE

Rabbi Shlomo Kugel 212.864.5010

OCEANSIDE

Rabbi Levi Gurkow 516.764.7385

OSSINING

Rabbi Dovid Labkowski 914.923.2522

OYSTER BAY

Rabbi Shmuel Lipszyc
Rabbi Shalom Lipszyc 347.853.9992

PARK SLOPE

Rabbi Menashe Wolf 347.957.1291

PORT WASHINGTON

Rabbi Shalom Paltiel 516.767.8672

PROSPECT HEIGHTS

Rabbi Mendy Hecht 347.622.3599

ROCHESTER

Rabbi Nechemia Vogel 585.271.0330

ROSLYN

Rabbi Yaakov Reiter 516.484.3500

ROSLYN HEIGHTS

Rabbi Aaron Konikov 516.484.3500

SEA GATE

Rabbi Chaim Brikman 347.524.3214

SOUTHAMPTON

Rabbi Chaim Pape 917.627.4865

STATEN ISLAND

Rabbi Mendy Katzman 718.370.8953

STONY BROOK

Rabbi Shalom Ber Cohen 631.585.0521

SUFFERN

Rabbi Shmuel Gancz 845.368.1889

WEST BRIGHTON BEACH

Rabbi Moshe Winner 718.946.9833

YORKTOWN HEIGHTS

Rabbi Yehuda Heber 914.962.1111

NORTH CAROLINA

ASHEVILLE

Rabbi Shaya Susskind 828.335.4604

CARY

Rabbi Yisroel Cotlar 919.651.9710

CHAPEL HILL

Rabbi Zalman Bluming 919.357.5904

CHARLOTTE

Rabbi Yossi Groner
Rabbi Shlomo Cohen 704.366.3984

GREENSBORO

Rabbi Yosef Plotkin 336.617.8120

RALEIGH

Rabbi Pinchas Herman
Rabbi Mendy Wilschanski 919.847.8986

WILMINGTON

Rabbi Moshe Lieblich 910.763.4770

WINSTON-SALEM

Rabbi Levi Gurevitz 336.756.9069

OHIO

BEACHWOOD

Rabbi Moshe Gancz 216.647.4884

CINCINNATI

Rabbi Yisroel Mangel 513.793.5200

COLUMBUS

Rabbi Shea Kaltmann 614.935.2804
Rabbi Yitzi Kaltmann 614.294.3296

DAYTON

Rabbi Nochum Mangel 937.643.0770

TWINSBURG

Rabbi Mendy Greenberg 440.465.2063

OKLAHOMA

OKLAHOMA CITY

Rabbi Ovadia Goldman 405.524.4800

TULSA

Rabbi Yehuda Weg 918.492.4499

OREGON

PORTLAND

Rabbi Mordechai Wilhelm 503.977.9947

SALEM

Rabbi Avrohom Yitzchok Perlstein 503.383.9569

TIGARD

Rabbi Menachem Orenstein 971.329.6661

WEST LINN

Rabbi Shimon Wilhelm 503.753.4744

PENNSYLVANIA

AMBLER

Rabbi Shaya Deitsch 215.591.9310

BALA CYNWYD

Rabbi Shraga Sherman 610.660.9192

CLARKS SUMMIT

Rabbi Benny Rapoport 570.587.3300

DOYLESTOWN

Rabbi Mendel Prus 215.340.1303

FAIRMONT

Rabbi Hirshi Sputz 267.332.1321

FREEDOM

Rabbi Yosef Feller 612.275.6438

GLEN MILLS

Rabbi Yehuda Gerber 484.620.4162

LAFAYETTE HILL

Rabbi Yisroel Kotlarsky 484.533.7009

LANCASTER

Rabbi Elazar Green 717.723.8783

LEWISBURG

Rabbi Yisroel Baumgarten 631.880.2801

MECHANICSBURG

Rabbi Nissen Pewzner 717.798.0053

MONROEVILLE

Rabbi Mendy Schapiro 412.372.1000

NEWTOWN

Rabbi Aryeh Weinstein 215.497.9925

PHILADELPHIA

Rabbi Berel Paltiel 718.288.8574

PHILADELPHIA: CENTER CITY

Rabbi Yochonon Goldman 215.238.2100

PITTSBURGH

Rabbi Yisroel Altein 412.422.7300 EXT. 269

PITTSBURGH: SOUTH HILLS

Rabbi Mendy Rosenblum 412.278.3693

READING

Rabbi Yosef Lipsker 610.334.3218

RYDAL

Rabbi Zushe Gurevitz 267.536.5757

UNIVERSITY PARK

Rabbi Nosson Meretsky 814.863.4929

WYNNEWOOD

Rabbi Moishe Brennan 610.529.9011

PUERTO RICO

CAROLINA

Rabbi Mendel Zarchi 787.253.0894

RHODE ISLAND

WARWICK

Rabbi Yossi Laufer 401.884.7888

SOUTH CAROLINA

BLUFFTON

Rabbi Menachem Hertz 843.301.1819

COLUMBIA

Rabbi Hesh Epstein

Rabbi Levi Marrus 803.782.1831

GREENVILLE

Rabbi Leibel Kesselman 864.534.7739

MYRTLE BEACH

Rabbi Doron Aizenman 843.448.0035

TENNESSEE

CHATTANOOGA

Rabbi Shaul Perlstein 423.910.9770

KNOXVILLE

Rabbi Yossi Wilhelm 865.300.8012

MEMPHIS

Rabbi Levi Klein 901.754.0404

NASHVILLE

Rabbi Yitzchok Tiechtel 615.646.5750

TEXAS

AUSTIN

Rabbi Mendy Levertov 512.905.2778

BELLAIRE

Rabbi Yossi Zaklikofsky 713.839.8887

CYPRESS

Rabbi Levi Marinovsky 832.651.6964

DALLAS

Rabbi Zvi Drizin 214.632.2633

Rabbi Mendel Dubrawsky 214.215.1540

Rabbi Boruch Hecht 310.704.5403

Rabbi Moshe Naparstek 972.818.0770

EL PASO

Rabbi Levi Greenberg 347.678.9762

FORT WORTH

Rabbi Dov Mandel 817.263.7701

FRISCO

Rabbi Mendy Kesselman 214.460.7773

HOUSTON

Rabbi Dovid Goldstein

Rabbi Zally Lazarus 281.589.7188

Rabbi Moishe Traxler 713.774.0300

HOUSTON: RICE UNIVERSITY AREA

Rabbi Eliezer Lazaroff 713.522.2004

LEAGUE CITY

Rabbi Yitzchok Schmukler 281.724.1554

PLANO

Rabbi Eli Block 214.620.4083

Rabbi Mendel Block 972.596.8270

ROCKWALL

Rabbi Moshe Kalmenson 469.350.5735

ROUND ROCK

Rabbi Mendel Marasow 512.387.3171

S. ANTONIO

Rabbi Chaim Block

Rabbi Levi Teldon 210.492.1085

Rabbi Tal Shaul 210.877.4218

SOUTHLAKE

Rabbi Levi Gurevitch 817.451.1171

SUGAR LAND

Rabbi Ari Feigenson

Rabbi Mendel Feigenson 832.758.0685

THE WOODLANDS

Rabbi Mendel Blecher 281.865.7242

UTAH

LEHI

Rabbi Chaim Zippel 801.674.4566

PARK CITY

Rabbi Yehuda Steiger 435.714.8590

S. GEORGE

Rabbi Mendy Cohen 862.812.6224

SALT LAKE CITY

Rabbi Benny Zippel 801.467.7777

VERMONT

BURLINGTON

Rabbi Yitzchok Raskin 802.658.5770

MANCHESTER

Rabbi Menachem Andrusier 518.506.8678

WATERBURY CENTER

Rabbi Boruch Simon 518.360.7337

VIRGINIA

ALEXANDRIA/ARLINGTON

Rabbi Mordechai Newman 703.370.2774

FAIRFAX

Rabbi Leibel Fajnland 703.426.1980

GAINESVILLE

Rabbi Shmuel Perlstein 571.445.0342

LOUDOUN COUNTY

Rabbi Chaim Cohen 248.298.9279

NORFOLK

Rabbi Aaron Margolin
Rabbi Levi Brashevitzky 757.616.0770

RICHMOND

Rabbi Shlomo Pereira 804.740.2000

WILLIAMSBURG

Rabbi Mendy Heber 234.770.0306

WINCHESTER

Rabbi Yishai Dinerman 540.324.9879

WASHINGTON

BAINBRIDGE ISLAND

Rabbi Mendy Goldshmid 206.397.7679

BELLINGHAM

Rabbi Yosef Truxton 360.224.9919

ISSAQUAH

Rabbi Schneur Matusof 347.775.7069

KIRKLAND

Rabbi Chaim S. Rivkin 425.749.8512

LYNNWOOD

Rabbi Berel Paltiel 425.286.7465

MERCER ISLAND

Rabbi Elazar Bogomilsky 206.527.1411
Rabbi Nissan Kornfeld 206.851.2324

NORMANDY PARK

Rabbi Moshe Wolff 206.946.2477

OLYMPIA

Rabbi Yosef Schtroks 360.867.8804

SEATTLE

Rabbi Yoni Levitin 206.851.9831
Rabbi Shmuel Levitin 347.415.2271
Rabbi Shnai Levitin 347.342.2259
Rabbi Yossi Rodal 310.382.0868

SPOKANE COUNTY

Rabbi Yisroel Hahn 509.443.0770

WISCONSIN

BAYSIDE

Rabbi Cheski Edelman 414.439.5041

BROOKFIELD

Rabbi Levi Brook 925.708.4203

KENOSHA

Rabbi Tzali Wilschanski 262.359.0770

MADISON

Rabbi Avremel Matusof 608.335.3777

MEQUON

Rabbi Doobie Lisker 323.216.6139
Rabbi Menachem Rapoport 262.242.2235

MILWAUKEE

Rabbi Levi Emmer 414.277.8839
Rabbi Mendel Shmotkin 414.961.6100

WYOMING

LARAMIE

Rabbi Yaakov Raskin 307.920.2613

ARGENTINA

BAHIA BLANCA

Rabbi Shmuel Freedman 347.300.2779

BUENOS AIRES

Rabbi Abraham Benchimol 54.11.6048.5333
Rabbi Yossi Birman 54.11.5334.6606
Mrs. Chani Gorowitz 54.11.4865.0445
Rabbi Menachem M. Grunblatt 54.911.3574.0037
Rabbi Mendy Gurevitch 55.11.4545.7771
Rabbi Mendel Levy 54.11.3687.8258
Rabbi Shlomo Levy 54.11.4807.2223
Rabbi Yosef Levy 54.11.4504.1908
Rabbi Yosef Yitzjok Levy 54.11.6292.4125
Rabbi Tzvi Lipinsky 54.11.5249.2693
Rabbi Yossi Ludman 54.11.3935.0214
Rabbi Yoel Migdal 54.11.4963.1221
Rabbi Mendi Mizrahi 54.11.4963.1221
Rabbi Shiele Plotka 54.11.4634.3111
Rabbi Itzjak Safranchik 54.11.3699.3977
Rabbi Shniur Zalmen Schvetz 54.11.3552.5208
Rabbi Shloimi Setton 54.11.4982.8637
Rabbi Pinhas Sudry 54.1.4822.2285

CORDOBA

Rabbi Menajem Turk 54.351.233.8250

ROSARIO

Rabbi Shlomo Tawil 54.93.4152.0039

S. MIGUEL DE TUCUMÁN

Rabbi Ariel Levy 54.381.473.6944

SALTA

Rabbi Rafael Tawil 54.387.421.4947

AUSTRALIA

NEW SOUTH WALES

BELLEVUE HILL

Mrs. Chaya Kaye 614.3342.2755

DOUBLE BAY

Rabbi Yanky Berger 612.9327.1644

DOVER HEIGHTS

Rabbi Motti Feldman 614.0400.8572

MAROUBRA

Rabbi Schneur Goldstein 614.3476.0722

NEWTOWN

Rabbi Eli Feldman 614.0077.0613

NORTH SHORE

Rabbi Nochum Schapiro
Rebbetzin Fruma Schapiro 612.9488.9548

SYDNEY

Rabbi Levi Wolff 614.2162.2622
Rabbi Meir Wilenkin 614.4886.9153

THE HILL

Rabbi Yossi Rodal 614.2573.0412

QUEENSLAND

BOKARINA

Rabbi Asher Goodman 898.6763.0334

BRISBANE

Rabbi Levi Jaffe 617.3843.6770

TASMANIA

SOUTH LAUNCESTON

Mrs. Rochel Gordon 614.2055.0405

VICTORIA

EAST S. KILDA

Rabbi Sholem Gorelik 614.5244.8770

MOORABBIN

Rabbi Elisha Greenbaum 614.0349.0434

WESTERN AUSTRALIA

PERTH

Rabbi Shalom White 618.9275.2106

AZERBAIJAN

BAKU

Mrs. Chavi Segal 994.12.597.91.90

BELARUS

BOBRUISK

Mrs. Mina Hababo 375.29.104.3230

MINSK

Rabbi Shneur Deitsch
Mrs. Bassie Deitsch 375.29.330.6675

BELGIUM

ANTWERP

Rabbi Mendel Gurary 32.48.656.9878

BRUSSELS

Rabbi Shmuel Pinson 375.29.330.6675

BRAZIL

CURITIBA

Rabbi Mendy Labkowski 55.41.3079.1338

S. PAULO

Rabbi Avraham Steinmetz 55.11.3081.3081

CANADA

ALBERTA

CALGARY

Rabbi Mordechai Groner 403.281.3770

EDMONTON

Rabbi Ari Drelich
Rabbi Mendy Blachman 780.200.5770

BRITISH COLUMBIA

COQUITLAM

Rabbi Mordechai Gurevitz 604.787.5667

NANAIMO

Rabbi Benzti Shemtov 250.797.7877

RICHMOND

Rabbi Yechiel Baitelman 604.277.6427

VANCOUVER

Rabbi Dovid Rosenfeld 604.266.1313
Rabbi Shmuel Yeshayahu 604.738.7060

VICTORIA

Rabbi Meir Kaplan 250.595.7656

MANITOBA

WINNIPEG

Rabbi Menachem Altein 204.869.7631
Rabbi Shmuel Altein 204.339.8737

ONTARIO

BAYVIEW

Rabbi Levi Gansburg 416.551.9391

EAST THORNHILL

Rabbi Mendel Zaltzman 647.998.7105

GREATER TORONTO REGIONAL OFFICE & THORNHILL

Rabbi Yossi Gansburg 905.731.7000

INNISFIL

Rabbi Zevi Kaplan 705.970.7074

KINGSTON

Rabbi Yisroel Simon 613.770.1884

MAPLE

Rabbi Yechezkel Deren 647.883.6372

MISSISSAUGA

Rabbi Yitzchok Slavin 905.820.4432

NORTH YORK

Rabbi Sruli Steiner 647.501.5618

OTTAWA

Rabbi Menachem M. Blum 613.843.7770
Rabbi Moshe Caytak 613.902.4394

RICHMOND HILL

Rabbi Mendel Bernstein 905.303.1880
Rabbi Yosef Hecht 416.837.0962

TORONTO

Rabbi Menachem Gansburg 647.409.6480
Rabbi Shmuly Grossbaum 648.677.0665
Rabbi Sholom Lezell 416.809.1365
Rabbi Shmuel Neft 647.966.7105
Rabbi Moshe Steiner 416.635.9606

WATERLOO
Rabbi Moshe Goldman 226.338.7770

WHITBY
Rabbi Tzali Borenstein 905.447.8215

WOODBRIDGE
Rabbi Shalom Bakshi 647.982.3419

QUEBEC

CÔTE S.-LUC
Rabbi Levi Naparstek 438.409.6770

DOLLARD-DES ORMEAUX
Rabbi Leibel Fine 514.777.4675

HAMPSTEAD
Rabbi Moshe New
Rabbi Berel Bell
Mrs. Chanie Teitlebaum 514.739.0770

MONTREAL
Rabbi Ronnie Fine
Pesach Nussbaum 514.738.3434

MONTREAL WEST
Rabbi Mendy Marlow 514.632.9649

OLD MONTREAL/GRIFFINTOWN
Rabbi Nissan Gansbourg
Rabbi Berel Bell 514.800.6966

S. LAURENT
Rabbi Schneur Zalmen Silberstein
514.747.1199

S. LAZARE
Rabbi Nochum Labkowski 514.436.7426

TOWN OF MOUNT ROYAL
Rabbi Moshe Krasnanski
Rabbi Shneur Zalman Rader 514.342.1770

SASKATCHEWAN

SASKATOON
Rabbi Raphael Kats 306.384.4370

CAYMAN ISLANDS

GEORGE TOWN
Rabbi Berel Pewzner 717.798.1040

COLOMBIA

BOGOTA
Rabbi Chanoch Piekarski 57.1.635.8251

COSTA RICA

S. JOSÉ
Rabbi Hershel Spalter
Rabbi Moshe Bitton 506.4010.1515

CROATIA

ZAGREB
Rabbi Pinchas Zaklas 385.1.481.2227

DENMARK

COPENHAGEN
Rabbi Yitzchok Loewenthal 45.3316.1850

DOMINICAN REPUBLIC

S. DOMINGO
Rabbi Shimon Pelman 829.341.2770

ESTONIA

TALLINN
Rabbi Shmuel Kot 372.662.30.50

FRANCE

BOULOGNE
Rabbi Michael Sojcher 33.1.46.99.87.85

DIJON
Rabbi Chaim Slonim 33.6.52.05.26.65

LA VARENNE-S.-HILAIRE
Rabbi Mena'hem Mendel Benelbaz
33.6.17.81.57.47

MARSEILLE
Rabbi Eliahou Altabe 33.6.11.60.03.05
Rabbi Mena'hem Mendel Assouline
33.6.64.88.25.04
Rabbi Emmanuel Taubenblatt
33.4.88.00.94.85

PARIS
Rabbi Yona Hasky 33.1.53.75.36.01
Rabbi Acher Marciano 33.6.15.15.01.02
Rabbi Avraham Barou'h Pevzner
33.6.99.64.07.70

PONTAULT-COMBAULT
Rabbi Yossi Amar 33.6.61.36.07.70

VILLIERS-SUR-MARNE
Rabbi Mena'hem Mendel Mergui
33.1.49.30.89.66

GEORGIA

TBILISI
Rabbi Meir Kozlovsky 995.32.2429770

GERMANY

BERLIN
Rabbi Yehuda Tiechtel 49.30.2128.0830

DUSSELDORF
Rabbi Chaim Barkahn 49.173.2871.770

HAMBURG
Rabbi Shlomo Bistritzky 49.40.4142.4190

HANNOVER 49.511.811.2822
Chapter founded by Rabbi Binyamin Wolff, OBM

GREECE

ATHENS
Rabbi Mendel Hendel 30.210.323.3825

GUATEMALA

GUATEMALA CITY
Rabbi Shalom Pelman 502.2485.0770

HUNGARY

BUDAPEST
Rabbi Shlomo Kovesh 361.268.0183

IRELAND

DUBLIN

Rabbi Zalman Lent 3538.7419.5354

ISRAEL

ASHKELON

Rabbi Shneor Lieberman 054.977.0512

BALFURYA

Rabbi Noam Bar-Tov 054.580.4770

CAESAREA

Rabbi Chaim Meir Lieberman 054.621.2586

EVEN YEHUDA

Rabbi Menachem Noyman 054.777.0707

GANEI TIKVA

Rabbi Gershon Shnur 054.524.2358

GIV'ATAYIM

Rabbi Pinchus Bitton 052.643.8770

JERUSALEM

Rabbi Levi Diamond 055.665.7702
Rabbi Avraham Hendel 054.830.5799

KARMIEL

Rabbi Mendy Elishevitz 054.521.3073

KFAR SABA

Rabbi Yossi Baitch 054.445.5020

KIRYAT BIALIK

Rabbi Pinny Marton 050.661.1768

KIRYAT MOTZKIN

Rabbi Shimon Eizenbach 050.902.0770

KOCHAV YAIR

Rabbi Dovi Greenberg 054.332.6244

MACCABIM-RE'UT

Rabbi Yosef Yitzchak Noiman 054.977.0549

NESS ZIONA

Rabbi Menachem Feldman 054.497.7092

NETANYA

Rabbi Schneur Brod 054.579.7572

RAMAT GAN-KRINITZI

Rabbi Yisroel Gurevitz 052.743.2814

RAMAT GAN-MAROM NAVE

Rabbi Binyamin Meir Kali 050.476.0770

RAMAT YISHAI

Rabbi Shneor Zalman Wolosow 052.324.5475

RISHON LEZION

Rabbi Uri Keshet 050.722.4593

ROSH PINA

Rabbi Sholom Ber Hertzel 052.458.7600

TEL AVIV

Rabbi Shneur Piekarski 054.971.5568

JAMAICA

MONTEGO BAY

Rabbi Yaakov Raskin 876.452.3223

JAPAN

TOKYO

Rabbi Mendi Sudakevich 81.3.5789.2846

KAZAKHSTAN

ALMATY

Rabbi Shevach Zlatopolsky 7.7272.77.59.49

KYRGYZSTAN

BISHKEK

Rabbi Arye Raichman 996.312.68.19.66

LATVIA

RIGA

Rabbi Shneur Zalman Kot
Mrs. Rivka Glazman 371.6720.40.22

LITHUANIA

VILNIUS

Rabbi Sholom Ber Krinsky 370.6817.1367

LUXEMBOURG

LUXEMBOURG

Rabbi Mendel Edelman 352.2877.7079

MEXICO

PUERTO VALLARTA

Rabbi Shneur Hecht 52.32.2141.7279

S. MIGUEL DE ALLENDE

Rabbi Daniel Huebner 52.41.5181.8092

NETHERLANDS

ALMERE

Rabbi Moshe Stiefel 31.36.744.0509

AMSTERDAM

Rabbi Yanki Jacobs 31.644.988.627
Rabbi Jaacov Zwi Spiero 31.652.328.065

EINDHOVEN

Rabbi Simcha Steinberg 31.63.635.7593

HAGUE

Rabbi Shmuel Katzman 31.70.347.0222

HEEMSTEDE-HAARLEM

Rabbi Shmuel Spiero 31.23.532.0707

MAASTRICHT

Rabbi Avrohom Cohen 32.48.549.6766

NIJMEGEN

Rabbi Menachem Mendel Levine
31.621.586.575

ROTTERDAM

Rabbi Yehuda Vorst 31.10.265.5530

PANAMA

PANAMA CITY

Rabbi Ari Laine
Rabbi Gabriel Benayon 507.223.3383

RUSSIA

ASTRAKHAN

Rabbi Yisroel Melamed 7.851.239.28.24

BRYANSK

Rabbi Menachem Mendel Zaklas 7.483.264.55.15

CHELYABINSK

Rabbi Meir Kirsh 7.351.263.24.68

MOSCOW

Rabbi Aizik Rosenfeld 7.906.762.88.81
Rabbi Mordechai Weisberg 7.495.645.50.00
Rabbi Mendel Wilansky 7.916.572.22.41

NIZHNY NOVGOROD

Rabbi Shimon Bergman 7.920.253.47.70

NOVOSIBIRSK

Rabbi Shneur Zalmen Zaklos 7.903.900.43.22

OMSK

Rabbi Osher Krichevsky 7.381.231.33.07

PERM

Rabbi Zalman Deutch 7.342.212.47.32

ROSTOV

Rabbi Chaim Danzinger 7.8632.99.02.68

S. PETERSBURG

Rabbi Shalom Pewzner 7.911.726.21.19
Rabbi Zvi Pinsky 7.812.713.62.09

SAMARA

Rabbi Shlomo Deutch 7.846.333.40.64

SARATOV

Rabbi Yaakov Kubitshek 7.8452.21.58.00

TOGLIATTI

Rabbi Meier Fischer 7.848.273.02.84

UFA

Rabbi Dan Krichevsky 7.347.244.55.33

VORONEZH

Rabbi Levi Stiefel 7.473.252.96.99

SINGAPORE

SINGAPORE

Rabbi Mordechai Abergel 656.337.2189
Rabbi Netanel Rivni 656.336.2127
Classes in Hebrew

SOUTH AFRICA

JOHANNESBURG

Rabbi Dovid Masinter
Rabbi Ari Kievman 27.11.440.6600

SWEDEN

STOCKHOLM

Rabbi Chaim Greisman 46.70.790.8994

SWITZERLAND

LUZERN

Rabbi Chaim Drukman 41.41.361.1770

ZURICH

Rabbi Mendel Rosenfeld 41.44.289.7050

THAILAND

BANGKOK

Rabbi Yosef C. Kantor 6681.837.7618

UKRAINE

BERDITCHEV

Mrs. Chana Thaler 380.637.70.37.70

DNEPROPETROVSK

Rabbi Dan Makagon 380.504.51.13.18

NIKOLAYEV

Rabbi Sholom Gotlieb 380.512.37.37.71

ODESSA

Rabbi Avraham Wolf
Rabbi Yaakov Neiman 38.048.728.0770 EXT. 280

ZAPOROZHYE

Mrs. Nechama Dina Ehrentreu 380.957.19.96.08

ZHITOMIR

Rabbi Shlomo Wilhelm 380.504.63.01.32

UNITED KINGDOM

ALTRINCHAM

Rabbi Mendel Chein 44.793.589.5600

BOURNEMOUTH

Rabbi Bentzion Alperowitz 44.749.456.7177

CHEADLE

Rabbi Peretz Chein 44.161.428.1818

ESSEX

EPPING

Rabbi Yossi Posen 44.749.650.4345

LEEDS

Rabbi Eli Pink 44.113.266.3311

LONDON

Rabbi Moshe Adler 44.771.052.4460
Rabbi Boruch Altein 44.749.612.3342
Rabbi Mendel Cohen 44.736.640.8244
Rabbi Mechel Gancz 44.758.332.3074
Rabbi Chaim Hoch 44.753.879.9524
Rabbi Mendel Kalmenson 44.758.592.0195
Rabbi Dovid Katz 44.207.625.2682
Mrs. Esther Kesselman 44.794.432.4829
Rabbi Mendy Korer 44.794.632.5444
Rabbi Baruch Levin 44.208.905.4141
Rabbi Eli Levin 44.754.046.1568
Rabbi Yisroel Lew 44.787.987.1571
Mrs. Chanie Simon 44.208.458.0416
Rabbi Bentzi Sudak 44.781.211.1890
Rabbi Yisroel Weisz 44.797.652.2807
Rabbi Shneur Wineberg 44.745.628.6538

MANCHESTER

Rabbi Levi Cohen 44.161.792.6335
Rabbi Shmuli Jaffe 44.161.766.1812

NOTTINGHAM

Rabbi Mendy Lent 44.759.005.1261

RADLETT, HERTFORDSHIRE

Rabbi Alexander Sender Dubrawsky 44.794.380.8965

The Jewish Learning Multiplex

Brought to you by the Rohr Jewish Learning Institute

In fulfillment of the mandate of the Lubavitcher Rebbe, of blessed memory, whose leadership guides every step of our work, the mission of the Rohr Jewish Learning Institute is to transform Jewish life and the greater community through the study of Torah, connecting each Jew to our shared heritage of Jewish learning.

While our flagship program remains the cornerstone of our organization, JLI is proud to feature additional divisions catering to specific populations, in order to meet a wide array of educational needs.

THE ROHR JEWISH LEARNING INSTITUTE

A subsidiary of Merkos L'Inyonei Chinuch,
the adult education arm of the Chabad-Lubavitch movement

Torah Studies provides a rich and nuanced encounter with the weekly Torah reading.

The Rosh Chodesh Society gathers Jewish women together once a month for intensive textual study.

Participants delve into our nation's past while exploring the Holy Land's relevance and meaning today.

Equips youths facing adulthood with education and resources to address youth mental health

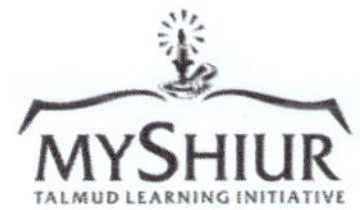

MyShiur courses are designed to assist students in developing the skills needed to study Talmud independently.

A crash course that teaches adults to read Hebrew in just five sessions

Jewish teens forge their identity as they engage in Torah study, social interaction, and serious fun.

TorahCafe.com provides an exclusive selection of top-rated Jewish educational videos.

This yearly event rejuvenates mind, body, and spirit with a powerful synthesis of Jewish learning and community.

Select affiliates are invited to partner with peers and noted professionals, as leaders of innovation and excellence.

This rigorous fellowship program invites select college students to explore the fundamentals of Judaism.

Machon Shmuel is an institute providing Torah research in the service of educators worldwide.